Hindsights

the autobiography of an unknown artist

Stan Erisman

Hindsights

Published by Stan Erisman
Publishing partner: Paragon Publishing, Rothersthorpe
First published 2020

© Stan Erisman 2020

The rights of Stan Erisman to be identified as the author of this work have been asserted by him in accordance with the Copyright, Designs and Patents Act of 1988.

All rights reserved; no part of this publication may be reproduced, stored in a retrieval system, or transmitted in any form or by any means, electronic, mechanical, photocopying, recording or otherwise without the prior written consent of the publisher or a licence permitting copying in the UK issued by the Copyright Licensing Agency Ltd. www.cla.co.uk

ISBN 978-1-78222-765-6

Book design, layout and production management by Into Print
www.intoprint.net
+44 (0)1604 832149

Cover illustration: *Man with Guitar*, oil painting #8, by Stan Erisman, 1964

FOREWORD

Hindsights – *the autobiography of an unknown artist*

Until 1988 I'd never really thought I'd write a book, let alone a six-part series called *Hindsights*. My first piece of serious writing came in 1978, when the greatest tragedy in my life – the death of Jeanette in 1977 – engulfed me and brought me to the brink of suicide. I set out to write a lengthy explanation to those I felt might need one. Although I wasn't writing for the purpose of freeing myself from agony, the writing of it had the serendipitous effect of a catharsis. By imposing a grammatical structure on my chaotic thoughts, I coincidentally imposed a structure on that chaos, enabling me to survive, to crawl and claw and scrape my way out of an abysmal depression, pull myself back from the brink, and start to move beyond it.

When my next major crisis began unfolding a few years later, I'd learned that writing about deeply troubling events and chaotic situations gave me crucial balance, so I began keeping records and writing notes about what was happening, what was being said, how I felt at the time. When that crisis came to a head and erupted in 1988, I also had the needs of my two precious small daughters to consider; I couldn't "afford" another year of debilitating depression and chaos. Writing became my therapy, my preemptive catharsis, my way not to go under.

Other major upheavals earlier in my life – escaping from suffocating religious indoctrination, finding a new moral compass, fleeing my homeland due to Vietnam, adopting and adapting to a new life in a new country, finding a unique friendship, enduring the arduous freedom of painting – left me with a storehouse of anecdotes that friends and acquaintances kept urging me to write down. One told me my stories about loss helped him greatly in dealing with the tragic loss of his own wife. Others told me that the account of my liberation from religious brainwashing had helped them deal with their own similar struggles. When I began to weave my stories and anecdotes into a more comprehensive and coherent work, I thus had a substantial cache of researched material about the development and interrelatedness of the events that have shaped my life.

I started turning my writings into book form in around 2008, as I was approaching retirement. My intention then was not to publish. The thought of publication might have made me too inhibited to strive for total honesty, and I could see no point in striving for anything less. Even after I began to consider publishing, I continued to write *as if* I were *not* going to publish in order to avoid compromising honesty. Some things I've related might cast certain people (not least myself) in an unflattering light. One early reader of my first book protested vociferously about a minor detail, despite acknowledging that it was true, because he felt I had no right to write it, even though it had impacted me as well. I can only say *sorry* for mentioning things that have had an important influence on me, but may be uncomfortable for anyone I care about.

When I started this project, I felt a compelling need to make sense of how my convoluted journey from infancy in Texas in 1945 led to the septuagenarian version of myself in the countryside of southern Sweden where I've done most of my writing. I also wanted to explain the background of my vocation as an artist, what my paintings are about (what they might mean to others may or may not say anything about my paintings!), and why I was unable to go on painting.

The writing process itself proved to be a moving target; the structure, scope, contents and purpose have morphed and evolved monumentally along the way. And towards the end of this project I started to change my mind about publishing (although I abhorred the prospect of finding a publisher!). Several of my friends and acquaintances heard I'd completed my first book and asked if they could read it. I agreed, on condition that they provide feedback (and tell me about my *spielling* [sic] and other mistakes). Four of my friends have read all six parts; they've all insisted that I publish.

Many years ago, Jeanette earnestly admonished me to "teach art to the world, to help us all." *Hindsights* is probably as close as I can ever get to heeding that admonition. I feel (as she felt) that many of my paintings, if they were understood, might help others. And yet those same paintings (again, if they were understood) might offend a lot of people. I side with and address those who are willing to have their ideas challenged – even if it means being offended initially – in order to achieve greater understanding and honesty. In my view, most important art inevitably challenges us to look at and think about the world in a different way, even if it means taking us outside our comfort zone. My 86 paintings, which I describe and refer to throughout the *Hindsights* series, are to be published in a separate volume.

Each person has a unique set of fingerprints, just as each person has a unique set of experiences that comprise the journey of his or her existence. I decided to write about mine. I've pointedly avoided filtering out things about my past selves of which I am not proud. Now that I'm in my 70s, why should I bother about vanity?

I frequently hear people say that one shouldn't dwell on the past – that one should let things go, move on, look forward, and focus on the future. As I now see it, that view is a younger person's perspective and prerogative, when one's life looking forward seems so big, so unending. I no longer have the privilege of that youthful perspective – a narrow brush with death in January 2015 made a major contribution to changing it. Rather, I want to be able to feel that I have learned something from what I've been through, from the many things I've done wrong and the few I've done right. And I'm keenly aware that "those who don't learn from the past are condemned to repeat it."

I've observed a striking similarity between writing my memoirs and doing connect-the-dots puzzles of the type found in children's coloring books – a page that is blank except for many seemingly randomly placed numbers accompanied by dots. Connecting the dots in numerical order gradually leads to the emergence of an image. Writing about the events in my life has illuminated their interrelatedness; things make more sense (or at least achieve more clarity and context) than before. I found this phenomenon thrilling, challenging, exhausting, revealing, sometimes alarming – and always valuable.

In writing my memoirs, I frequently found myself not merely *relating*, but *reliving* the events I was writing about. Sometimes it made me laugh, or cry, or feel embarrassed, proud, sad, disgusted and/or reproachful. I've frequently shaken my head in disbelief at my own naiveté or outright stupidity.

While writing the very first chapter, I experienced a phenomenon I'd never before experienced personally to such a great extent: the more I wrote about old memories, the more long-forgotten ones began popping up. Yes, there's good reason to be skeptical about the accuracy of memory. But since I wasn't interested in turning an autobiographical work into one of fiction, I did my best to verify those pop-up memories as well as all other memories of people, events, conversations etc that remained in my consciousness since they first took up residence there.

To this end, I've been fortunate to have access to most of the letters I wrote to my parents and/or my mom for close to half a century. (My mom saved nearly every letter I ever wrote to her and my dad; she handed them all to me in a box in the mid-1990s.) I've also had access to much of the correspondence between me and my cousin Bob Krause, my closest friend and mentor for nearly three decades, from our first correspondence in December 1969 until his death in April 1999. Bob's influence on my life was and remains huge.

I still have access to some of the correspondence between me and my two brothers, as well as rather detailed travel journals kept by Jeanette from some of our major trips. I've also been able to confirm or correct stories pertaining to certain milestones in my life by talking to several key people, particularly my mom, whose memory remained amazingly sharp almost until her death in 2014 at the age of 101.

Altogether, I've thus had access to a significant cache of reliable material that has given me a great deal of clarity about the development and interrelatedness of the events that have shaped my life, and thus through hindsight I've gained insights into my life. In the words of British author Alan Bennett, "You don't put yourself into what you write. You *find* yourself there [italics mine]." And I've made good use of the internet, fact-checking in the archives of various newspapers as far back as the late 1940s. Using Google Maps' street view, I've made virtual tours of my old neighborhoods, haunts, and other places of personal importance that I haven't been able to revisit in person.

I've frequently noted that some of the events in *Hindsights* – and the timing of those events – might seem too good or coincidental to be true. I can only say that to the best of my ability, I did not "fiddle" with facts to achieve dramatic effect, and did my best to corroborate everything I wrote. But I was admittedly astonished about the number of coincidences there turned out to be.

As my focus began shifting more and more from writing only about my paintings to writing about my whole life, the more I realized how unpredictable a work like this was likely to turn out to be. Obviously, I cannot *ever* complete a work that runs to the very end of my life. That consideration, and the wish to avoid an increasing number of sensitive toes upon which I have no desire to tread, led me initially to select a cutoff date in 1983, one that coincided with the end of my vocation as a painter. That would have meant five books. On further consideration, however, I decided against concluding *Hindsights* in 1983, a year in which my life was once again in mounting turmoil. Although

Foreword

I've experienced a couple of deep depressions, on the whole I don't think I'm a negative, pessimistic or chronically depressed person – on the contrary. Thus I chose not to end my opus on the partially low note I was experiencing in 1983, but on a very high one in 1988. *Hindsights* thus comprises six parts:

1. *Natural Shocks* – from my birth (1945) and earliest memories until I fled the extreme religious indoctrination of my childhood home (1964)

2. *The Undiscovered Country* – from my journey to San Francisco (1964) and the beginning of my life with Jeanette, my muse, to our year in Canada before moving to Sweden (1969)

3. *No Traveller Returns* – from our voyage to Sweden (1969), settling in, and beginning to paint in earnest (1972)

4. *Slings and Arrows* – from my most intensive period of painting (1973-75) to our almost-completed conversion of a ruin into a home, and the unfathomable tragedy of Jeanette's death (1977)

5. *A Sea of Troubles* – from the depths of depression (1977) and cathartic recovery to new love, new despair, and the end of my painting (1983)

6. *Perchance to Dream* – from the first pregnancy (1983) and the arrival of my children to the breakup of my family, a new miracle of love (1988), and a summarizing Afterword.

The chronology of *Hindsights* – like my life itself – is largely but not entirely linear. The books and chapters appear in the order they do for a reason, and build upon each other. I feel that "skipping around" would diminish the understanding of the work as a whole, as it would if one were to rearrange the order of the movements of a symphony or concerto.

The primary purpose of *Hindsights* is not to entertain – my writings are not intended to be best-selling page-turners – although I am aware that many (but certainly not all) of the incidents in my life might today be seen to have some entertainment value. There are elements of adventure, tragedy, absurdity, passion, love, struggle, naiveté, hope, despair, outrage and reflection. There are also details that may seem tedious and laborious to others, but are important to me.

Sometimes life does seem to imitate art. When I set out to paint my last major painting, based on having recently re-read Voltaire's *Candide*, I was struck by the similarities in my own life of a naive young man processing layer upon layer of indoctrination, through difficult twists and turns, and ultimately finding peace in a pastoral setting. I didn't know at the time that mine would be Glimminge.

In closing this introduction, I want to thank Karin – my wonderful and loving partner, wife and friend of the past 30 years and more – for her unfailing and uncomplaining patience, even throughout the most intensive and moodiest phases of my writing, when I would frequently disappear into my past, leaving only my physical presence behind like the smile of a Cheshire cat.

I also wish to extend my special thanks to my four "readers", who volunteered to plow through my six books (sometimes more than one version) and offer me valuable feedback and encouragement during the writing process: Norm Denton (my long-time friend), Lee Whitehead (my former professor of English and newfound friend), Brian Erisman (my close friend and nephew) and Bengt Schager (my former client and good friend). I will relate more about these guys in the Afterword at the end of Book Six.

Just as I was completing the writing of the six books that comprise *Hindsights*, the world was struck by the COVID-19 pandemic, with its profound existential impact on humankind.

I wonder where we'll all go from here ....

Stan Erisman
Glimminge, 2008-2020

Foreword

To be, or not to be, that is the question:
Whether 'tis nobler in the mind to suffer
The *slings and arrows* of outrageous fortune,
Or to take Arms against *a Sea of troubles*,
And by opposing end them: to die, to sleep
No more; and by a sleep, to say we end
The heart-ache, and the thousand *natural shocks*
That Flesh is heir to? 'Tis a consummation
Devoutly to be wished. To die, to sleep,
To sleep, *perchance to Dream*; aye, there's the rub,
For in that sleep of death, what dreams may come,
When we have shuffled off this mortal coil,
Must give us pause. There's the respect
That makes Calamity of so long life:
For who would bear the Whips and Scorns of time,
The Oppressor's wrong, the proud man's Contumely,
The pangs of despised Love, the Law's delay,
The insolence of Office, and the spurns
That patient merit of the unworthy takes,
When he himself might his Quietus make
With a bare Bodkin? Who would Fardels bear,
To grunt and sweat under a weary life,
But that the dread of something after death,
The undiscovered country, from whose bourn
No traveller returns, puzzles the will,
And makes us rather bear those ills we have,
Than fly to others that we know not of.
Thus conscience does make cowards of us all,
And thus the native hue of Resolution
Is sicklied o'er, with the pale cast of Thought,
And enterprises of great pitch and moment,
With this regard their Currents turn awry,
And lose the name of Action.

– William Shakespeare, Hamlet's soliloquy
from *Hamlet*, act III, scene I

Hindsights

Natural Shocks

Book one in the Hindsights series

Stan Erisman

CONTENTS

Chapter 1: Glendale 1
How I was born in 1945 in Dallas (Texas) into an insular fundamentalist family of Plymouth Brethren, as the youngest of three brothers, and how my earliest childhood memories from Glendale (California) sought to instill in me that fundamentalist Christianity was the only Right Way (I knew no other).

Chapter 2: The Meeting 13
How the beliefs and practices of the Plymouth Brethren (aka the Meeting) determined and restricted my upbringing, and how layer upon layer of indoctrination defined not merely something we did, but how we lived, behaved, thought, breathed; and how our place was explicitly to be "in the world, not of the world."

Chapter 3: Pets 57
How the execution and murder of my beloved pet dog and pet ducks were sanctioned by my parents and how this presumably influenced my future desire to own pets – and my innocent trust in my parents and their proclaimed values.

Chapter 4: Dad 64
How I came to recognize that my dad grew up to be a decent guy despite his deeply Christian influences and his deference to my mom and his parents, and how sorry I came to be about never having known him well.

Chapter 5: The Trapper 92
How I sought escape by aspiring to become a fur trapper in a remote part of Alaska, then a taxidermist; and how I abandoned such ideas in a flurry of humiliation.

Chapter 6: Red Eagle 109
How I attempted to channel my alleged traces of Cherokee blood and my boyhood outrage at the treatment of Indians into a new life as a full-blooded Indian; how I began to doubt and circumvent my strictest prohibitions; and how my pre-pubertal introduction to genitalia left me confused but curious.

Chapter 7: Mom at Home 123
How I began to understand the twofold nature and personality of my mother and the dominant role she played in my childhood and in our family, and would continue to play in all our lives until and beyond her death at the age of 101; and how I began to question more of what I'd been taught, on several levels.

CHAPTER 8: Crumbling 148

    How the combination of my extremely strict upbringing and my entry into painful adolescence as an involuntary outsider began to disintegrate the wall my parents had attempted to confine me within, planting the seeds of furtive rebellion.

CHAPTER 9: The Thursday Night Massacre 158

    How my parents totally destroyed the mildly rebellious behavior of my beloved brother and broke his spirit as a young man; and how I observed this with horror and vowed I would never let it happen to me, thereby launching my own far greater rebellion.

CHAPTER 10: The Countdown 175

    How my friend Norm and I forged plans to leave home at all costs as soon as he finished high school; how we began the countdown to our day of departure at around 1000 days; how I realized I'd have to forego the financial support my brothers got for their college educations; how I fell for ultra-right-wing political influences, suffered my mom's dirty tricks, and began to paint.

CHAPTER 11: The Final Year 196

    How my life at home became an open war of attrition while I continued to paint and Norm and I fined-tuned our plans to leave; how we left, on schedule, precisely at the end of the countdown; and how on June 6th, 1964, Norm and I joyously and nervously boarded a Greyhound bus bound for San Francisco.

APPENDIX 1: My boyhood home 213
APPENDIX 2: Paintings 1-8 214

CHAPTER 1

Glendale

My life began in Dallas on September 13th, 1945, at St. Paul's Hospital. My dad was born on Staten Island in New York in 1911 and moved to Oak Park, Illinois, as a boy, where he grew up and became the first in his family to obtain an academic degree. My mom was born in Des Moines, Iowa, in 1913, the fourth of six daughters, whose grandparents were Swedish immigrants. After my parents married, Mom joined Dad in Oak Park, where my eldest brother John, the pre-war edition of us brothers, was born in September 1937; and Al, the wartime edition, was born in February 1941. My parents were both raised in the Meeting, a small group of pious Christian fundamentalists who believed – or rather believed that they *knew* – that our lives are but pilgrimages through a spiritual wilderness (otherwise known as planet Earth), that our dwelling is a camp, and that our true Home is in heaven, however much they strove to delay going there.

In 1943, Dad's job transferred him to Dallas for two years. With seven months to go of his stint there and the war at last safely over, I was born, thus becoming the post-war version of us brothers. I've sometimes told people that Mom got pregnant with me two years earlier, but that I flatly refused to come out until the war was over and the last treaty signed. In any case, Mom had an excruciating time delivering me; the doctor warned my parents not to have any more kids. The soundness of that advice probably wouldn't achieve full clarity for them until I became a teenager.

For some inscrutable reason I was given the name Stanley, possibly because of the contemporary popularity of "Stan the man" Musial, an all-star player for the St. Louis Cardinals baseball team, although my parents never displayed any interest in sports at all, but could provide no other explanation for giving me my moniker. Since my mom's father's name was John Albert Larson, I might otherwise have been called Larson, or at least Lars, but instead I got Larson as a middle name (something that would puzzle and amuse Swedes many years later).

I knew nothing of all this, of course, during my time in Dallas. The venue for the birth of my consciousness and memory was much farther west, in Glendale,

California, where we moved when I was seven months old, when Link-Belt again transferred Dad, this time to its Los Angeles branch. I lived in Glendale until I was five years and four months old, in a pleasant, single-story stucco house at 919 Patterson Street. My memories of Glendale are few, but mostly happy.

The lawn part of our back yard was rectangular, the long side parallel with our house. Along the back edge of the lawn was a small rose garden, and beyond that a few small trees or big bushes. Sometimes a huge, dew-laden spider web appeared in the morning, stretched between the rose bushes, with a monstrous spider parked in the middle. That was enough to keep me on the grass and out of the roses. There was a fairly high wall of whitewashed cinder blocks on the right-hand side. I remember it as a completely private yard, but perhaps that's only because I was too short to see over the walls, or too unaware to register anything beyond them, whether the walls had been there or not. There was a path from the back yard to the front along one side of the house, in deep shadow at all times. It was here I remember Mom taking a broom to kill a black widow spider one day.

My first birthday was celebrated in the back yard. I'd already been walking for about four months, one of my few somewhat precocious achievements. The gift that made the deepest impression on me was a teddy bear. It immediately became my constant companion, day and night, until half of the stuffing was gone (some of which I allegedly consumed) and I was obliged to set it aside when it was time for kindergarten. My first birthday was also when Mom baked me my first Treasure Chest cake (as she continued to do for most of my childhood birthdays), from a batter containing lots of nuts, raisins and oranges (including peels), all ground up together; the same mixture was used for the frosting, but with the addition of extra butter and plenty of powdered sugar. (Mom's recipe – obviously the only true Treasure Chest Cake – has absolutely nothing in common the recipes found online.) Without Treasure Chest cake, it would never truly seem like my birthday. Jeanette would one day learn to make Treasure Chest cake for me, and still later I would learn to make it myself until its stratospheric calorie content in combination with my middle-age metabolism obliged me to forego that particular avenue of pleasure. I would also make them, using my mom's recipe, for my kids every year until they left home.

I reportedly never sucked my thumb, and as far as I know, my parents never gave me a pacifier. Instead I'm told I sucked the middle and ring fingers of my right hand (imagine how precocious I might have been if I'd sucked only my middle finger!) until one day when I was about two or three and had to accompany Mom to the doctor's. While the doctor was examining her, he looked over at me sucking my fingers, and with theatrical alarm announced to me that if I didn't stop, he'd have to cut them off. Eyes wide with terror, I immediately withdrew my fingers and never sucked them again. Mom told me that for some time after that, when she would go in to check on me at night, I'd start moving my extended fingers towards my mouth in my sleep, and when they got close to my mouth, I would suddenly jerk them away, far from the looming amputationer's knife.

Our neighbors across the street – whose last name was my first – had a son around my age whose first name was Tommy. They got a TV when I was around four. Television was so new at the time that the unofficial hierarchy of the Meeting hadn't yet declared it to be an instrument of Satan. Not that we had a TV anyway; the device hadn't been explicitly approved either.

I remember the bird-of-paradise flowers outside our front door, and a bee there that stung me on my arm. I remember having to go to the emergency room to have a peanut removed from my nose after I'd stuck it there because I got bored sticking them in my mouth while Mom was on the phone. The doctor who removed it with his tweezers might have been the same one whose threat removed my fingers from my mouth.

I remember the tall and stately palm trees of southern California and the dry heat and the rustling of the breeze in the gray-green eucalyptus trees. I remember the large avocado tree in crazy Aunt Marion's back yard. Aunt Marion lived within walking distance of us. She was the only one of Mom's sisters who ever left the Meeting, and that was because she didn't find it holy enough. But somehow she had a TV and had Easter egg hunts in her back yard, where the avocado tree stood. When she left the Meeting for another even wackier group, her husband Fred stayed with the Meeting. Fred and Marion then became estranged but were still living under the same roof until he went back to live with his mother quite some time later. Aunt Marion hid us all – and herself – whenever Uncle Fred came to the house. He was such an incredibly timid little man, in total contrast to the gaunt, intimidating, histrionic Aunt Marion, who always looked as if she were perched in the prow of a pirate ship, sternly glaring forward, leading it into battle. Uncle Fred looked little to me then, even as a four-year-old.

I don't remember much about Marion's two kids, my cousins Winnie and Sterling, during our years in Glendale. They were even older than my brother John, so we never had much in common. It was years before I learned that "Winnie" was short for "Winifred". She was born when Marion and Fred were still together, and in Aunt Marion's typically exaggerated ebullience, she wished for her daughter to "win a Fred"; hence the name, and hence it was never, ever used once Marion and Fred separated.

I remember watching Hopalong Cassidy on the Stanleys' TV (which my parents didn't forbid or even discourage during our time in Glendale). I instantly became an avid "Hoppy" fan and coaxed my parents to get me a whole Hoppy cowboy outfit – black suit, black hat, black boots, toy pistol and even spurs, whose purpose I had no clue about. I had never been wild about bread. In fact, I gagged on it – particularly the standard American white, square, spongy, tasteless sandwich bread that was a staple in our home and households nationwide. I could only endure it toasted. But then a big commercial bakery in LA came out with "Hoppy bread" – emblazoned with the image of my cowboy hero – and I succumbed to the wiles of marketing. I remember helping to bring the groceries into the kitchen that evening, and I could hardly wait to have a sandwich with peanut butter and jelly on *untoasted* Hoppy bread. I solemnly and with full, innocent conviction declared that "Hoppy bread is good bread."

Affection was expressed spontaneously and frequently in our home. I was loved and secure, as long as I did what I was told, by which I mean that I might not have felt as loved and secure as I would have felt if I had been able to feel I would be loved no matter what I did. I was spanked into repentance if I didn't do what I was told, so I tried my earnest little best to follow the rules, even while my reportedly naturally impish nature – surely the purest evidence of my innate wickedness? – was compelling me to test the limits. I didn't realize that I was already being poured and pressed into a mold that was significantly stricter than the molds into which the neighbor kids were being pressed.

Mom often told me that once when I was about two, the phone rang while I was sitting on my potty. When she went to answer, I leaped up from the potty and broke for the front door. With Mom in hot pursuit, I made it all the way down the street, around the corner, and halfway up Highland Avenue towards a busy street called Glenoaks before she caught up with me. I was stark naked and squealing with delight. It's likely that I got a spanking for that. I spent nearly every minute of those five years in Glendale with my family. My world was almost entirely defined by my parents and brothers. I didn't yet see *our* world as being different. It was the *outside* world – the world of the Stanleys and other neighbors – that was different, worldly (whatever that meant), and categorically *wrong*.

I was constantly being told by my parents that I was a sinner and had to be "saved" by "putting my trust in Jesus", or I would end up in the Lake of Fire forever. What was my "trust"? Where did I keep it? Where was I supposed to put it? Was there a box somewhere called "Jesus" that I should put it in if I ever figured out what and where it was? It never occurred to me to question why the God who loved me so much would find it necessary to threaten three-year-olds with eternal torture.

Mom claimed that when I was about three, I told her that I had done this trust-putting thing that I didn't understand, but which she was demanding of me every day. At that moment, according to her, my "soul" (whatever that was) was "redeemed" (whatever that meant), and my name was written forever (however long that was) in the Book of Life (and I hadn't yet learned to read). She frequently reminded me of this moment throughout my childhood and for many years afterwards. I have no memory of the occasion myself, but it seems reasonable that a three-year-old could recite any not-too-complex combination of words or phonemes that he was constantly being told were expected of him, especially ones that his mother was so emotionally dependent on hearing and had made them my password for accessing her unconditional affection.

Mom also frequently reminded me that in my early childhood she got me to sing along with her, as she played the piano, "*Now I belong to Jesus / Jesus belongs to me / Not for the years of time alone / But for eternity.*" I remember wondering who "Ty Malone" was. My brother Al spoke in awe of Ty Cobb, the all-time all-star third baseman for the Detroit Tigers, who was the only other "Ty" I'd heard of. So I believed there was this Ty Malone guy who somehow had something to do with being "saved". You can get kids to believe almost anything. Kids don't have to become as little children – that's what they already are. Then, once they've been guided, steered, duped or threatened into believing things, it can take years for them to "dis-believe" them – if it ever happens, if they ever get that much courage.

The air in southern California was warm and dry. There were avenues of palm trees, there were brown-green-gray, hazy sage-covered mountains and blue skies; smog hadn't yet become a plague. And there was the vast Pacific Ocean. I couldn't get enough of the ocean. Uncle Ralph was early to acquire a home movie camera and when he and his family came out from Oak Park to Glendale to visit us one year, he filmed a scene at one of the beaches. My dad is barefoot, with his trousers rolled up, standing close to where the onrushing waves finally give up, thus only occasionally getting a slight lapping of wetness over his bare feet. As Ralph's film shows, Dad is standing talking to someone off-camera, with his back to the sea, firmly holding my hand. All the while I'm struggling like mad to throw myself into the waves. Then, I see something coming (also off-camera) and I stop struggling, allowing Dad to relax his grip slightly. In the next second, one of the afternoon's larger waves reaches halfway up Dad's calves, while I, having timed it perfectly, fling myself at his feet, jubilantly immersing myself completely – fully clothed – in the foaming brine.

I remember Kathy Fiscus, a little girl about my own age, who one Friday fell far down a narrow abandoned well shaft somewhere in the LA area, and whose cries could be heard during massive rescue efforts for two days. Everyone seemed to be glued to their radios, including us, and fervent prayers and hymns were heard everywhere, not only from the Chosen Few. But Kathy Fiscus died just before the would-be rescuers reached her on Sunday evening, and I got my first taste of how things work. If God had willed her to be rescued, it would have been proof of His goodness and mercy, and all those prayers would have been proof that He listens. But since God did not will her to be rescued, it was proof of His goodness and mercy anyway. And if you don't understand that equation, it's just because He is greater than you.

When I started writing about my earliest childhood, I thought I only had a handful of memories from the well-defined period of living in Glendale. As I began to write, dormant memories began popping up, things I'd assumed were long forgotten. I had just written about Kathy Fiscus when I began to doubt the reliability of my memory, and then I realized I could try to Google it to verify the story or delete it as false. There I found the story, in the archives of a newspaper at that time, identical to what I'd just written, and to my great surprise discovered that I was just three years and seven months old at the time. I only needed to correct the spelling of her name; I was illiterate at the time.

I remember the iceman delivering blocks of ice to our neighbor's icebox, even though by this time most homes in our neighborhood had refrigerators, which were often still called iceboxes. I remember the milkman in his white uniform and white, black-patent-leather-brimmed cap (I would encounter such caps again in Sweden one day, but not on milkmen) bringing to our doorstep bottles of milk and cream in accordance with the rolled-up paper note from Mom stuck in the top of one of the empties he would pick up. I remember a baseball player named Wayne Terwilliger, only because of his name, which was almost as funny to me as Peleg (see Genesis 10:25). I remember Dad's business trips to Mexico, usually to Mazatlán, and him coming home after days or weeks looking pale and sick. I remember him getting snowbound onboard a train near Green River, Wyoming, for several days in March 1950, when there were legitimate fears for the survival of those on board. I remember getting home delivery of Bob's Big Boy hamburgers. They were delivered in a tiny little van (I believe it was a Crosley), one of the smallest ever made in America. The hamburgers were sensational – at least they seemed that way to me at the time: double-deckers, toasted sesame seed buns, special sauce. It would take another hamburger chain a quarter of a century to make that idea their own.

Throughout my childhood, I was an avid drawer (the two-syllable kind who wields pencils and crayons, not the monosyllabic kind of box you slide out of desks or cabinets). As far as Mom remembered (and she remembered a lot), my earliest passion was drawing trains, on whatever paper Mom found to let me draw on. Often it was brown paper, perhaps saved wrapping paper or shopping bags from the grocery store. Trains played a bigger role in my childhood than they probably would have played if they hadn't played an even bigger role for Dad. Between the ages of three and six, probably influenced by his great interest in trains, I would draw trains everywhere, making them in several roughly parallel lines across the paper. I don't remember much about real trains until we moved to Oak Park, although trains would have been involved in one or more family trips back east. I know we were in Des Moines when I was three, because photos tell me so, as did my eldest cousin Bob many years later.

I remember riding the little trains in Griffith Park, where I also have some vague memories of family picnics, as well as visits to Knott's Berry Farm, where they had a small-scale train you could ride. My parents weren't much for amusement parks, since the name itself suggests that they are intended for worldly amusement, but berry farms and other parks were fine, especially if they had trains in them. Dad could be highly pragmatic, but I was far too young to realize how profoundly perceptions of things or people can be influenced by the values ascribed to their names.

I remember going to Meeting, of course. We usually went to the Meeting assembly in Burbank, the closest of the three in the LA area. We occasionally also visited the gathering in Pasadena, but seldom the one in Fullerton. I don't remember them individually. The Meeting was who we were, what we did, how we lived, what we thought, where we went, where I was taken, where all my parents' friends were, where we connected with the people who would join us for Sunday dinner, or those to whose homes we would sometimes be invited. The Meeting rooms were places where I had to keep quiet. I often fell asleep, which was permitted at my tender age. I remember the smell of eucalyptus trees and cypresses and cedars near the Meeting room. And there were always old ladies with wicker hats and lacework veils that seemed designed more to blur their vision than to hide their faces.

I don't remember becoming left-handed because I was never anything else. Nor do I remember anyone trying to make me right-handed. It was one thing they just let me be.

I started kindergarten at Mark Keppel Elementary School in September 1950. Mark Keppel was the Superintendent of Schools of Los Angeles County from 1902 to 1928, which earned him the right to have schools named after him. Tommy Stanley also went to Mark Keppel, and so did another neighbor boy whose name I've forgotten, but I do remember how different he was. He was a towhead blond with extremely pale skin. He might have been an albino – I wouldn't have known at that age. He was extremely shy and nervous and embarrassed about everything, especially about his mother, who seemed to think he was a Strasbourg goose. After a hearty breakfast, she would send him off to the half-day kindergarten session with a bag of doughnuts to eat along the way. She would also come to the school with additional food to get him through the recess, and she met him on the way home with a snack, in case he might get hungry before he could get home to his lunch. My memory of this boy is that he wasn't at all fat, so perhaps he had a metabolic disorder that his mother was trying to compensate for. I never understood it. What I did understand was that he and his family were weird. We, on the other hand, were normal. We were always normal in my early childhood; we defined the word.

In kindergarten, and throughout elementary school, I was among the smallest of the boys. But I was also among the quickest, fastest runners, and the most athletic. When we played a tag game called pom-pom during recess, I was usually the last one to be "it". Although many in my kindergarten already had a TV, not everyone did, so I wasn't completely left out yet, especially since I often went over to the Stanleys' to watch various programs, like Hoppy and baseball. From watching baseball, but perhaps mostly from having a brother named Al, I developed an interest in sports and had good enough coordination to do well for my age.

When it became clear in the autumn of 1950 that we would be moving from Glendale to Oak Park in the beginning of 1951, my parents must have had lots of arrangements to make about selling our house in Glendale and building a new one in Oak Park. I don't remember being involved in any of those arrangements. Our house on Patterson was sold quickly, well over a month before we were ready to move to Illinois, so we had to rent a small apartment for the interim period. That apartment was in a U-shaped, 2-storey building on Highland, just around the corner from our house. There was some sort of aspiring Hollywood acrobat who lived in the same building, and he would walk around on his hands, even up and down the stairs that way. I don't remember what he looked like or whether I ever saw his face right-side-up. Perhaps I wouldn't have recognized him. I didn't know a thing about Hollywood back then, but I knew that this guy was "different" in yet another different sort of way. The word was acquiring nuances.

We moved by train from LA to Chicago just after New Year's, arriving on January 5th, 1951. It was the first full-scale train ride I remember, and the most luxurious I would ever experience, since Link-Belt was footing the bill for Dad's transfer back to Chicago. I could tell that my parents had never traveled in such style either. And here's this 5-year-old kid, arriving at the cathedralic Los Angeles Union Station, people bustling everywhere, half of the Burbank Meeting there to see us off, as well as from the other Meetings in the LA area, plus Aunt Marion, and we were so excited as we set off to start a new life, a change more profound than any of us were probably aware of at that moment, and certainly not me – I being the only member of our family who had never lived in Oak Park, and would thus be traveling to a complete unknown. The station hall was a symphonic cacophony of announcements, shouts, cries, singing, whistles, bells, as well as the closer, more urgent exchanges among my family members as to where we should go, and when, and sometimes how.

We hurried more than we had to. We always tended to arrive early – incredibly early – for everything, a trait particularly strong in my mom, who at least once, on one of our many later train trips from LA to Chicago, took out her house key and sat clenching it until we got home to 1231 N. Euclid. The point at which she took her key out and began clenching it was, however, in connection with crossing the Mississippi River into Illinois, which meant she sat there clenching that key for hours, across the entire state, to the Union Station in the Chicago Loop, then out to Oak Park and to our home.

But we were not so early that we couldn't board the train, which was standing there waiting for us, emitting small puffs of steam from under each of the cars. It may have been the El Capitán or the Super Chief – the name was less important to me than the silvery, glistening cars and the mighty, rumbling engines. There were porters in white starched uniform coats, with special caps and baggage trolleys to help us with our bags, and other porters at each car, standing by the special foot-high step placed in front of each open door, ready to lend passengers a hand to climb up into the train. All these porters were black. Although I have no memory of ever having encountered black people before, they seemed to me as matter-of-fact as white starched uniforms and baggage trolleys and white people. I had apparently not yet been exposed to racial prejudice either.

My dad found our car, and saw that the porters got our bags on board, and got their tips, but we didn't board just yet ourselves. There were too many hugs to be exchanged, blessings to be intoned, *"journey mercies!"* to be proclaimed, tears to be shed, reminders to write to be issued, and the chorus of *"Till we meet again"* to be sung. Traveling – especially moving – was such a bigger, more final deal in those days, when it meant that conversations and face-to-face encounters would no longer be normal parts of the relationships that had been founded on them.

As the train started to fill and the dark-blue-uniformed conductor started looking at his pocket watch, we went through a final round of hugs and boarded the train, making our way along the corridor so that we could wave at those we were leaving behind, through the half-open windows. Dad lifted me up to see, till the conductor at last blew his whistle and shouted *"BOAAAH!"* which I was told meant "all aboard" – which we already were. The last of the stragglers boarded quickly, the steps were hauled up into the train, the doors closed with a solid *"thunk"*, people waved furiously, anxiously, sadly, and excitedly. The faint roar of the powerful diesel engines, sounding proud to be powerful, could be heard up the tracks, and our train lurched into motion, slowly at first, so that some of those on the platform began to walk in pace with the train, but only for a moment. Out of the station and from the sight of those we had known, we turned from the windows, Dad put me down and raised the windows up to the closed position. Mom and Dad had wet eyes. We all went to investigate our quarters, the only time any of us had experienced a stateroom on a train – an entire suite – complete with two bedrooms, our own bathroom and shower.

It wasn't long before my brothers and I went exploring the train, to find out how many cars forward and backward we could go. Struggling to open the doors between cars – the sudden release with a roaring *psssst*, and then stepping into a noisy, gusty, dimly lit, scary, often chilly no man's land, crossing the overlapping, bouncing, swerving floor plates to get to the heavy door of the next car, letting the door *thunk* hard behind us – got the adrenalin going and made it easier for my brother John to open each successive door. Each transition from one car to the next was a decreasingly scary experience, until I gradually got used to it, particularly with the 13-year-old John and the nearly-10-year-old Al in charge of the doors. My brothers and I would explore the entire train, from the baggage car in front (no admittance), through all the coach cars and sleeping cars, smoky lounge cars and pristine dining car, with strangers milling around in corridors, the coach cars full of them, people with picnic baskets and magazines and comic books and smells, families, couples, groups and loners, all the way back to the end of the train, with its rounded end windows where we could stand and watch the rails speeding away from us, the parallel lines of the rails slowly converging behind us and California disappearing beneath our feet.

Meals onboard were another comparative luxury; the only restaurants I'd ever eaten at were diners or hamburger establishments. We ate in the dining car at tables with crisp white linen tablecloths and napkins, with exceptional 3-D entertainment just outside the window, starting with the American West and its spectacular deserts and awe-inspiring mountains' majesty. The breakfast smells of pancakes and maple syrup and coffee and link sausages and bacon combined with the magic of the ever-changing landscape whizzing by, punctured and punctuated by the Doppler-shifting clang of an occasional level crossing bell as we roared straight through what seemed like hundreds of small towns that failed to merit a stop from the likes of our auspicious cross-country silver beauty of a train.

Using the toilet was another surprise; flushing it meant opening a hole in the bottom of the train, where I could see the blur of the railroad bed racing by. The sudden noise was less scary to me once I grew used to the sudden noises of moving between cars, and not nearly as startling as the flushing suction on airliners, which I would not experience until I was nearly 20. I could easily become totally absorbed looking down through the hole to the ground below, but I kept those viewings short in case it meant missing something outside the windows.

As we raced eastward through the West in those early days of 1951, it felt like we were moving in the wrong direction, against the amber waves of grain, although most of the grain was east of the West anyway, so we were moving with the grain, or at least towards it. But it felt wrong. We were leaving, not reaching.

CHAPTER 2

The Meeting

Our new house in Oak Park was a snow-covered concrete slab when we first saw it in January 1951. Snow was new for me, although I must have seen snow when we drove up into the mountains from Glendale on various late- or early-year Saturday excursions. But there had never been snow you couldn't drive away from in half an hour or so. When we arrived at the train station in the Chicago Loop, we thus had to make our way to a temporary residence in a huge rented house in River Forest, a suburb on the western border of the northern half of Oak Park, until our new home was finished.

At this house in River Forest – a two-storey frame dwelling that was probably four times as big as our house in Glendale – I invented a couple of fictional characters, possibly because I didn't have any "real" friends yet, possibly as a vent for the dramatic side of me I seemed to have inherited from my mom (or crazy Aunt Marion), and probably at least to get some attention. These characters' names were *Seezboolahboolah* and *Uhm-ime-the-dairdy*. They lived in the ceiling light fixture. Seezboolahboolah spoke with a deep growling voice I'd learned to produce, a kind of inverse falsetto. I entertained the family with stories of their adventures, doing the growly voice till my throat got sore. I could be a real show-off.

I'd begun kindergarten in Glendale before transferring to one in River Forest for a couple of months. Then, when we finally moved into 1231 North Euclid in May, I started my third kindergarten, for the last month only, at the dark-red-brick Horace Mann Elementary School, where I would continue throughout the eight grades of elementary school. Although I was blithely unaware of it at the time, it turned out that Horace had done quite a bit more for educational progress than Mark Keppel. In the early 1800s in Massachusetts, Horace Mann was a highly progressive leader in educational reform, promoting non-sectarian public education for everyone, with a broader curriculum and a ban on corporal punishment – a real pioneer.

Oak Park was an "upstanding" community, the self-proclaimed world's largest village (around 64,000 inhabitants), a bit posh – although less so than River Forest. Oak Park is tucked in about halfway along Chicago's zig-zag western city limit, such that the boundaries of Oak Park to the east (Austin

Avenue) and north (North Avenue) are formed by Chicago's own borders. Across most of the southern boundary of Oak Park is Berwyn, adjacent to and west of Cicero. Both of these suburbs had a history of notoriety as the haunts of Al Capone. Across the western boundary (northern half) is River Forest, which shares the township high school with Oak Park. To the west of the southern half is Forest Park, which had the nearest office of the Selective Service, as well as a big outdoor swimming pool, thankfully accessible by bus and open to the public during the sweltering Midwestern summers. The Lake Street L – the elevated train between the Loop of Chicago and the western suburbs – dissects Oak Park into northern and southern halves. Our house was at the northern edge of Oak Park, with just one vacant lot and a commercial property (a small hamburger joint with a huge parking lot) between us and North Avenue. In fact, at the time our house was completed, and for quite a few years thereafter, we had vacant lots on all four sides. Our garage was behind our house, accessible from an alley – a zoning configuration that applied to most of the blocks in Oak Park and much of Greater Chicago.

Oak Park and the surrounding suburbs are almost completely flat, consisting mainly of straight, parallel, tree-lined streets (mostly elm in Oak Park at that time, the name of the village notwithstanding) intersected perpendicularly by other straight, parallel tree-lined streets, creating rectangular blocks that are longer in the north-south direction, like the village itself. Each block is neatly divided into lots, most of which are much deeper than they are wide, and in Oak Park the homes on them range from pleasant to stately, nearly all of them brick, most of them built in the early half of the 1900s. The lots are biggest, ritziest and most varied just north of Lake Street (where the number of homes designed by Frank Lloyd Wright is sufficient to put Oak Park on the map of most architecture buffs), then become somewhat more modest and uniform towards North Avenue. Some of the neighboring blocks were divided into nine lots on each side of the street. Our block was divided into eleven. It also had an extra east-west alley, separating the residential part from the commercial part along North Avenue. Oak Park Avenue (the principal thoroughfare bisecting Oak Park in the north-south direction, constituted the western boundary of our block, with LeMoyne Parkway to the south.

Parallel to each side of each street was a sidewalk consisting of about three-by-three-foot concrete plates. Between the sidewalk and the street, evenly spaced elm trees grew from a section of lawn that separated the sidewalk from the street by about six feet. It was the civic duty of each homeowner to keep this lawn trimmed. Keeping one's own front lawn trimmed was "voluntary", though no statutes wield more power than peer pressure. The houses along the north-south streets were set back about 35 feet from the sidewalks, and the front yards were not fenced off; fences were not the custom in Oak Park, whether by zoning law or by the ubiquitous pressure of conformity, I don't know.

"The Meeting" was the only name ever used by my parents and their ilk for their tiny branch of a tiny religious group, founded principally by John Nelson Darby (the Nelson part is the surname of his godfather, Lord Nelson, the guy on the pillar in Trafalgar Square in London) in the 1830s in Plymouth, England, and eventually officially called the Plymouth Brethren by outsiders and the authorities. If necessary, they called their group "non-denominational", i.e. having no name, but they *did* use a name: the Meeting.

They prided themselves on their humble devotion to literal interpretation of the Bible in its entirety. This forced them, however, to suppress the fact that the more they took the Bible literally, the fewer of its hundreds of grotesque commandments and socialist injunctions they were prepared to live by. But they remained firm in the belief that their duty was to forsake the temporal pleasures of sin (which included just about everything that their "worldly" peers found enjoyable) for the sake of an eternal reward that would only be attained by a Chosen Few, humbly admitting that they themselves were foremost in this select gathering.

They *knew* that every word in the Bible was the immutable Word of God, directly given and inspired by Him and representing Absolute Truth. Not a word could be added or taken away on pain of eternal damnation and torment. For mainstream Christian denominations, the only refuge from literal interpretation of a book as antiquated, anachronistic, brutal and self-contradictory as the Bible, however, was to interpret more and more things figuratively. Not even the Plymouth Brethren (nor any other denomination I've ever heard of) could stomach going the whole way – interpreting *every* brutality and horror in the Bible literally. But they quibbled about who interpreted more of it literally than others.

This led to a sort of holier-than-thou one-upmanship among the members and local gatherings, resulting in numerous divisions and schisms. My parents' branch was one of the many "closed" or "exclusive" branches of the Plymouth Brethren, with further complexities in its dendritic structure erupting continuously. Theirs was also, in their own assessment, of course, the only branch, the only faith, the only doctrine, to follow the *true* Path fully, as laid down in the King James Version of the Bible, which in turn was and is – in their own assessment, of course – the only source of Truth on earth, it being the Word of God. (A "new" translation by Darby himself was allowed for reference purposes; Darby's version gave some insights that were hidden by the more archaic forms of pre-Elizabethan English. King James's crew of translators used variants of the language that were already antiquated back in his day, to give it a more authoritative ring.) The Meeting people seemed convinced that the original language of the Bible, and indeed of the Lord Himself, was 16th century English, occasionally pointing out, for various purposes, the number of times a certain word appeared in the Bible, forgetting or ignoring the fact that words that are the same in one language may be translated with several different words in another, and vice-versa, and the Bible involved translations from Hebrew, Greek, Aramaic, and Latin. They also ignored the fact that the canon of the Bible was not finally agreed upon until centuries after the fact, when whole books (not just single words), probably having already undergone numerous revisions and embellishments, were selected for inclusion or exclusion from the text that predated John Nelson Darby and the English language itself. Indeed, the Meeting seemed to regard Biblical scholars (and all other scholars) with suspicion, as though they were lacking in faith, and were in fact questioning the "true" version. They certainly regarded other English-language versions (apart from Darby's) than King James's as departures from the True Word.

The terms "church" and "religion" were mostly used pejoratively within the Meeting. The Meeting was *not* a church according to them, and absolutely *not* a religion (cf. the Merriam-Webster definition, "the service and worship of God or the supernatural"). To them, religions were man-made constructs, while their own beliefs were Absolute Truth. Everyone else was wrong, to varying degrees. Even the term "Christian" – in its truest sense – applied only to them. That others called themselves Christians was mostly a measure of their spiritual blindness.

There were no crosses or crucifixes, no paintings of Jesus, no Catholic idols. Nobody in the Meeting ever wore a cross around his or her neck. The practice of wearing a common means of execution around one's neck is, after all, bizarre, but only if one stops to think about it. A gas-chamber bracelet? Guillotine earrings? (This turns out not to be as far-fetched as I thought it sounded when I wrote it. Some people in France allegedly did wear guillotine earrings during the so-called Reign of Terror during the French Revolution!) A firing-squad belt buckle? An electric-chair tiara? As if the means and tools of execution are somehow laudable.... The Bible says *"By their works ye shall know them"*, not by their jewelry, and that was proof enough.

The Meeting was a state of mind, a way of life, not a building or a Sunday activity. Most Meeting people seemed sincerely to believe that they were constantly endeavoring to do what was Right in the Sight of the Lord, and since they believed they *knew* the Truth, this often led to a profound disinterest in learning anything else about what truth might mean.

The Meeting had no official clergy, no altars, no organs or pianos, no decorations, no taste. People often addressed each other (mercifully in private only) by names like *Brother Wilson* and *Sister Brown*. At most of the Oak Park Meeting's meetings, there were 20-50 people sitting in concentric rectangles around a small central table, with long periods of silence not greatly enlivened by somnambulant singing *(a capella)*, reverent reading, pious praying, or indoctrinating and indoctrinated interpretations of the Word.

There was a sternness about the Oak Park Meeting that was different from the Meetings in Greater LA. It may have been partly due to the lack of a California sun to loosen people up. But I think it was mostly because the Oak Park Meeting was unofficially ruled with a poorly concealed iron hand by my paternal grandfather, John Lockhart Erisman, a cold, humorless man whose few words were Law.

To better understand the impact that the Meeting – my "third parent" – had on my childhood and youth, bear in mind that back in the 1950s and 60s, the Meeting constituted a kind of lunatic fringe in the US; a huge gap existed between them and nearly all the rest of society, for whom religion was much more of a social activity, while faith was a personal, private matter at that time. Mainstream Christians didn't go around declaring that they were "born again". The big impact of the Religious Right would not come until decades later. The first self-proclaimed born-again US President did not appear until the mid-1970s. Only rarely in my day would there be a baseball player who in a half-hidden gesture would cross himself before coming to bat, and then I knew he was a wicked Catholic anyway. Nobody pointed at the sky in the belief that God had somehow helped him hit a home run. I never heard of anybody dropping to his knees in the end zone because God had thrown a key block to enable him to score a touchdown.

Not that the Meeting people did such things either! But we were drenched in the belief that God was interested in, and knew, and kept a record of, every little thing we did, said, or *thought*. By thinking about Him, we sincerely believed we were in fact talking to Him, and that He was listening, and we were expected to endeavor at all times to harken unto His replies, His Plan, His will for us in everything. No plans of ours were stated without the codicil "Lord willing". We always "gave thanks" (said a prayer) before eating anything, whether we were in public or not, and we had Bible verses crashing around inside our heads from morning to night, mindful and continuously reminded that God saw our every move and knew our every thought, day and night.

My multi-layered indoctrination began before I had the slightest awareness of it or of anything else, when I was an infant, with my baptism by Grandpa Larson in the bathtub of our home in Dallas. In my usage of the terms, *indoctrination* means teaching someone that a particular doctrine constitutes the only ideas or beliefs worthy of consideration, and thus does not allow open-mindedness towards the possible merits of any others. I use *brainwashing* to mean a more coercive form of indoctrination, usually involving forcibly eliminating one set of ideas or beliefs in order to supplant them with another. In both cases, an attempt is made to eliminate or severely curtail free thinking, open-mindedness and doubt.

Anyway, the Meeting believed in baptism by immersion, not sprinkling, but didn't seem to have a fixed position on baptism in infancy or at the request of the "baptee" years later. I suppose my parents found the earlier occasion a way of ensuring that I would make the right decision. The Meeting had no clear policy, or doctrine, for or against circumcision either, but as it was common practice in the US at that time for medical reasons, and some Brothers offered doctrinal arguments supporting it, this was done to me, too.

Becoming "saved", or "born again", was supposed to be a specific, life-changing event, and *the* prerequisite in the personal life of anyone calling himself a True Christian. We were all born into Sin, and even the first sign of stubbornness in an infant was evidence of innate wickedness and the power of the Devil already taking hold in the little one's life and soul. Some Meeting parents would literally try to beat this out of their beloved toddlers at the slightest sign of disobedience to incomprehensible commands; my parents were not quite that harsh, but they certainly felt entitled – indeed *commanded* by the Word – to administer corporal punishment of a kind that, if administered to another adult, would have had them up on assault charges.

For children born into Meeting families, when the pressure to believe things one couldn't possibly understand began so early as to be inseparable from learning to walk or commencing the acquisition of one's native language, it was difficult to ascertain any point in time for the actual life-changing salvation. How can one's life change dramatically from what one had already been inculcated with, any deviation from which was met with severe punishment? The only way to satisfy the demands of being born again was to learn, at as early an age as possible, to "confess" some sort of internal wickedness from which one's "acceptance" of the Lord had brought one's little self into the Light.

Since the parents of such children were so urgently predisposed to believe in the salvation of their own loved ones, and then rejoice that this had happened, and greatly relieved that their particular little one would not face the eternal wrath of *I Am That I Am*, they did not normally challenge the child's claim to having been born again. At least not directly. But it allowed parents to take it to the next level, giving them new leverage whenever any disobedience arose, enabling them to go on browbeating (not necessarily involving or limited to the brow) their children in the lifelong struggle against the Evil One.

We generally attended at least five Meeting sessions a week, which I will now describe. I realize that this long and complicated description might seem tedious. Then try also to imagine how utterly and mind-numbingly tedious this indoctrination process was to me as a little boy, over and over, on and on through most of my teenage years.

The first of these weekly sessions was Sunday School, on Sunday mornings. Meeting people collectively referred to themselves as "Saints" (but, again mercifully, never went so far as "*Saint John*" or "*Saint Erisman*"; theoretically, they might have gone for "*Saint Brother John*", but that was perhaps deemed too pretentious, even for them). They usually avoided the term "Sunday", preferring "Lord's Day" instead (but for some reason, it was always "Sunday School", never "Lord's Day School"). Mercy upon mercy, this linguistic drivel was also for internal use only. They had a whole vocabulary of it, with roots in pre-Elizabethan English, echoing the language of the King James Bible. They did not, however, refer to each other with "*thee*" and "*thou*" as the Quakers and a few others did; that form of address was reserved for the Lord – never "*you*" to Him.

For Sunday School, kids were divided into groups by age and gender. I was one of about five or six of the youngest group of boys who went down to one corner of the Meeting Room basement with Matilda Johnson. To me she was an ugly, overbearing, and unpleasant-smelling spinster with blue-tinted gray hair, whose mission in life was to make small boys like me tremble with guilt about how wicked we were. The greatest sin of all, she seemed to think, was being too hard-hearted to admit that we *were* evil sinners, and since it was hard for us to come up with any guilt feelings based on *real* deeds of evil, we were instead left to struggle with guilt due to pride in *not* having done the things we weren't supposed to do and would have had to feel guilty about. It was bewildering. We were all supposedly "saved" already, all our sins had supposedly been "washed away" forever, yet here we were being made to feel like guilty, lowly, hell-bound sinners after all. I didn't know what brimstone was, but I was convinced that it smelled like Matilda Johnson.

After our session in the basement with Matilda, we and the other small groups of pre-teens and teens, as well as the adults, convened in the Meeting Room itself, upstairs. The small kids were asked, one by one, to recite the Bible verse we'd been assigned to memorize the week before. And we were once again reminded of how sinful we were and how short we fell of the Glory of God and how only a loving God could save us from the hell that He had lovingly created for those who failed to recognize how loving He was. And there were more hymns, *a capella*, as always. Since musical instruments weren't specifically mentioned in the Bible as being part of the early Christians' worship, that made musical instruments sufficiently suspicious to bar from the Meeting Room. Many of the Meeting people did, however, have pianos in their homes (they also had cars, eyeglasses, refrigerators, stuff like that, despite the lack of holy Biblical references to such things) for playing hymns and singing His praises.

Later in life I would discover piazzas in Rome with four or more churches, all Catholic, all facing the same square. I would wonder whether people feared that they would start losing their religion during the short walk from one side of the piazza to the other. It was, in any case, that kind of need for pianos in the homes of the Saints.

Technically speaking, there were in fact pianos in a few of the Meeting Rooms;

some local gatherings were so small that they couldn't afford separate premises, so the living room of one of the locals had to serve as the local Meeting Room, and if that living room had a piano in it, it meant that that Meeting Room had a piano in it. But such breaches of protocol could be overlooked, unless the piano in question was played at inappropriate times, like during Meeting meetings. We visited a number of these tiny local gatherings during our family trips around the country. The Meeting published a *List of Gatherings* (strictly confidential and with highly restricted distribution), so that no Meeting person would ever have to spend the Lord's Day without True Christian Fellowship. The smaller gatherings served as a reminder of a frequently quoted Bible verse, that *"where two or three are gathered together in my name, there am I in the midst of them"* (Matthew 18:20). The smaller the gathering, the more it reinforced the notion that we were indeed the "Chosen Few".

After Sunday School in Oak Park, there was just enough time for a leg-stretcher before the "Breaking of Bread", the holiest and most pious of the meetings, starting at 10:30. The small central table was laid with crisp white linen (like on a dining car), on which a loaf of bread about the size of a football (baked by Grandma Erisman the day before) was placed in the upper of two small nesting baskets lined with white linen napkins. Two goblets of red wine also stood on the table, each with a wooden coaster as a lid. The Breaking of Bread began with a few minutes of total silence, to allow an ambience of deepest reverence to build up and prevail.

If there were a visitor present, there would first be an announcement: a letter from the visitor's "home" Meeting would be read aloud by one of the Brothers. The salutation inevitably followed a strict, liturgical formula: *"To the Saints gathered to the name of our Lord Jesus Christ in Oak Park, beloved brethren...,"* followed by a Biblical reminder of our duty to welcome this visitor as one who belonged to the "righteous" faction of the splintered Plymouth Brethren (the letter expressed this somewhat differently). The visitor could then partake of the bread and wine, prayers and hospitality, etc. The visitor was also entitled to speak, provided he had a penis (no body searches were conducted). The letter of introduction was thus a kind of passport – with password protection to keep all deviants from hacking into their bread and wine.

The letter-reading was followed by more silence. Any Brother might then "give out" a hymn, which meant that he would audibly propose that we should all sing a certain hymn from the *"Little Flock"* hymnbook, compiled by none other than John Nelson Darby himself. Since my dad was one of the few local Brothers who both knew the appropriate tunes to all 426 hymns in that book, and could also carry a tune pretty well, he would normally lead the singing – leading with his voice only, and hoping that those gathered would fall in without covering too many of the surrounding keys or too many different tempos and tunes simultaneously, in their often pathetic attempts to "make a joyful noise unto the Lord". (They always got the noise part right, at least.) Sometimes we would all rise to sing these hymns (*"Shall we rise and sing hymn number..."*), sometimes we would remain seated. This probably depended on how lethargic people were becoming as the meeting dragged on. Once in a very great while, if the hymn was running slow or comprised too many verses, the key (or keys) it was being sung in would be overcome by gravity, or the gravity of the situation, and slip down several tones. Dad would then have to come to the rescue by assertively restarting us, belting out the opening notes of the following verse slightly ahead of the rest, and often quickening the pace again as well.

There were occasions when another Brother challenged Dad's unofficial role as *Kapellmeister* and beat him to the draw by starting the hymn instead, startling my dad. On several such occasions, the zeal of the renegade outweighed his talent; the selected tune was an impossible match for the selected hymn, and Dad would have to intervene and restart the hymn after all. After the hymn, there was again silence.

Then one of the Brothers would stand up to pray. There were no assigned duties or roles here, just as there were no assigned seats. But people always played the same roles and sat in the same seats. Any visitor who arrived somewhat early would usually know enough to discretely ask a local which of all the empty seats was "available", and it was never, ever, the seats belonging to Grandpa and Grandma Erisman. It was the same with the giving out of hymns and saying of prayers: no official assignments, no official pecking order, no official liturgy. But you always knew what was coming. The prayers were nominally extemporaneous, but were so full of pre-Elizabethan clichés that they might just as well have been liturgical. Depending on the personality of the person praying, the prayer might be long or short, emotional or somber – or just plain excruciatingly boring. And it was followed by more silence.

Sometimes a prayer could be bizarrely comical, at least to my best friend Norm Denton and me. One of the Brothers who sometimes rose to pray in the Oak Park Meeting was a colorfully drab fellow, about my dad's age, named Richard Evans, a man of no discernible intelligence, wit or comeliness, which he endeavored to compensate for with large dollops of zeal. He was so full of himself when he prayed, that he would literally rock back and forth from his heels to his tiptoes, eyes solemnly and piously closed. Norm and I kept waiting for him to tip over. Brother Evans prayed with a degree of affectation in his voice that might make an amateur poetry reader's diction sound downright conversational. His favorite word was "glory", which he pronounced *"gluddy"*, apparently because he thought it sounded more pious that way in a prayer. He would work it in at least twice in every prayer (*"Oh, the gluddy!"*). By the time we reached our late teens, Norm and I would audibly clear our throats each time the magic word was spoken, then smirk and snigger because our simultaneous throat-clearing *could* have been coincidental (although the sniggering wasn't). In fact, Norm and I compiled a long list of Meeting "buzzwords" (long before that term was widespread). Apart from Richard Evan's *"gluddy"*, most of them were part of the Meeting's anachronistic vocabulary: fain, nigh, lo, e'en, harken, divers, sundry, succor, etc. In our teens, Norm and I were always trying to find some lasses willing to give us succor, but – alas! – to no avail.

It was during this period that I invented my first advertising slogan, albeit for a fictitious product. There is a Meeting-approved hymn, stemming from a Bible text, that goes something like *"But for a moment, only a moment, light our affliction, 'twill soon pass away."* My fictitious product was a brand of extremely short cigarettes I called Affliction, and my slogan was "Light up an Affliction, have a butt for a moment." It was enough to amuse me; being able to play with words was not only great fun, it also helped to keep me sane. I created a cliché-based map that Norm and I wept with laughter about. Unfortunately, my mom discovered and destroyed the only copy, but I do remember there was an Admonition Avenue in there, and you could meet on the corner of Fain and Nigh Streets. Just outside the town there was a place called Oddball Lake, paraphrasing the real Otter Lake, to which the Meeting's unmarried young people (ages 16-25) could be invited for a two-week stint each summer, provided they submitted a piously written request for an invitation. Otter Lake was located deep in the woods somewhere in Ontario, and was run by Gordon Hayhoe, the eldest son of Harry Hayhoe, a patriarch so revered that I suppose my grandpa was grateful he almost never visited the Oak Park Meeting. Harry Hayhoe had a horrible habit, probably due to some form of pulmonary condition, which caused him to aspirate loudly "*Hhhhhhh!!*" at sudden and unpredictable intervals during Meeting sessions, as if he were undergoing spirometry.

But I have strayed from my account of how a Morning Meeting unfolded. After the opening prayer, often followed by several minutes of silence, another Brother would read something from the Bible, usually related to the crucifixion of Jesus, from one of the Gospels. There was no way of knowing exactly what he would read or exactly which Brother would read it – all this was allegedly the workings of the Holy Ghost (who apparently could stomach the singing). If no one made a move fast enough, it would be my grandfather. His power was subtle; he didn't hog the floor. When he had to step in, an almost invisible scowl told the others that someone else should have.

It seemed to me quite clear that crucifixion had been expressly invented for the execution of Jesus, and that no more than two others were ever subjected to that gruesome punishment. Not until many years later did I discover that it was a fairly common form of execution perpetrated by the ancient Persians and adopted centuries later by the lovely Romans and others. Its widespread usage did nothing to make it less horrendous, of course, but I had to admit there was nothing unique about it.

The reading might be followed by another hymn, another prayer, or both (not simultaneously; there were no operatic prayers). And then more silence. At around 11:18, it was time for the actual and literal Breaking of the Bread. One of the Brothers – sometimes my dad, sometimes Uncle Ralph, sometimes my grandfather, sometimes someone else – would rise, leave his seat, and go to the central table, where he would stand and pray a quasi-extemporaneous "this is my body" kind of prayer that was pretty much identical week after week. Then he would pick up the loaf, literally break it in half, and place one half in each basket, broken side up. Two other Brothers would act as ushers, coming forward to receive the baskets and deliver them to the person sitting in the front row of each "half" of the Meeting Room, while the "bread-breaker" would take a temporary seat nearby. As the baskets were being solemnly passed up and down the rows, each member would pinch off a small piece of bread (the size of the pinch covered anything from a large crumb to a hefty wad, as long as it all fit in the mouth in one go) and slowly chew it with bowed head, after having passed the basket to the next Brother or Sister along the row. When the baskets had made the rounds, the ushers would return them to the table and cover them over with the napkins.

Then the "bread-breaker" would again stand at the central table and say another prayer, this time the "this is my blood" version. The ushers would come forward again and the uncovered goblets would make the rounds, with each member taking a sip of the wine – real wine, mind you – the only alcohol any Oak Park Meeting person would ever admit to imbibing. And there was none of that wicked Roman Catholic transubstantiation stuff going on.

Not every attendee got a pinch and a sip. First you had to "take your place at the Lord's Table" (become a member), which you were discouraged from doing before the age of 12, encouraged to do until the age of 14, then increasingly pressured to do thereafter. "Taking your place" meant solemnly approaching one of the senior Brothers and solemnly announcing your solemn wish to undergo that solemn rite of passage. A small group of Brothers would confer on the matter in closed session, interview (or cross-examine) you as to your zeal, and if satisfied, announce your request at a subsequent Morning Meeting. Finally (usually), you would be officially received into the fellowship of the Brethren a few weeks later.

But once there, you could also be "put away from The Lord's table" for having behaved extra sinfully. This was the equivalent of excommunication or ostracization, and it was dramatic (by Meeting standards), as well as awesome and horrifying (from the perspective of a small boy like me). It not only meant that you could not break bread with the others, you were also frozen out socially, and treated like a pariah (although not quite to the extreme extent of official shunning, as practiced by the Amish and others). Since the Meeting was your only real social network (unnecessary contact with "the world", i.e. neighbors, colleagues, classmates, etc, was discouraged), you were out there in the cold, a kind of solitary confinement in plain view. If you wanted back in, you were expected to attend Meeting anyway, but you had to sit at the back and remain silent. You had to plead for forgiveness to various Brothers, and demonstrate your longsuffering piety, contrition and submission. Sometimes you would be invited to a special prayer session, just for you, with a number of key Brothers making you the object of their vocal prayers, and where you were expected to pray aloud too, confessing your sinfulness, showing true repentance and abject humility.

Unmarried couples in their late teens or early 20s were "put away" at the first sign of fornication, which was usually revealed by a bulging abdomen. Even newly married couples whose first babies were born "too soon" were put away. The first in my memory to undergo this were John and Betty Nunnikhoven. John was a friend of my brother John's, which brought it close to home, even though the excommunication didn't take place at the Oak Park Meeting. Another couple I knew, Butch and Stearly Holt, were not officially put away, but were obliged to stand aside for a period of "observation" after having eloped to Idaho. Nobody in the Oak Park Meeting except me and one or two others had a clue that they were even interested in each other, yet suddenly they were off to Idaho and got married. So they were under suspicion of premature pregnancy until time proved otherwise. This happened when I was about 17. Butch and Stearly later bought two of my paintings.

 But I digress again. After the bread and wine had made the rounds, it was time to pass closed wooden collection boxes, which moved fairly swiftly up and down the rows in total silence. Only the youngest members of this Little Flock made audible contributions. A full-fledged adult Brother didn't put mere coins into the box. My dad's contributions were substantial. Contributions inserted into the boxes were not documented in any way, since this would have been a sinfully prideful way of proclaiming to the other Brothers and Sisters how generous one had been. But it was all right to make a mental note of the magnitude of one's own contribution and then go for a tax deduction, despite the ostensible separation of church and state in the Land of the Free. The collection money was used to finance the modest Meeting Rooms, the Laboring Brothers, and the Bible Conferences.

 In one respect, the Meeting was a refreshing departure from the practices of the few other religions I would ever experience directly. The Meeting didn't harp about money. They didn't require tithing. They did all kinds of things to ensure a high level of guilt feelings in all other areas of life, but making monetary contributions wasn't one of them. Collections were taken at Morning Meetings only, on Sundays. There might possibly be an announcement about a major upcoming expenditure, for a Conference, urgent support for a Laboring Brother, etc, but no admonitions to *"Dig deep into your pockets! Give till it hurts!"* That might have been understood, but was never spoken.

 After the collection, more silence. Maybe a little more Bible reading. Another hymn or two. A prayer. And it was over. After Morning Meeting, people would mill about for a while, gossiping (they didn't call it that, but information about everyone's private lives spread instantly), and deciding who was going to be invited to whose house for Sunday dinner. My parents were probably the most socially generous of anyone at the Oak Park Meeting. We seldom had a Sunday dinner at home on our own, and often had five or six guests, which was the full capacity of our small dining room.

The meetings were the entire fabric of social interdependency. People in most other Christian religions are like cows in a pasture: often eating, chewing the cud, and lying down at the same times, often facing in the same direction, but technically independent of each other. The Meeting people were more like bees in a beehive, or ants in an anthill – tantamount to a single organism. Outside the Meeting, you had nothing, a "wilderness wide". The whole worldview of the Meeting was that "we are *in* the world, but we are not *of* the world", we are strangers just passing through on our way to heaven, and should definitely *not* be "laying up treasures for ourselves here below" in the form of worldly goods, but focusing on our heavenly rewards.

The fact of the matter was, however, that most of the Meeting people I ever knew or knew of lived materially comfortable lives. Self-denial could only be construed when comparing with the very wealthy, who would never get their camels through a needle's eye anyway. Giving to the poor was pretty much limited to their *own* poor, and since few of their own were poor, the definition might be stretched to the African and South American objects of the efforts of the relevant Laboring Brothers, from whom alms came with plenty of strings attached.

The third of the regularly scheduled Meeting meetings each week was also on Sunday, this one in the evening. It was called Gospel Meeting, from 7:30 until 8:30 or sometimes, if the speaker was long-winded or exceptionally zealous, until nearly nine. It was often – except during harsh winter weather – preceded by "street preaching" on the corner of Austin and Madison, on the Chicago side (perhaps they couldn't get a permit to shout at passers-by on the Oak Park side), on the bustling northeast corner of this intersection, where there was a bus transfer point that brought more passers-by than most other intersections around. At this corner, about an hour before Gospel Meeting, a few of the Brothers (no Sisters) would gather, and several Meeting kids were conscripted to pass out Gospel tracts to whomever might accept one. Then one of the Brothers would open his Bible and start roaring earnestly at whomever would listen or was obliged to hear, informing them that they were on their way to hell and other friendly, comforting, loving messages like that.

I used to take my required handful of tracts and set off, seeking to stay close enough to the corner so Dad wouldn't think I was shirking my duty, yet far enough away so that if anybody I happened to recognize from school came by, I could quickly hide my fistful of tracts and not be immediately associated with the ranting going on at the nearby corner. This usually put me in a zone about 30 paces from the corner, where I would do my best to evade and endure. Technology eventually added a battery-powered bullhorn to this scene, but fortunately not before the tail end of my days in Oak Park, by which time I had become a distinct liability for the Meeting as a tract-passer-outer.

Hardly anybody ever seemed to stop and listen to this street-corner ranting (Norm and I used to call it "street screeching"), but we're talking about 1955-63, before religious browbeating became commonplace in my fatherland. The ideal scenario was that if a passer-by stopped, one of the "spare" Brothers would move in and talk to this stranger privately, so that the current ranter could continue bringing the loving words of hell to additional passers-by. Of the few rantees who ever stopped, I can only remember one or two who subsequently agreed to come along to the Gospel Meeting. When that happened – or when, on equally rare occasions, a pedestrian on Harrison Street had the gall to take the *Welcome* sign literally – it created quite a stir of what seemed like discomfort among the Meeting folks. It's definitely inhibiting to evangelize when you're so convinced that you're a Little Flock, part of the Chosen Few, just the *"two or three gathered together in my name."*

So outsiders were welcomed, but more with open Bibles than open arms. Furtive, suspicious, or condescending glances were cast from every direction. Sometimes the outsider satisfied his curiosity long before the presidential-strength Gospel message was fully developed, and he or she would leave prematurely. The undercurrent of a sigh would be felt (not heard) throughout the Meeting Room, not so much of disappointment as of relief, but relief that knows it *should* have been disappointment, and so, in order to compensate, the undertone of a sneer would also be felt: a hardened sinner had left the room; Satan obviously felt too uncomfortable here, and what else could anyone expect? I've met few people as proud of their humility as these Saints.

In spite of the rare presence of outsiders in attendance, the Gospel Meetings were held in exactly the same way, which meant they were held for exactly the same audiences as all the other Meeting meetings, which meant that everybody there was already supposedly "saved". Yet no Gospel Meeting worthy of the name could exclude the threat of the Lake of Fire, the gnashing of teeth forever, and the earnest calls to be in time. Being in time was a double-edged sword. You could be "too late" by dying before you repented and turned to the Lord. But you could also be too late if "the Rapture" came, and that could come *at any moment*. The only escape from God's wrath was to confess your sins and wicked ways.

How could anybody in that company ever hope to get away with anything wicked, with all the Brethren ready to pounce at the first sign of worldliness? Yet how was anyone supposed to turn to the Lord if they had already turned to Him? It could only mean that some hadn't *really* turned. Who might that be? *Might it be me?*

Neurosis and paranoia were built into that equation. Everyone had their "sure and certain hope" of redemption; everyone was snugly and smugly nestled in among the Chosen Few. But the slightest deviation from the unwritten bylaws, Grandpa Erisman version, immediately cast doubt on whether you *really* were one of them after all. They believed in Eternal Security – once you were saved, you were saved forever, and could not become "unsaved", unless you committed the Sin against the Holy Ghost, which nobody really knew what it was, so you could never be sure you hadn't committed it. But if you strayed from the True Path of Righteousness, the question immediately arose as to whether you had ever *really* been on it, and whether your Salvation was just a sham. So you sat through Gospel Meetings with fearful eyes, heart pounding, wondering, *Am I really saved?*

Eternal *in*security was for the kids. It bites at your soul, your heart, your mind, eats away at your character and leaves you desperate, the flames of hell lashing at your heels, the eternal agony rushing towards you. The only way out is to be sure, to "know" that what you've been told to believe is the Only Truth, and the only way to "know" that is to keep switching off all the little questions that arise, until they stop arising. By the time you're well into adulthood, raising your own family, you've invested too much of your life and your mind and your emotions and your being into the Way you were once compelled to choose, so that you can no longer allow yourself to call it anything but the True Way, and the little questions stop coming, and all doubt and the will to question has been gnawed away. It has become your sacred duty to participate heart and soul in pushing it onto and into the next generation; you're one of the Chosen Few.

Or the chosen not-so-few. The Meeting could never have remained as small as it did in the face of a burgeoning surrounding population, if many of its younger members had not decided to leave it, especially during the 60s and 70s, for something they could regard as less fundamentalist, less lunatic fringe. But most of those who left the Meeting, to my knowledge, did not stray far, relatively speaking. The basic "knowing" that one is right, possessing the "Truth", and the flat refusal to truly question first premises almost always remained intact.

The grounds for a literal, fundamentalist interpretation, however, were eroding all around the Faithful. Many young educated types were becoming hard-pressed and even embarrassed to cling to that, but new religious waves were making it acceptable to be less rigid. Some left for a new and essentially parallel path that allowed some "cool" stuff (like dancing and drinking wine), but Eternal Security still absolutely had to be part of the deal. Even the old fundamentalism required considerable cherry-picking to arrive at a functional doctrine. The new, less-fundamentalist evangelicalism was different: different cherries, but still all carefully picked from the same basket.

The Oak Park Meeting Room shaped so much of my childhood that it behooves me to convey some idea of what the physical premises looked like. The building the Meeting occupied for nearly all my time in Oak Park didn't exist when we arrived in early 1951, so for the first year or so, our meetings were held somewhere on California Avenue in Chicago, but I have no clear memory of what that place looked like.

The new Meeting Room at 237 Harrison Street in southern Oak Park was half of a brand-new building also comprising number 239. The building was set back from Harrison Street by the width of the sidewalk. It was built by Bruce Goodman, who also built our home. I don't know why he got the honors, but I suppose his surname name wasn't a disadvantage. My dad was a practical enough man to have done his homework, so presumably Bruce-built buildings had a solid reputation and a solid, well-engineered foundation. (I would later find it strange that Dad required evidence regarding whom to trust to build his buildings, his cars, his appliances, but not the beliefs that would steer his life.)

The Harrison Street location also put it within walking distance of my grandparents' home, certainly no coincidence. The other half of the building occupied by the Meeting Room was the headquarters of the Bible Truth Publishers (BTP), owned and operated by the Meeting. The BTP published and sold gospel tracts, supplied Bibles, as well the spiritual writings of John Nelson Darby and his patriarchal cohorts and successors who, in proud abasement of their splendidly lowly selves, tended to publish their thoughts and ministries under their initials only: JND, CHB, CHM, etc.

The aesthetically disastrous, flat-roofed, one-storey building was clad in off-white stone at the base, massive storefront windows, and red brick cladding above them. The window of the Meeting half was mostly covered by a slightly translucent off-white curtain that kept out peering eyes. In one corner of the window was a small sign with the word *Welcome*, a Bible text, and the times of the Gospel Meetings and Reading Meetings. The other meeting times were not announced – and were tacitly not included in the welcome (or perhaps even less so).

I never saw a black person at the Meeting; non-whites were represented in Oak Park by one Japanese family, the Hoshinos, who only came on Sunday mornings. But there was no overt discrimination; nobody would ever have admitted to any racial prejudice. We even read *Uncle Tom's Cabin* at home, which was our proof that we knew that black people *could* be True Christians and beloved of the God who has His special mysterious ways of showing it, just as the Meeting people had their special and mysterious ways of showing their vague distrust of blacks: a shudder here, a subtly sarcastic lilt there, a raised eyebrow or scowl whenever a black person was seen or mentioned; that was all it took. After all, slavery was clearly and repeatedly condoned in the Bible, however embarrassing it had since become (not one of those cherries most Believers like to pick any longer). After all, weren't black people the sons of Ham, who uncovered his father Noah's nakedness and was forever cursed, along with his progeny (which is what we were taught)? Or maybe blacks were just too smart to go to Meeting.

The interior of the Meeting Room, our cathedral and basilica, our temple, mosque, tabernacle, chapel and sanctuary, was about as drab as a customs building in a small coastal town in Poland in the early 1970s. The room was about 24 x 36 feet. The ceiling was flat, dull white, about 10 feet high, and punctuated with fluorescent light fixtures that provided ample but harsh lighting. The floor was covered with light gray linoleum tile squares, offset with occasional squares of charcoal gray. The walls were a pale grayish-green. On the walls there were a few framed Bible verses in a pseudo-gothic font, and a large round clock on the wall opposite Grandpa Erisman's seat, where he could keep an eye on it.

The high-backed seats, made of some sort of dark-brown molded plywood, considerably older than the building, came from a waiting room or auditorium (*could they – shudder – have come from a movie theater?!*), that someone from the Meeting got cheap. They were bolted together in rows of six, and arranged in rectangles around the central table – except for Gospel Meetings, when some were moved so that all would face in the same direction. The little table became the closest thing we had to a pulpit for the speaker. They never used terms like *pulpit* and *pew* for their own furniture, since those terms signified religion, and the Meeting people did not see their faith as a religion. Seriously. Other people's faiths were religions, but the Meeting was Truth. Religion and Truth were seen as polar opposites. You get to do things like that with language when you're the Chosen Few.

Many people outside the Meeting referred to it as a sect or cult, so it might be useful to define terms. A *religion* is defined in the English language as an organization or institution of beliefs and ceremonies based on belief in one or more gods. A *sect* is the same as a religion, but has fewer followers – few enough to be called a sect (usually condescendingly) by the established religions. A *cult* is an institution of beliefs with very few followers; religions *and* sects seem to find cults whacky and scary. Then there are *myths* – tales no longer held to be true and gods no longer worshiped – though myths often retain great value as parables and symbols.

Although the Meeting didn't officially practice shunning (they seldom used that particular word to describe similar behavior), it was there in many forms and to many degrees. Within their own group, a Brother could be "silenced" – forbidden to speak during any of the sessions – for various reasons, such as doctrinal error, inappropriate behavior or other unmentionable and mysterious offenses. (The Sisters were automatically silenced for failing to have penises.) I only observed one instance of silencing, however. It was Mr Soonyay (spelling?), a poor slob in his late 50s, with a constant look of great and unctuous pain on his face, a slightly stooped posture, and slicked-back black hair, who showed up for Morning Meeting about one Sunday a month for several years. I always wondered why he did, and perhaps he eventually got around to asking himself that same question, because he stopped showing up.

Towards outsiders, shunning was a matter of degrees, loosely based on the seven churches of Revelation, chapters 2 and 3. We, the Meeting, were, of course, Philadelphia: *"...thou hast a little strength, and hast kept my word, and hast not denied my name."* Assessments of the others varied from "room for improvement" to "utter wickedness".

Many individual Lutherans, Baptists and Presbyterians might be considered to be True Christians, albeit not fully aligned with The Word, and on some points sorely misguided. Such individuals were generally treated with reserved kindness, probably more condescendingly than either party quite realized. However, none of these religions was perceived as fully on the True Christian Path, in the Meeting's exclusive sense of the term. But our neighbor lady, Mrs Burtness, was a Lutheran who, my mom was convinced, was truly saved, a "real" Christian, with whom she could quote Bible verses and talk glowingly about Him. She was, in any case, a nice matronly lady, while Mr Burtness was a retired railroad bigshot, a somewhat gruff, pot-bellied tycoon in whom I would later see a likeness to Edward G. Robinson minus the cigar, and who seemed less than enthusiastic about discussing spiritual matters with my parents, so there was some considerable doubt about where he would spend eternity. Social congress was limited to Mom and Mrs Burtness occasionally having cups of coffee together.

The Burtnesses were of Norwegian ancestry (their name was most likely Americanized from *Bjørknes*). They practiced a form of Lutheranism that was the official religion in the Scandinavian countries. My mom's own ancestors had been members of the Swedish Mission Church (aka the Swedish Covenant Church), a breakaway branch of mainstream Lutheranism that retained its separate identity on settling in America. It was much closer to the Truth, of course, but not close enough, so my Grandpa Larson pulled up his family's roots and replanted them in the Meeting in Des Moines, Iowa, when my mom was about four. Apparently his mother-in-law was heartbroken by this, and his wife Sarah (my grandma) refused to follow him into the Meeting until after her own mother died in 1919, when my grandma was 32. (Sarah died the year before I was born.)

Congregationalists, Episcopalians and other such non-fundamentalist, non-evangelical Protestant denominations were deemed lukewarm, neither hot nor cold, about whom God says *"I will spue thee out of my mouth"* (Revelation 3:16). There was a distinct coldness in the extremely limited social relations one might be obliged to have with such people. In fact, one of the favorite Bible verses of the Meeting people was the injunction *"Be ye not unequally yoked together with unbelievers"* (II Corinthians 6:14), defined in the broadest possible way – essentially everyone else in the human race.

The Roman Catholic Church held a special place in the Meeting's spectrum of abhorrence. As an institution, it was the Whore of Babylon, the Beast, the Great Abomination, almost as wicked as you can get, what with the Spanish Inquisition as depicted in Foxe's *Book of Martyrs* with its morbidly fascinating and horrific drawings of the torturing of True Christians who had turned from the evils of Catholicism. We had the book at home, in the same bookcase as the *Compton's Encyclopedia*. We *knew* Catholic monasteries and convents to be virtual prisons. Gullible young Catholics, having once entered their walls, were doomed forever, and few could escape. Nuns always went about in pairs, we were told, so they could prevent each other from escaping the clutches of their evil Church. Their Douay Bible was not the real King James Bible; it had added Books to its canon, and thus perverted the Word. As individuals, it was acknowledged that there nevertheless could be a *few* True Christians among them, albeit extremely misguided or oppressed. Johnny, my best neighbor friend for a couple of years, was being raised in a Catholic home, but our parents never met socially (if at all). I don't think they ever had a conversation, apart from our mothers' occasional phone calls to learn of our whereabouts or to inform the appropriate party that it was time to come home.

The Mormons, Jehovah's Witnesses, Unitarians and Christian Scientists were among those who were even worse than the Catholics. Whenever my parents spoke of those religions, it was with a palpable shudder, like the personification of Evil had cast its shadow over them. They had perverted the Word far more than the Catholics, and they were in the fast lane on the freeway to hell. Back in those days, the world had not yet been introduced to the brilliant plan of a mediocre science-fiction writer to capitalize on his fantasies by creating an extremely lucrative religion out of nothing; otherwise Scientology would certainly been on that list.

The Jews had a place in this pantheon that was special in every way. Jesus was a Jew, or at least half Jewish if God Himself was his father (kind of hard to imagine Jehovah being circumcised) and got Mary pregnant out of wedlock. But the Bible doesn't say that God was Jewish. It does say that Jesus was not Joseph's offspring, yet it's *Joseph's* lineage – *not* Mary's – that Matthew and Luke traced forwards and backwards, through King David and all the way to another Son of God, Adam. (You get to play around with genealogy and facts and stuff like that when you're religious, even if you don't call your religion a religion.) Anyway, the indelible bad marks for Jews stem less from their insistence on Jesus' crucifixion and more from their rejection as Jesus as the Son of God.

The series of Old Testament prophets who played key roles in the mysterious prophesies – ones that the Meeting's mystical experts would weave magical stories around – were also Jews. Everything about the rebirth of the modern state of Israel was prophesied in the Word, we were told; the Jews were *needed* to fulfill the prophecies; indeed, they were blessed by having God's special attention. They were God's Chosen People, but were cursed because they had denied their Savior. And now *we* were God's Chosen Few. So there.

In my elementary school in Oak Park, close to a third of my classmates were Jewish. As far as I can remember, it was not until the mid-1950s, when I was in the middle grades, that a few of their traditions – Bar Mitzvah and Hanukkah – began to come to the attention of us gentiles. It was never an issue for anyone, as I recall. I think we assumed that Hanukkah was a recent invention to give Jewish kids an excuse to get presents when the others were getting Christmas presents. I was the only one getting "holiday presents", although I told my classmates that they were Christmas presents – ah, the importance of branding!

We hardly ever spoke of non-Judeo-Christian-based religions. The most important thing was that God had created all these people, and yet only the Chosen Few were going to be spared eternal agony – and *we were among those chosen few! O happy day!* Since God knew the past and the future, He knew that He was going to doom nearly everyone but us, which made us so incredibly special. (As kids, we didn't learn a lot about empathy, justice and psychosis.)

Islam, Buddhism, Hinduism and many others had no role that I was aware of in American society in the 1950s and I knew nothing about them other than that they were totally wrong. Perhaps it was because they were still too unknown and irrelevant in America. When they were mentioned at all, their followers were dismissed as backward heathens and pagans, to be preached at if we ever came in contact with them, which we never did, then shunned completely if they refused our particular brand of Salvation.

All actual contacts with such barbaric peoples were left entirely to the little clique of Laboring Brothers. This select group was the *crème de la crème* – missionaries, Meeting-style. When any of these fellows came to town out of

Africa or South America, there would be a Special Meeting (in addition to the regular five sessions per week) in honor of their missionary positions, sometimes even an All-Day Meeting, if we knew of their arrival well enough in advance to arrange it. These men had clout, even more than my grandpa. They would usually get to sit in the same row as he did. And they carried more than just a Bible: they had Bible *bags*!

A Bible bag was a small leather satchel, about a third of the size of a briefcase, kind of like those traditional construction workers' lunch boxes, only in black leather, preferably well worn. It usually contained at least one Bible, a *Little Flock* hymnbook, an *Echoes of Grace* hymnbook, a *Cruden's Concordance*, and a volume or two with initials on it. As a kid, it gave me the sense that it might also contain other Mysteries that were not for me to know. (Harry Hayhoe had a Bible bag.) The *Cruden's Concordance*, by the way, was an amazing tool, the original search engine (and has remained so throughout my life. My parents gave me one when I was in my teens, perhaps not realizing that it would become invaluable to me after my childhood, as a way of quickly finding what the Bible actually said when my brothers challenged me on topics of faith). You could look up practically any word or name used in the Bible and find every reference to it: book, chapter and verse.

The Laboring Brothers were the Meeting's only "employees" (apart from the employees of the Bible Truth Publishers), but were by no means "clergy". They had no official training or investiture. Nor did they have a regular salary, but relied solely on donations from the collections that were taken up each Sunday, i.e. Lord's Day. When they weren't saving the souls of Incas in the Andes or savages in the Congo, they would make the rounds of the various gatherings in North America, full of sound and fury, rustling up cash to finance their next foray.

Preaching at a Gospel Meeting to the same Chosen Few was ultimately pretty futile in terms of saving more souls. But the Laboring Brothers were out there, in the midst of heathendom, in the Latin American strongholds of Catholicism and the demon worship of Africa, preaching to people who'd never heard The Word before, at least not Meeting style. This was one of the reasons the Laboring Brothers commanded special respect: they actually went around saving souls, or so they claimed. Strangely, not one of the newly redeemed Incas or Congolese ever turned up on the doorstep of any American Meeting Room I've ever heard about.

But I was describing the Oak Park Meeting Room. On entering from Harrison Street – which we seldom did (we parked in the parking lot behind the Meeting Room and entered through the back door) – there was a large plywood partition, stained dark brown like the seats. The partition screened off any direct overview of the premises from anyone in the doorway who may have entered the building inadvertently or unadvisedly. I always suspected that this partition had the additional function of screening Uncle Ralph from view when he rounded it to bring back the goblet of wine to the table during the Breaking of Bread; there was often, in my already corrupted perception, a longer-than-expected lapse between the time he disappeared on one side and emerged on the other. Having an extra swallow? Probably just my wicked imagination, my fantasy finding some source of amusement amidst the insufferable boredom.

Anyway, the street side of this screen also served as a bulletin board. In the left-hand corner of the room, parallel with the front wall, was a bookcase for hymnbooks and a coat rack for use by those who came in the front door. In the rear, left-hand corner of the Meeting Room there was a stairway. In the rear, right-hand corner of the upstairs was a partition that served both as a coat rack for use by those who came in by the back door, and as a screen for the entrance to the small men's room. (Architecturally, the Bible Truth Publishers' half of the building was essentially a mirror image of the Meeting Room half, so there was another restroom there, for the Sisters, sharing a common firewall with the Brothers' at the back of the Meeting Room.)

The two long walls had no windows at all. But the right-hand wall as seen from the street entrance – the one shared with the BTP – had a door in the rear corner leading directly into the BTP from the Meeting Room. The back wall of the Meeting Room had a couple of bedroom-size windows facing the parking lot.

The basement had several functions. It wasn't divided by a wall, but the half of the basement that was beneath the BTP consisted of the stockroom: rows of metal erector-set-style bookshelves. It was always dark and dusty and sometimes the younger kids would play hide and seek there when it was Tea Meeting Sunday – an extra (6th) meeting that was thrown in about once every month or two, so that on those Sundays we had the privilege of spending the entire day and evening at the Meeting Room. The half of the basement under the Meeting Room consisted largely of tables that were used for sorting the BTP's wares, but also served as dinner tables on Tea Meeting Sundays, or for the occasional wedding dinner, if two became one there, and didn't have a baby that was born too soon.

I can't remember more than three or four weddings there in the 13 or so years I attended the Oak Park Meeting, starting with Norm's big sister's wedding in the newly (or almost) finished Meeting Room when I was about seven. This was partly due to the lack of eligible brides and grooms at this local Gathering. Some of those from Oak Park who did get married during this time (including my brothers) chose to have their weddings elsewhere. The basement, with its naked rafters, concrete walls and gray painted concrete floor, bare light bulbs, musty odor, cobwebs and dustballs, was not always the venue sought by romantic young people for their wedding party, wilderness wide or no wilderness wide. And since the Meeting had no clergy, nobody was authorized to perform a legally binding marriage ceremony, so a Justice of the Peace had to be called in anyway. There were no Brothers who were Justices of the Peace, which meant that the Meeting Room, in spite of not looking anything like a church, and consciously made to look conspicuously *un*adorned in every way, was nevertheless in some way sullied by the presence of this outsider, this Justice of the Peace, who spoke at what was, after all, a meeting of sorts, and yet he wasn't "gathered" and had no letter of reference from the Saints at city hall, since there were none there, but were all most likely on the broad road to destruction and hellfire. So I think most people at the Oak Park Meeting were kind of relieved when their younger generation managed to do their marrying elsewhere, like at some other Meeting Room or in somebody's back yard or living room.

The basement also had small, open-plan kitchen facilities at the parking lot end of the building, with a big fridge, a gas stove, and some cupboards for dishes. This was where the gallon jug of Mogen David Ruby Red was carefully stored. At a pace of one tiny sip per person per week (on average, Uncle Ralph notwithstanding), the long-since-opened jug would last long enough to be capable of doing serious damage to anyone's notion that wine could be sipped for pleasure.

Also connecting the basement with the upstairs was a dumb waiter that was used to transfer boxes and cartons between the BTP and its basement storage room. It was operated by ropes and pulleys, and was large enough for one of us boys to take a short, exciting, eerie ride down into the darkness, while another pulled on the ropes from upstairs. It used to make Clem Dear furious. Clem ran the BTP and lived right next door to it. His house was set towards the back of his lot, farthest from Harrison Street, in line with the Meeting Room parking lot.

The basement had one other function. It was where Brothers' Meetings were held. I never attended these (although I did pick up numerous snippets of information from Dad's insufficiently hushed comments to Mom over the years), since they were limited to those who had "taken their place", but even boys in their early teens who had taken their place were not expected to attend. Females were, of course, banned. The regular Brothers' Meetings were normally short, consisting of 15 minutes or so of earnest prayer right before a Gospel Meeting. They probably also served to identify any potential unsaved or straying targets among those gathered (the Meeting never used words like parishioners, congregation, or devotees) upstairs. When Gospel Meeting was about to start, the Brothers would solemnly file up the stairs and join everyone else already seated and speaking in muffled whispers, or staring piously at something.

So much for the basement. The BTP itself (upstairs) had a number of tables along the front for displaying featured books and Bible-verse-adorned paraphernalia such as key chains, plaques, coin purses and bookmarks, as well as some even kitschier stuff like little loaves of bread in brightly colored cast aluminum, filled with little cards with Bible verses for passing around at dinner tables for everyone to read from. And of course there were racks for tracts and pamphlets of approved messaging. These tables could, with a different business plan, have served well for mounds of second-hand T-shirts, or bric-a-brac in the best flea market style. Farther in from the tables were several rows of bookcases containing volumes of the more advanced doctrinal material, and the advanced tomes whose authors were well known, but who displayed their initials only.

Beyond the shelves was an open office area with several desks where orders were taken, invoiced, paid and sent, as well as a large table where material from the basement was sorted. At this table Clem Dear ran the Sunday School for the boys who had grown too old for Matilda Johnson, i.e. had become pubertal but had not yet necessarily "taken their places".

Behind the Meeting Room was the parking lot, with space for around ten gas-guzzlers, a catalpa tree, and the BTP warehouse that also included Clem Dear's garage. Although Oak Park, Illinois is mostly flat as a pancake, there are a few slight level differences. One of these was between the parking lot and the Meeting Room, a difference of around a foot. About a yard out from the wall of the Meeting Room there was therefore a kind of curb, and a one-foot-high step down to the level of the door. At the far end of the blacktop-covered parking lot was the alley. On one side was an ivy-covered brick wall and on the other was Clem Dear's house, which was directly adjacent to the parking lot. His front yard was bordered on one long-side by the wall of the BTP, also ivy-covered. Meeting people used Clem's front sidewalk to go between the front (Harrison Street) and back of the building, for example when mothers sitting at the back with crying babies had to get out to the front and didn't want to cross the Meeting Room indoors. Clem's two-storey house was clad with tarpaper shingles embossed to look like brick if you didn't look too closely or in daylight. Clem was married to Olga, the aunt of my brother John's future wife.

My brother Al scared the shit out of me in this parking lot. He was about 17 or 18 at the time, and still fairly new at driving. Ralph Buchanan was up from Lawrenceville on his huge Harley-Davidson. Ralph impressed me as being an even huger young farmer with a barrel chest, short strawberry blond hair above a round freckled face, and a slight, tight-lipped, perpetual trace of a smile. The Buchanan's were in some way distantly related to the eponymous US President. They were hard-working, god-fearing farmers who, together with a few neighbors and locals, had started their own Meeting-accredited Gathering of the Saints, down in Lawrenceville, in southeastern Illinois, close to the Indiana border. There was no way anyone was going to doubt their faith.

Anyway, Ralph offered my non-huge, non-barrel-chested brother to take the Harley for a short spin around the block between meetings, so Al climbed aboard, his outstretched toes straining to balance the big machine. Ralph started it for him, and showed him where the gas and the brakes were. Al took off with a bigger roar than he or I expected, but his speed didn't match the roar, so as he rounded the turn from the parking lot to the alley, leaning far too much for his low speed, the whole machine came sliding down over him, pinning his leg beneath it. Worse, the gas tank cap came loose, and gasoline was pulsing out in small splashes onto Al's trapped leg. I was frozen in horror, watching from across the parking lot. Fortunately, Ralph was not frozen, and immediately hurried to the rescue, lifted the machine by the handlebar with one hand, switched it off, and quickly led it a few paces away, so as to separate my gasoline-drenched brother from any more gasoline or possible sources of ignition from the engine. I was about 13 at the time; my lust for motorcycle-riding was nipped in the bud.

In this same parking lot, Norm and I used to "ride" Mr Petrequin's big Packard. The car was equipped with torsion-bar suspension, a kind of hydraulic mechanism to compensate for big loads in the trunk (or removal of them) by raising (or lowering) the back end. It worked even when the engine was off.

When the car was parked in the Meeting Room parking lot, we would jump on the back, wait for the torsion bar to kick in and level out the car again, then run around to the front and repeat the procedure, only this time it would be a double ride – a double compensation. We made the most of our opportunities to get a few kicks.

The Petrequin's were an unusual couple, contemporaries of my grandpa. Maurice was of French extraction, so he pronounced his first name More-*eece*, unlike my dad, who pronounced his identically spelled name *More*-iss. He was about the hugest man I've ever met, and definitely had the hugest hands. Whenever I shook hands with him, my hand felt totally *engulfed* in his thick, gargantuan, extremely soft palm and thick fingers. He was about 6'8", not fat, but with a thick frame, thick lips, thick everything, including his glasses. He had only one non-glass eye and tended to use the center line in the street as a guide for steering his thick Packard, like a pilot landing a thick plane. His voice was thick too – at once booming and soft. His wife Pearl was of an equally astonishing size, but in the opposite direction, seemingly only about a quarter of Maurice's body mass. There was no way anyone would guess she was nearby if she were standing behind him.

My small group of peers at the Meeting, in addition to Norm, comprised Norm's cousin Dave Henderson (like Norm, a year younger than me) and my double cousin Howard (17 days younger than me). I used to enjoy stumping my classmates with a riddle: I have 16 cousins on my mom's side and 3 on my dad's side, making a total of 16. Few could figure out that my dad's brother Ralph married my mom's sister Maxine, giving me three double cousins to whom I am as genetically related as half-siblings. Dave and Howie also lived in Oak Park, while Norm lived in Elmwood Park, which shares only an intersection with Oak Park, namely the corner of North and Harlem avenues.

Back to the Meeting. I was describing the Sunday evening Gospel Meetings, the third of the five regularly scheduled Meeting meetings we went to every single goddamn week. (Sorry, I'm getting a bit ahead of myself....) Gospel Meetings were the only ones of these five that had a "preacher" – one individual who ran the show, gave out the hymns, did the praying and did all the other talking. The speaker would sometimes be asked in advance to speak, or would sometimes volunteer. This gave an opportunity for an up-and-coming younger Brother to take it to the next level and strut his stuff. Once in a while, when no speaker had been asked and the Holy Ghost didn't call upon any new Brother, one of the more experienced Brothers would be obliged to fill in on short notice. This was no problem, however, since nearly everything they said consisted of the clichés they'd been practicing at least five times a week for their entire lives.

There was another exceptional feature of Gospel Meetings, besides the rows of seats all facing the front: we didn't use the *Little Flock* hymnbook, but the *Echoes of Grace* instead. The *Little Flock* was almost always bound in black leather and was only about 3 x 5" in its standard form. It contained no musical notes. The *Echoes of Grace* was larger, about 6 x 8", with a red hardcover, and it contained notes as well. It was used exclusively for Gospel Meetings (*a capella*) and young people's Hymn Sings (piano accompaniment permitted!). The *Echoes of Grace* was considered somewhat more modern and not sufficiently solemn to use for the Breaking of Bread. I would discover later that a number of the tunes had been usurped from previously existing songs – including some from old English drinking songs (e.g. *How Dry I Am*).

Many of the hymns used by the Meeting are also used by most other Christian religions, and let it be said that I have come to find some of the melodies absolutely beautiful. Much later in life I would learn to enjoy operatic music, particularly Mozart's, before I had a clue what the usually ridiculous librettos were about, by which time my appreciation of the music had already inoculated me against adverse reactions to the silliness of the text. With the hymns, it would be the opposite: I would have to overcome my aversion to the texts in order to learn to appreciate the music. Handel's *Messiah* and Bach's *Mass in B minor* were a big help in this. When I discovered that one of the Meeting's melodies had been lifted from the chorus in Sibelius' *Finlandia* – a totally secular piece, beautiful enough to turn anyone into a raving patriot for that Nordic nation, I was able to stop simply salivating and decide for myself whether I enjoyed the music or the text of a piece, or both, or neither.

The fourth regularly scheduled meeting was Reading Meeting, on Tuesday evenings from 7:30 to about 9. The procedure was more or less identical to the Breaking of Bread, but with the bread-breaking replaced by the reading of a chapter from the Bible, followed by a somewhat timid discussion, which tended to be dominated by my grandpa informing the rest of us what it meant, with the support of the writings of JND et al. They would normally pick a particular book of the Bible and discuss one chapter a week. The one time they picked

Psalms, it took about three years to get through. They never picked the *Song of Salomon*. But I was excited when they had *Revelation*, my first taste of science fiction, with all the beasts and mighty vengeance of the Lord and bloodthirsty horsemen and massive slaughters and all those other righteous and holy ways of their merciful and loving god. If I'd had any exposure at all to information about drugs, particularly hallucinogenic ones, I would probably have wondered what its alleged author John was smoking when he wrote his revelatory reveling in mayhem.

On Thursday evenings it was Prayer Meeting, which was like Reading Meeting in terms of the opening and closing hymns from the *Little Flock*, but between them, everybody got down on their knees on the cool, hard linoleum floor, and various Brothers took turns praying aloud. Since the seat backs were high and slightly backward-leaning, and the rows were close together, the arrangement in concentric rectangles around the central table meant that the people on their knees were facing four different directions, all away from the central table. (The elderly were allowed to remain seated for the sake of their knees, when cushions no longer sufficed.) You couldn't see anyone but the few in your own row, or partial glimpses between the seatbacks, but of course everyone knew whose voice it was.

They could go on and on. Each prayer might last from one to 10 minutes, depending on the verbosity and fervor of the Brother in question; then there would be silence until another Brother felt moved by the Holy Spirit to start droning, usually saying basically the same things as the previous prayer, all in quasi-pre-Elizabethan, thee-and-thou King James English. (I had a comparatively easy time with Shakespeare in my later school years!)

Prayer Meeting had the lowest attendance. Sometimes only 10-15 people would show up, partly owing to the fact that the Oak Park Meeting served as a substantial catch basin; it was the nearest Gathering for people living up to 100 miles away (depending on the direction and Lake Michigan), like the Keislings from Milwaukee. There seemed to me to be an unspoken view, in our family at least, that people who chose to live that far away were not entirely harkening unto God's Plan for them. Prayer Meetings were the first meetings I would be allowed to skip "due to homework".

But the five regularly scheduled Meeting meetings were not the only meetings we attended. Every couple of months or so, sometimes more often, there would also be a Young People's Meeting, held on Fridays in the informal atmosphere of someone's home, usually the Dentons' in Elmwood Park. These meetings might take the form of an additional Reading Meeting. But if one of the younger zealot Brothers was moved by the spirit, or if a Laboring Brother happened to be in town, the young people would be railed at by him. There would be a little extra singing (from the *Echoes of Grace*, mind you, so this was cutting loose). And refreshments would be served: juice, Kool-Aid, Rice Krispie squares, cake, and sometimes *krumkake*, a delicious Norwegian cone-like cookie that Norm's mom (of Norwegian lineage) made in a special kind of baking iron. The Dentons' house was small, so it got pretty cramped, even if we were only around 20 people.

Also about once a month, perhaps less often in the winter, there would be a young people's Hymn Sing after the Gospel Meeting, at Clem Dear's house next door to the BTP. The Dears had a piano, and it was permissible to use it to accompany the hymns from – you guessed it – the *Echoes of Grace*. Once, when I was in my late teens, a guy my age called Richard Macy was in town from the Gathering in Delavan (central Illinois). When he took over the keyboard during the refreshment break, the place unexpectedly rocked – to my and Norm's utter joy, and to the utter outrage of many others, including Clem. Richard could play hymns with boogie arrangements like Jerry Lee Lewis, foot on the keyboard and all. I was thrilled beyond belief.

And then there were Tea Meetings, between Morning Meeting and the evening Gospel Meeting. All the women would bring something – casseroles, Jello desserts, Jello salads, rolls, more Rice Krispie squares, fried chicken, mashed potatoes, potato salad, corn on the cob, corn bread. The ladies would heat things and whip them together down in the basement immediately after Morning Meeting. Everyone would sit and eat at two long tables on either side of a long buffet-style central table with all the food, and there would be an hour or so until the extra Afternoon Meeting and before the street preaching, so it was possible to take a walk or something. But no ball playing. This was, after all, the Lord's Day. The afternoon Meeting would normally be like yet another Reading Meeting. I used to like the orange Jello with shredded carrots and pineapple in it, and the Rice Krispie squares and fried chicken.

Was that the sum of all our total immersion in this unsubstantiated and utterly repressive worldview? Far from it. At home we of course prayed – "gave thanks" – before breakfast, lunch, and dinner, and sometimes even before snacks. Seven days a week, we read a chapter from the Bible, aloud, all of us taking turns reading a verse or two, either at the dinner table, or in the den or living room immediately after dinner. I'm sure this gave our reading skills a boost when we were learning to shed our illiteracy. We read the Bible systematically, from the first chapter of *Genesis* to the last chapter of *Revelation*. We didn't even skip the tedious enumerations of *Numbers*, nor the mysteriously poetic and semi-erotic *Song of Salomon*, but we did skip Genesis 38. After all, getting us kids to read about a guy who jacks off so he won't have to follow God's orders and get his late brother's wife pregnant, or about the upright elder who tries to screw his daughter-in-law, would be a bit too much to swallow – too embarrassing! – when you're trying to prove that the Bible is the bastion of morality. And when we finished the entire Bible, we started over. Over and over for as long as I lived at home.

In this way, I ended up reading the entire Bible, cover to cover, several times during my youth and childhood. Not until much later would I realize, to my astonishment, what kinds of things I'd been reading without understanding or registering: God demonstrating his Might, leading the Israelites out of Egypt, slaying the first-born in every household in Egypt except in the homes where the Israelites had smeared their doorposts in blood, as instructed. How could I have read stories of such slaughter, over and over, and failed to summon up enough empathy to realize the horrible injustices, for example to every single Egyptian family who were the victims of the vengeance of a psychopathic being because of the behavior of the autocratic Pharaoh – whose will He also explicitly controlled? How could I have read a text that clearly stated that it was God Himself who repeatedly intervened and hardened the Pharaoh's heart just so He could show off His unlimited power by killing more innocent Egyptians? Much later in life, when Jehovah's Witnesses came knocking on my door, they usually started their pitch by asking whether I knew anything about the Bible. I've had great fun with them.

Back to our after-dinner family sessions. After reading our chapter, we would sing a hymn from the *Little Flock* (that's how serious), then all get down on our knees and each of us would have to pray out loud. I'm sure our audible prayers were an excellent indicator to our parents of just how well my brothers and I were adopting the clichés and jargon, and whether our tone of voice reflected sufficient earnestness, solemnity, righteousness and piety. There was absolutely no tolerance of mirth in these contexts (except for an uncontrolled giggle or two at the mention of Peleg), nor of questioning the benevolence of God. Before going to bed, we also had to kneel by our bedsides and pray to Him again.

There was an annual Sunday School Picnic, usually held in Thatcher Woods, a forest preserve just past River Forest, west of Oak Park. This was supposed to be the big event of the year for the children, with a picnic, hotdogs and hamburgers, Kool-Aid and Rice Krispie squares, roast marshmallows, preaching, prayers, hymns and softball. Some of those who attempted to play ball, especially the girls (all in long skirts, of course), didn't know which end of the bat to hold and which direction to run if they ever managed to hit the ball, which was irritating to those who loved sports and were competitive like me. My dad, to my embarrassment, was among the more inept players, as were my cousin Howard and his entire family. John (my eldest brother) was OK, Al was my coach and hero. Al taught me everything about sports.

The worst thing about the Sunday School picnic, which was on a Saturday, was that it was so public. We didn't own Thatcher Woods. We reserved one of the many designated picnic spots along the perimeter of a huge clearing, provided with numerous picnic tables and barbecue pits, but there were other groups nearby, in and around the clearing, at the same time, groups who would stare curiously when we began singing our hymns. I always hoped to avoid having anyone from school see us there (see *me* there). I would keep an eye out for anyone approaching, and if they looked remotely like anyone from my school, I would try to hide behind my baseball glove or pull my cap down low until they had passed or until I could ascertain that I didn't know them.

At one of these picnics, a particularly zealous (as new converts often are) younger Brother had been asked to speak to us kids (actually to everyone, but ostensibly to the kids). His name was Chuck Hendrix, and he wowed me with his prowess at the softball game earlier in the afternoon. He had reportedly been a professional Minor League baseball player, with high hopes of entering the Majors with the Chicago Cubs, when he got "saved" and left the worldly world of professional sports forever. I later learned that Chuck regularly belted his children (literally), but since he did so "as unto the Lord", it was OK. What effect it had on his children is another story entirely.

His talk to us was based on the biblical text *"Without the shedding of blood, there is no remission"*, and he drew upon God's rejection of Cain's vegan offering. Then he made a claim that was so ludicrously false that even my not-yet-doubting pre-pubertal mind could accept it: "*Every* garment we wear requires the shedding of blood." OK, leather does, I conceded to myself. But I was wearing rubber-and-canvas sneakers, a cotton T-shirt and denim jeans. I looked around to see whether the other Brothers were squirming in embarrassment at a statement so criminally stupid – or blatantly ignorant – but I saw no reaction. I was baffled.

God hadn't informed Cain or his brother Abel beforehand, yet He scorned Cain's veggie offering in favor of Abel's meat dish ("*Without the shedding of blood....*") Then He moved the goalposts, allowing Esau the hunter to be bested by his vegetable-growing brother Jacob.

I've now covered the Meeting meetings I was wont or forced to attend in Oak Park. But it still wasn't enough. Every year, my family would attend three or four Bible Conferences. These were annual 2-3-day events hosted by different local Gatherings. The Memorial Day weekend was for the Des Moines Conference. In August it was the Oak Park Conference, which during my earlier childhood was held in the gym at Concordia Teachers' College (Lutheran) in River Forest, then (as I was entering my teens) switched to the gym at Wheaton College (Fundamentalist Christian). At Thanksgiving it was the Detroit Conference. And at Christmas it was the LA Conference. These were the ones we attended almost every year. Once or twice we also attended the Walla Walla Conference in June, or a 2-day Conference in Toledo, Ohio, and once or twice an All-Day Meeting or mini-Conference, for example in Lawrenceville, Illinois.

Each day of such Conferences comprised back-to-back Meeting meetings from morning to evening. These included two Reading Meetings a day (morning and afternoon sessions), each lasting about two hours. The afternoons would also have a Young People's Address, and in the evening there would be a Gospel Meeting, followed by a young people's Hymn Sing. The latter served a crucial social function at Conferences, because they were one of only two unequivocally legitimate venues for dating someone from a different Gathering, the other being the Otter Lake summer camp, by requested invitation only. These two venues were the Meeting's spawning grounds, the mating parlors. A piano was allowed at the Hymn Sings. Couples who went to a Hymn Sing together might wind up sitting together at the Reading Meeting the next day. Then you knew it was serious. If they held hands openly, it was definitely serious, with an engagement announcement to be expected. If they kissed and were seen, they would be reprimanded. (If unseen, I suppose they would just get hot.)

Since Conferences provided the opportunity to meet kids from other Meetings, we could also compare notes. Some of the kids from other Gatherings might come from homes that had TVs, and some kids even went to the movies without having to sneak off, but they stayed quiet about it at the Conferences, because the lowest common denominator of morality prevailed: if any Meeting bigshot disapproved, nobody could disagree. Conferences without bigshots were unheard-of. As a result, there would always be several Laboring Brothers in attendance, as well as the patriarchs of the whole shebang, like a selection of Hayhoes.

Grandpa Erisman, I discovered, was relatively small potatoes in this company, although he did occasionally contribute a few comments at a Reading Meeting, probably in order to bolster his stature back home. At the Oak Park Conferences, at least, my dad would often retain his role in leading the singing, still *a capella*, a much greater task when it involved up to 300 unwieldy sets of vocal chords, mostly belonging to people who had little interest in any music apart from hymns or any assurance of talent apart from looking pious, which consisted of acting and dressing as drably and old-fashioned as possible, so as to stand apart from the rest of the human race by not standing out.

The Wheaton Conference in August 1960 was where I got – or rather gave – my first kiss, just a month before my 15th birthday. In June, we had been to Idaho for John and Marj's wedding. Al was the Best Man and I was a "man of honor" (living up to my surname). Marj's two younger sisters, Joan and Nancy (about Al's and my ages respectively) were the Maids of Honor. Marj's whole family came out to Wheaton for the Conference two months later, and I decided to ask the shy, 13-year-old Nancy to the Hymn Sing at the end of the first day's session. She reluctantly agreed, perhaps feeling she was obligated, our respective siblings being newlyweds and all. Afterwards, about six of the young people – including me and Nancy – were going to drive into town from the Wheaton campus to get sodas or something. I was sitting in the crowded back seat next to Nancy. Pretending to reach across her for something, I suddenly kissed her, meaning that I planted my lips flatly on hers. Her only response was alarm. It's hard to think of a less sexy moment. Afterwards, she apparently told one of her sisters what had happened, and the next day John came up to me to ask me sternly what I was trying to do, with the superfluous advice that I should be ashamed of myself.

Ralph Rule, a friend of my parents' from the Toledo gathering, distinguished himself by sometimes bringing to Meeting a few young people from the "outside", even to Conferences. Ralph had the somewhat stern, slicked-back-black-hair good looks of Lawrence Harvey or Christopher Plummer, but had a tic that from time to time would cause him to jerk his head once or twice sharply downwards and towards one side. He made a striking figure. One of the outsiders he brought to Wheaton several years in a row, when I was in my early teens, was a boy named Stanley Price, a few years older than me. He had the look and body language of a sullen, slightly sneering rebel, which intrigued me. He also wore his black hair slicked back, like Ralph's, but he had much more of it, so it gave him a sort of *West Side Story* (Sharks) look, matched by his preference for black clothes, including black T-shirts with the sleeves rolled up as high as he could get them towards his shoulders. I certainly wasn't allowed to dress like that!

Anyway, I tended to keep a lookout for Ralph Rule at the Oak Park Conferences, to see whom he might have brought along, and in 1960 he not only had Stanley Price with him, but a couple of distinctly non-Meeting girls, both of whom looked extraordinarily exciting to me. The day after my disastrously fumbling and unsuccessful attempt to extract a kiss from Nancy, I had a word with Stanley Price about his two outsider friends, not wanting to take the risk of flirting with his possible girlfriend, since he looked capable of making me regret it; but he was not interested in the one I was.

She had dark, short hair and also liked to dress in black. I eyed her and she eyed me back. Instead of asking her to the Sing, I asked if she'd like to go for a walk with me after the Gospel meeting, i.e. after dark, on the rolling campus hillock, a place of soft lawns, leafy lilac bushes, and few lights. She would. So we strolled away from the lights of the Wheaton College gym, far from the conglomerations of Meeting folk, with me almost holding my breath for fear someone would spot us, someone who knew me or my parents well enough to feel entitled to demand to know our business, until we had at last left them all behind us, safely out of sight and earshot.

We stopped walking on reaching a clump of tall lilac bushes. After carefully checking all around for prying eyes, I turned to her and she turned to me. We kissed, me at first hesitatingly – and she kissed back, delightfully and overwhelmingly exploring my mouth with her tongue, causing an instant response in my pants. Then we moved away from the path, to a patch of dewless grass shielded by more lilac bushes, and lay down, she on her back, I half over her, first from one side, then fully on top of her, kissing her wildly, feeling breasts for the first time ever, and dry-humping until a sudden explosion in my nether regions made me nearly faint with pleasure. Unlike my loins, the guilt that I should have been feeling at this point (according to a decade of indoctrination) never came. On the contrary, I was euphoric. I might have agreed to marry her on the spot had I not still been 14, which I didn't tell her. I did, however, feel some anxiety that there might be some noticeable leakage through my trousers, but that anxiety was a long time coming. I got the distinct impression that this was no big deal for her. She seemed to find my reactions oddly amusing. But she was an outsider, after all. We went back to the gym area, said goodbye, and never saw each other again. If I ever knew her name, I've forgotten it.

The Detroit Conferences were usually held at a union hall, the LA Conferences at the Odd Fellows Temple (fitting name). People from the local Gathering that was hosting a Conference were expected to open up their homes to as many overnight guests as possible. Often the older generation would stay at nearby motels and the kids would stay at the homes of the locals who had kids of similar age and gender. We once had 16 teenage boys sleeping over at our house in Oak Park, most of them on army-surplus cots in the basement, before the Oak Park Conference was moved from nearby Concordia (in River Forest) out to Wheaton, where everyone could stay in well-chaperoned student dormitories (gender-separated for the young people, of course).

The Conferences were not places for minor, fledgling Brothers to stick out their necks. The speakers at Young People's and Gospel Meetings were mostly Laboring Brothers. Those who opened their mouths during the Reading Meetings were the most revered and feared of all the Brethren. My grandpa Larson was occasionally invited to speak at a Gospel Meeting. He had served as a Laboring Brother, not in Africa, but in the hills of Kentucky. He was charismatic, even jolly sometimes. He was jovial and fat. He could laugh. He was the antithesis of an intellectual, but he could breathe hellfire, and so was chosen to address the gathered Saints at some of the Conferences. His fervor easily outshone his brightness.

Our family's trips to Conferences, especially the ones to LA, were combined with vacation time for Dad, and invariably included a visit to a National Park somewhere along the way. By the time I was 12, I had been in all 48 states.

Three years later, Alaska and Hawaii became states, and I've still never been there (after all, they had no Meetings, much less Conferences).

Meeting dogma included belief in the Rapture. According to several Bible verses, Jesus would return to the earth surreptitiously (well before the Second Coming) to snatch all True Believers – including living ones – up to heaven directly, leaving the rest of humanity (the Unchosen Many) behind to face the Great Tribulation, a period of general misery for mankind before eternal punishment would be meted out (see Matthew 16:28, Mark 9:1, Luke 9:27, and I Thessalonians 4:17). According to the Brethren, many of the Chosen Few who were alive in the 1950s and 60s would *never* die, but would be "*caught up in the clouds*" and taken directly to Heaven, "*to meet the Lord in the air*," and woe unto those who were left behind to face His judgment! This Rapture was definitely going to happen, I frequently heard, *before* the new millennium, *before* the year 2000. About this there was no doubt (unless He decided to "tarry"), despite the fact that the biblical references to it referred to those living nearly two millennia ago, all of whom *did* die. That the Rapture had not already transpired during the nineteen and a half previous centuries was explained by the "knowledge" the Meeting had of the Creation, aided by Bishop Ussher's chronology, that the world was created in 4004 BC. No evolution or geology here! Life as we know it would end in or around 2000 AD. From the perspective of all poor hell-bound sinners, the True Christians would one day just suddenly disappear without a trace, and the inaudible drum-roll of doom would begin for the billions left behind. This was a "fact" (religion-style, neither requiring nor admitting any evidence). End of discussion.

They *knew* they could see the "signs of the Last Days before His Coming", because they were revealed in the psychotic and psychedelic ramblings of the *Book of Revelation*, expounded by such Meeting prophecy luminaries as Paul Wilson from Southern California. I don't know whether this small select group of the Meeting's prophecy experts met or corresponded on their own in some way between Conferences; there were never any debates about their findings, the Conferences were simply the venues for disseminating those findings among the Brethren. But in the early 1960s, after the first satellites had already been placed in orbit, I did hear a couple of them state *categorically*, based on the Bible of course, that "Man will *never* set foot on the Moon!" They were also certain that the Common Market (later the European Union) was fulfilling some prophecy about the reinstatement of the Roman Empire in the Last Days, and that the Common Market would comprise *exactly* those countries that once comprised the ancient Roman Empire, and no others. (Perhaps there was a *"Revelation: the Sequel"* covering Finland, etc, that didn't make it into their canon.)

Sex was never an explicit topic at any Meeting meeting, nor at any Conference, but the official position, as it were, was made quite clear through the reading of choice Biblical warnings of stonings (instilling fear in me even when I had no clue what the fuck words like *fornication* meant). Sex was to be strictly hetero, and only after marriage, and it didn't seem to be associated with much joy; it was at best condescendingly benign (*"Marriage is honorable in all, and the bed undefiled"*, Hebrews 13:4). "Defiling oneself" was the euphemism for masturbation, which was also an abomination (although it took me longer to realize the meaning of the euphemism than it took for me to master the abominable technique, but perhaps this was because we skipped Genesis 38 at home).

In the Meeting, the word "pleasure" was so frequently used in the disparaging, contemptuous context of enjoying *"the pleasures of sin for a season"*, followed by eternal damnation, that it was best to lie low and not even think of anything in terms of pleasure. Divorce was highly frowned upon, and condemned unless one party was clearly guilty of adultery, apostasy, or heresy, or some offense of similar magnitude. Even then, remarriage was viewed with clear misgivings, and supported only by *"It is better to marry than to burn."* My mom and her sisters were horrified when their widower father, after some 15 years of burning, married my paternal grandmother's widowed sister Minnie. *"Can't he do without it?!"* his understanding daughters hissed to each other in harsh stage whispers.

The Meeting engulfed our lives, and since part of not being of this world meant not observing worldly holidays, it also generally frowned upon the celebration of Christmas, as no such celebration is mentioned in the Bible. So we never had Christmas trees – except when we lived in Glendale. As far as I know, nobody in the Oak Park Meeting observed Christmas in any way, and at Conferences some of the Big Guns were unequivocal about it being an evil observance of heathen, pagan winter solstice festivals, and that it had been introduced by the Emperor Constantine as a way to soften the blow to the ancient Romans upon whom he was trying to foist a false version of "Christianity" as the official religion of the empire, thus forcing them to give up their entire popular Pantheon of capricious gods and goddesses.

In this, the Meeting patriarchs were probably right – the Bible indeed makes no mention whatsoever about observing the birth of Jesus, and He was probably not born at the time of the solstice anyway; it *was* just a convenient festival time for Constantine to usurp. But I think the Meeting's main reason for not celebrating Christmas was that it gave them yet another opportunity to set themselves apart from the World and not to partake in its pleasures, but to condemn them, and to give themselves yet another reason to keep frowning. However, to ameliorate their strict non-observance, my parents gave me and my brothers "holiday presents" so that we wouldn't have to feel too bad when school resumed after the Christmas break, and all the kids were talking about their Christmas presents.

However, my parents were unable to suppress a certain curiosity about the pageantry of Christmas. Many of the residents of affluent Oak Park and even wealthier River Forest would decorate their homes with a stupefying array of lights, sleighs, Santas, mangers, snowmen, gingerbread men, wreaths and stars. Dad would sometimes take us all for an evening drive up one residential street and down another to take it all in. One home had a full-scale sleigh pulled by two or three actual stuffed reindeer, with a full-scale (probably not real and stuffed) Santa on the roof, with a leg up on the chimney. I'd never harbored even a secret belief in Santa Claus, because Santa's trip down our chimney would have landed him directly in the gas furnace in the basement.

Easter wasn't felt to have the same exclusively pagan origins, but we didn't celebrate it as such anyway. Its main Christian roots are in the Jewish Passover, which Jesus allegedly celebrated together with his disciples to mark the occasion when God in His mercy didn't kill, but passed over, the firstborn of the Israelites in Egypt who had followed instructions to paint their doorposts with blood. The fact that He *did* kill the firstborn in every single Egyptian household, an act that among rational people would earn Him the accolade of All-Time Psychopath, is apparently passed over in the minds of His worshipers. But the Meeting doctrine was that the Breaking of Bread every week was all that was needed to celebrate God making a human sacrifice of His son. Anyway, the celebration of Easter had already been corrupted with bunnies and decorated eggs, although we did have that Easter egg hunt in crazy Aunt Marion's back yard in Glendale.

As far as I recall, Meeting people somehow permitted their children to dress up for Halloween and go trick-or-treating, perhaps because Halloween's mid-20th century celebration in the US had no direct associations with religion, and thus didn't need to be set apart from it, or perhaps there were already so many prohibitions in place that a safety valve for young kids was deemed necessary. (In those days, Halloween was, as far as I knew, seldom observed by anyone of high school age or over.) So we always bought a large pumpkin and carved out a jack o'lantern and had costumes. I don't think I ever dressed up as a ghost or skeleton or wizard or anything like that, and probably would not have been allowed to do so; but I was content, first with cowboys and later with Indians, as long as it got me a shopping bag full of candy, which it did.

One March afternoon, Johnny and I had a severe craving for candy, and began nagging at our moms to give us some. That got us nowhere, so we surreptitiously put on costumes and went out ringing doorbells and greeted various surprised but amused housewife neighbors with *"Trick-or-treat, it's Halloween in Hawaii!"* Some had just been baking cookies, some happened to have candy in the house, one had just finished making candy apples. We were starting to make a respectable haul, when one of the less-amused neighbors blew the whistle, and we were reined in, chastised – and mighty pleased with our caper.

My family did partake in the American observance of Thanksgiving, in the sense that if we were at home, the Oak Park branch of our family (Aunt Maxine's family and my grandparents) would get together for a turkey dinner. We could hardly pray any more than we'd already been doing, or be any more thankful to the Lord for His bounty, so perhaps it was just the sudden abundance of turkeys in the grocery stores that made the dinner fare deviate from our norm, although my mom did make pumpkin pie at that time of year as well. But since she used canned pumpkin, which was available year-round, her tendency to make it only for Thanksgiving would seem to indicate some outside (worldly!) influence to conform.

There are many versions of how the celebration of Thanksgiving in the US originated. The most concise version – my version, not the Meeting version nor the most widely accepted version – would eventually make the most sense to me in terms of the ultimate factual outcome: the Pilgrims arrived in the New World in 1620 and, with the aid of the Indians, were able to grow, hunt, fish and store enough food to see them through that first harsh winter. Then, instead of giving thanks to the Indians, the Pilgrims shot the Indians and gave thanks to God.

Yet another aspect of our self-imposed *apartheid* from the World was politics. People from the Meeting were admonished not to vote – they "might end up voting against God's man". Money and taxes had a *"render unto Caesar"* seal of approval, but not voting. Nevertheless, there was little doubt of the positive view my parents took every time a Republican candidate won an election, a view generally shared by the residents of the village of Oak Park. That they as "True Christians" were emotionally supporting policies that overtly and extensively contradicted the repeated and explicit teachings of Jesus to care for the sick and feed the poor, whether through their democratically elected government or not, never seemed to occur to them.

To outsiders, the Meeting is one in a huge basketful of fundamentalist Protestant Christian sects, a "fundamentalist" being one who rigidly adheres to the founding principles of one's beliefs (in this case involving a literal interpretation of the Bible), and who is usually intolerant of other views, which would be a fair definition of what Meeting people claim to aspire to. However, the Meeting generally demonstrated considerably greater success with the intolerance part than with the strict adherence part. In fact, the Meeting shares with all other Christian religions, sects, cults or gatherings (at least those that use the Bible) a highly selective, cherry-picking process whereby those parts of the Bible they like are to be taken literally, while the parts they don't like are to be taken figuratively. Those parts where even the most figurative interpretation is still horrendous require the reader's total disengagement of logic, comprehension, critical thinking, empathy, common sense and decency.

It would seem that the only thing wrong with a fundamentalist position would be if that position were both considered incapable of being questioned and/or fundamentally wrong in the first place. Isn't playing by the rules fine if the rules are fine, especially if one is free to change them when they don't work or don't fit the available evidence?

***

My entire Meeting upbringing was a long and largely unbroken session of force-feeding, and I don't feel I can ever adequately convey what it was like to someone who has never experienced it firsthand. *What to believe* was the only important thing, not *how to think*, and definitely not how to think *critically*.

Obedience to the Word was the prerequisite for all approval of me, my very being, even by my parents, even when I was small. Indoctrination is about obeying, not questioning; absorbing, not learning; emotions, not evidence. It is based on endless repetition, until the right words or phonemes automatically come out in the right order, until healthy doubt is totally obliterated by mindless and ignorant certainty, and the concept of belief becomes hopelessly entangled and muddled with the concept of knowledge, when inquiry, logic and analysis may only be applied once the hard-sell doctrine has been accepted as axiomatic premises upon which any further reasoning must be based.

Deviations on my part were thus met with a variety of the worst psychologically manipulative techniques around: withdrawal of love, and being made to feel that by failing to believe I was inflicting severe pain on those I loved. Frightening outlines of the eternal agonies of hell were constantly being foisted upon me, emotional blackmail on every level was rampant. Every little step in the "right" direction, on the other hand, was met with thanks to Him, warm attention – and a ratcheting up to the next level of expectations of obedience to His Word.

I was pretty much forced swallow it all, to believe in the real existence of heaven, hell, God, Satan, resurrection, ancient miracles like Joshua stopping the sun so he could kill more people, eternal salvation, eternal damnation, being born again, all with a carefully picked cherry on top. This went on every year, every day, nearly every hour, from before my earliest consciousness until I finally began the long and arduous process of breaking free.

I have observed that few of those young people I knew in the Meeting, including my own brothers, were ever fortunate enough to manage to break completely free, but remained emotionally bound to the gravitational pull of an indoctrinated childhood, or in a low orbit of basic beliefs around it, at best picking somewhat different cherries from the same original tree. Moreover, one of the most unfortunate after-effects of childhood indoctrination and brainwashing tends to be a blissful unawareness on the part of its victims that they have been indoctrinated or brainwashed at all, causing them invariably to fail to recognize their role in perpetuating such non-thinking on their own children.

CHAPTER 3

Pets

This is the story about how my not-so-great uncle ate my ducks, and about one more childhood trauma involving a pet. A number of people (mostly pet-owners) have asked me in my adulthood if I've ever thought about getting a dog – usually it's a dog they ask about; I guess I don't seem to be as much of a cat person. Indeed, I've been dogged by the notion many times; I did think I might acquire a dog once I "settled down". Only I never felt I'd settled down, at least not until fairly late in life, by which time I had inundated myself with an array of the usual reasons against having a dog (yes, I guess it would have been a dog): being tied down with regard to travelling, the bother of walking a little shit-machine in freezing rain or slush in pre-dawn winter mornings, the self-imposed responsibility, the traumatic attachment. Oh yes, and I developed asthma when I was 38.

I don't remember my first pet experience. For some reason, Mitzi, the dog we had for a while in Glendale in the late 1940s never implanted herself among my earliest memories. Mitzi was mainly the charge of John and Al. She was run over by a car, so perhaps some of their trauma over that sad event stuck with me in some way. It may also have made my parents disinclined to have another pet in their home. But I did end up with two childhood experiences of having pets of my own; those experiences were both wonderful and horrendous.

When my folks started planning our move back to Chicago from the LA area in late 1950, they chose a "Bruce-built" home to be built to order by Bruce Goodman, a reputable local builder, in one of the few parts of Oak Park that still had vacant lots. Our front yard was fairly square. The position of our house on the lot, like Oak Park politics, was right of center. A section of fence with a gate extended from the front of our house to the left, then turned ninety degrees to enclose the back yard and garage, with another gate to the alley, forming an enclosed potential habitat for a dog. But the loss of Mitzi might have continued to make this notion unthinkable for my parents.

There was a pet store just down North Avenue, on the Chicago side, just beyond Oak Park Avenue. The song *"How much is that doggie in the window"* was popular in 1952, and although Mom and Dad were adamant about not listening to "worldly" music, or allowing us to do so, the tune was ubiquitous for a couple of years. At some point in 1953 or thereabouts, Al came home from school one day and said that one of his friends had a dog that just had puppies he'd just seen, and couldn't we please, please, *please* have one? I chimed in with all my natural intensity. After a lot of resistance – although perhaps the sight of the puppy once they gave in enough to go and take a look might have been persuasive – they finally acquiesced.

She was a mongrel bitch (even though nobody in our family used or knew the original meaning of that naughty word), primarily beagle and cocker spaniel, short-haired, with a mostly white body and a mostly black head, except for a white muzzle whose whiteness continued in a narrow white strip up to the top of her head. She was inquisitive and a bit high-strung. We named her "Ollie" (pronounced like "*only*" without the "*n*"), which was a suggestion from my Mom, based on a pseudo-Swedish name from her childhood. Not until many years later would I discover that it was a distortion of "Olle" (pronounced in a completely different way: *Oo*-leh), which is the diminutive form of the Swedish man's name Olof, thus being a distortion of Ollie's gender as well.

The principal care of Ollie gradually devolved to me. After a couple of early accidents on our wall-to-wall carpets, Ollie was confined to one of three places: the basement, the landing just off the kitchen, or the yard. The steps of the landing were her favorite place. Our kitchen was small compared to most of the kitchens in our neighborhood. To Mom's chagrin, it was a real corridor for human traffic. It was roughly square. Entering our house by the back door put you on a tiny landing from which you could continue on a stairway straight down to the basement or take three steps up to the right to the kitchen.[1] I almost always used this entrance when I came home from school, and we always used it when we'd been anywhere in the car and parked it in the garage. Ollie was allowed to perch on the highest of the three steps whenever we had meals in the kitchen. Most days the whole family had dinner in the dining room. But when it was just Mom and us boys (Dad usually had breakfast before the rest of us and driving all the way home for lunch was unthinkable), we ate at the kitchen table.

Facing the kitchen from the landing, there was a white porcelain sink along the wall to the right, beneath a window overlooking the narrow patio that separated our house from our dark red picket fence, painted with creosote to

---

1   See drawings of the layout of my boyhood home, Appendix 1

prevent rotting. Along the right-hand half of the wall straight ahead were a stove and a couple of cabinets. In the middle of that wall, a swinging door to the dining room divided it from table in the corner to the left. The wall to the left ended with an open doorway to the small downstairs hallway. Along the fourth wall – the one with the doorway to the landing – stood the big fridge and some more cabinets, one of which held a decoratively painted metal coffee pot with the inscription: "*Kaffetåren den bästa är av alla jordiska drycker*." My mom knew that this was Swedish, and that it meant "Coffee is the best of all earthly drinks". She could even pronounce it in a decidedly non-English way, but not in Swedish, as I would come to realize much later in life (most of her "Swedish" would remind me of the Swedish cook on the Muppets). In any case, this last kitchen wall separated the kitchen from the stairway up to "the boys' room" – the open dormer attic where I and my brothers lived.

Ollie and I had a mutual interest in her making the top step of the landing her spot. Her interest was having easy access to possible treats – food scraps that would otherwise have gone to the garbage. Mom liked to serve vegetables, because she thought they were good for us. They might have actually *been* good for us if they tasted good. But she boiled most of them far too long, as was the custom in those days, so I gagged. (In the 1980s, one of my brothers put it more colorfully: "She cooked the shit out of them!") But thanks to omnivorous Ollie, such vegetables were no problem, at least when we were eating in the kitchen.

I usually sat nearest the landing. Ollie would eat anything and she was quick. When I'd been forced to take a disgusting vegetable, I merely had to switch it from my plate to my hand, then hold my cupped hand under the table, and Ollie would dash up, instantly gobble it up, and whizz back to that top step before Mom could say "*Ollie! Out of the kitchen!*" I loved that dog.

Ollie was crazy about peanut butter. We loved to watch her eating it, smacking her jaws, opening her mouth as wide as she yawned, craning her head around as if to chase the inside of her mouth. Each blob of peanut butter meant about ten minutes of smacking. And then she'd be eagerly back for more. And more. She'd follow me around the enclosed back yard and we'd go for walks, but I was mostly supposed to keep her in our yard to prevent any risk that she might mess up the neighbors' yards. She would play with me and occasionally bark at neighbors or strangers who approached. Our back yard was, briefly, Ollie's turf.

The vacant lot to the south, outside our kitchen entrance, between us and our almost-Christian neighbors the Burtnesses, was a favorite place for the neighborhood kids to play impromptu games of baseball (normally with a wiffle ball to avoid broken windows). No parents objected, because it was preferable to the streets. One day, I believe it was in the summer of 1954, the Burtnesses' daughter and a couple of their young grandsons were visiting them. The boys, around my age and probably bored in the company of their elders, went out to the vacant lot between our homes to play.

I wasn't outdoors with Ollie at the time, but heard Ollie barking at them. I saw from John's window upstairs that one of the boys had come over to the picket fence and was teasing Ollie, poking aggressively at her between the pickets, deliberately working her into a frenzy. I cascaded downstairs to rescue Ollie from her tormentor just when she jabbed her paw between the pickets and scratched the boy in the face. The boy ran crying home to his mother and grandparents. Phone calls ensued. Emotions ran high. I was told to my horror that my parents felt they had no choice but to take Ollie to the vet and have her "put to sleep" – executed. "*What had she done?*" I wailed. "She was in her own yard, being tormented! Why couldn't they take that kid and put *him* to sleep?!"

Thus I lost my dog. But there was no mention of Ollie having gone to Heaven to be with the Lord, nor even of Ollie being in "a better place". Death was final and that was the end of it. There was no question of my questioning why it should be that way. The Lord had all the answers to Everything, and He would reveal as much as He felt like, when and if He ever felt like it. But to me, Ollie had just as much of a "soul" as anybody else – probably more than Grandpa Erisman. Ollie was a whole lot nicer to me.

A bit less than a year later, just before Easter in 1955, the show window of the pet store on North Avenue was filled with baby chicks and ducklings, newly hatched, yellow and fluffy, climbing and squirming over each other under the warmth of infrared lights. It was, of course, an Easter gimmick, but I fell for it and began pleading with Mom and Dad to be allowed to purchase two of those little ducklings. They were so tiny, I could easily have held both in one hand. Ducks don't bark, they have no claws, they don't need to be taken for walks, I can keep them in the basement, then in the yard when it's warmer, can't I, please, please, *please*? I took Mom to see them in the window. Then there was some talk between Mom and Dad, and finally, perhaps with the help of some residual guilt about the fate of Ollie, I got the go-ahead and we went to the pet store, me bursting with excitement, Mom more apprehensive, even though she readily admitted how cute they were.

I was fascinated with the two lively little yellow things, which I named Frank and Sally. They both turned out to be female. I have no recollection of where I got the names from, and I don't think I knew at the time either; I think I just liked them. The little ducklings soon began to follow me around, more or less, but they never stood still, never stopped their high-pitched peeping (it would take a while before the peeps became quacks). And there was no "off" button. A common expression gave me the idea that they might take to water, and Mom agreed that we could try letting them swim around in the bathtub. If they could have spoken, they might have said *"We LOVE this – let us do it ALL THE TIME!"* That, at least, is what their body language seemed to be pleading. How could I ever play with a rubber duck again?

For the first few weeks, they had to spend their nights in a small cage in the cool basement, perhaps wondering what happened to the infrared heat. But outdoors, April nights could still be downright cold, and the fence that enclosed the back yard was too sparsely picketed to contain them.

My ducks were the first things I went to see every morning when I woke up and the first things I would see when I came home from school every day. Their little yellow-fledged bodies grew and grew. The yellow began turning white. Bathtub sessions left the floor covered in puddles. But as weather became warmer, we had them out in the back yard during the day, and they loved it. They also loved Mom's tulips and mint plants, to her clear displeasure.

Until we had heavy rain for three days, we'd assumed that their growth had rendered the picket fence impenetrable. The rain transformed the still-vacant lot to the north into an irresistible pond; Frank and Sally somehow managed to squeeze through the fence or under it or over it or however they got out. We found them swimming and quacking merrily in that temporary pond. It took considerable effort to coax and lure them back into our custody. Once the pond had disappeared, however, they seemed content to forage in our back yard, and they followed me around whenever I came out. They didn't like it when I tried to leave the yard for school, so I'd have to wait until I had a clear shot at the back gate, then make a break for it from the back door and quickly secure the gate behind me as they came squawking and flapping after.

All summer vacation, from early June to the beginning of September, I had them in my charge and played with them every day. By now they were over two feet tall, snowy white with orange bills and feet. One day in late August, with the start of school rapidly approaching, Mom had a little talk with me. The ducks were now way too big to be indoors, she said. I didn't want to be convinced of that, despite knowing it was true. Chicago winters would be too brutally cold for them to be outdoors, she said. I knew that for sure. Here was a dilemma. Then Mom said that her Uncle Carl, who had a farm about 50 miles west of Chicago, had a hen house and might agree to take care of Frank and Sally during the winter. I looked anxious and skeptical. Mom added that we'd be able to drive out and visit my ducks from time to time, and I could get them back in the spring. As it turned out, she'd already talked to Uncle Carl about the arrangement, and he'd agreed. I reluctantly gave in. And so on September 4th, the Saturday before school started, we loaded the ducks into our car and Dad drove us out to Uncle Carl's farm.

Uncle Carl was Mom's father's youngest brother. We didn't see a lot of them, because they'd remained in the Swedish Covenant Church when Grandpa Larson left it to join the more pious and right-thinking (or at least right-believing) Meeting. Carl Larson and his wife made no real impression on me when we went there to leave off Frank and Sally. I hardly noticed them, I was so concerned about inspecting the hen house. I noted with disgruntled approval that there were plenty of chickens and a few other ducks. Frank and Sally seemed to find it all perfectly natural; they fit right in, and I felt a bit better about it, even though I cried when we had to leave. I seem to recall that the Larsons offered us lemonade and cookies or something, but not a meal.

School started, and every weekend I would ask if we couldn't go to Uncle Carl's to see my ducks, but my folks had other things to see to. Then one day when I came home through the empty yard after school, Mom was on the phone, speaking in an unusually hushed voice. When she hung up, she turned to me with a somewhat anxious look and said, "That was Uncle Carl. He's invited us to a duck dinner, but I said I thought you might not want to...?"

Anger, outrage, grief, incredulity, and panic pierced me, pounded me, swept over me in waves. What *utter* betrayal! How could that *mean, horrible* Uncle Carl (I hadn't learned any swear words yet) do such a thing?! Had he no heart at all?! I could not be solaced for days. I healed, slowly, from the outside in. The inside took many years.

Thus I lost my ducks. And, apart from a brief and futile attempt, in Sweden in the early 1970s, to keep some aquarium fish alive for more than a year, I also lost my desire to own a pet. I've often wondered whether the profound sense of betrayal I felt as a child on having my beloved pets so brutally ripped from me – that was my perspective – didn't on some subconscious level undermine my parents' credibility to me as purveyors of moral authority.

Later in life, when I was expecting my first child in late 1983, my great uncle Carl was still alive. If my first child had been a boy, the name of the murderer of my ducks was not to be considered. After he died in 1984, I removed "Carl" from my blacklist, but the issue turned out to be moot anyway – my second child was a girl.

I don't think my parents were expecting my grief to be greater than theirs, which was none at all where the ducks were concerned. But they did seem to feel bad about *my* grief and their role in it. During one of Mom's visits to our home in the early 90s, when she was nearly 80, I told her how long it had taken me to get over my underlying sense of hostility towards Uncle Carl. Then she confessed that all those years ago she had told Carl that it would be OK to turn Frank and Sally into dinner. By this time, I had no hostility left in me, at least not where my ducks – or my mom – were concerned. I just shook my head in amazement.

CHAPTER 4

Dad

I feel I never truly knew my dad, certainly not as well as I think I would have liked, which is a shame, because he was an exceptionally decent guy. He was, relatively speaking, the silent partner in my parents' marriage and in my upbringing. I don't think he ever had any enemies. Words not readily associated with him are: flamboyant, aggressive, manipulative, unkind, snobbish, dominant, intellectual, stupid, athletic, raucous, hilarious, insincere and powerful. Words easily associated with him are: friendly, calm, anxious, earnest, sincere, sensitive, smart, emotional, deferential, clever, gentle and amiable.

My memory – or perhaps only my impression – of his style of dress was a drab, solid-color suit (blue or gray), a starched white shirt and any of several non-spectacular ties. He wore black, well-polished, inexpensive shoes (only one kind), and – except in the summer – a gray felt fedora with a pinch-front teardrop-shaped crown. About the shoes: I was told that he had liked the look (in a catalog) of a pair of dress shoes of the type used by the Army, bought them, and found them to be sufficiently comfortable and thus appropriate for his every need for every occasion. Perhaps he figured that if these shoes would meet the criteria of the Army, they would also meet his.

That is pure speculation on my part, as everything will be that I write about what did or did not go on in his mind or his life out of my own eye- or earshot. I'm sure my brothers would have very different versions, which are probably valid for them. But my brothers didn't have the same father as I did, in the sense that, like most people, he was constantly changing and evolving as his youth left him and his parental experience taught or overwhelmed him, and thus he approached me in a way that can be presumed to be somewhat different from the way he approached John or Al. This account, this tale, this fiction attempting to be fact, represents *my* perspective and memory. If I got it all wrong, it is nevertheless what has shaped me.

Anyway, having found the Perfect Shoe, Dad wore no others. He bought two or three pairs at a time, replacing them as needed over the years. Those black army shoes, the suit, the white shirt (short-sleeved in sweltering summer weather), and the tie formed his normal attire six days a week. As he was severely myopic, he also wore glasses, fairly thick ones, usually wire-framed. In later years he would add a hearing aid. One day when my brother John and I were chatting about him some years after Dad's death at the age of 61, we both agreed that he'd *always* appeared to be in his 60s, even when we were kids. Looking back at the photos of him, even at the time of my birth when he was just under 34, our assessment hardly seems far-fetched.

On Saturdays, Dad would set aside the suit jacket, hat, white shirt and tie in favor of a more colorful shirt (never flashy, usually flannel except in the summer). I have a few vague memories that he did various chores around the house. I have no memories of repairmen, and yet our house was in impeccable shape, so he must have had some skills as a handyman.

What I do remember was some of his errands. He would go downtown Oak Park (the birthplace of Ernest Hemingway, who allegedly described it as "a town of wide lawns and narrow minds"), to the bank and the post office on Lake Street. As a child, I sometimes got to go with him on these errands, just him and me, and the great marble halls of those two imposing buildings would fascinate me. There was a certain smell of old paper, of an authority that was not the Meeting, not Grandpa Erisman, not my parents. There were photos of wanted criminals in the post office, and post boxes where people could pick up their mail if they didn't want it delivered to their door. And there were racks of information pamphlets from Army and Navy recruiters.

There were usually only a few people in the cavernous post office on Saturday mornings. Every sound of every voice could be heard, but none could be understood; the acoustics created echoes that commingled speech into unintelligible cacophony. Dad would transact his business and I would marvel at the ease with which he seemed to carry out his presumably important financial and postal tasks, and he would meet my awed gaze with a warm smile and tell me when it was time for us to move on to the next place.

On one side of the Post Office, across Kenilworth, was the striking Unitarian Church, designed by Frank Lloyd Wright, a pioneering architect whose work is exceptionally well represented in Oak Park, making the village a magnet for architectural buffs. The Unitarian Church (later called the Unity Temple) building is distinguished by its beautiful simplicity and by an almost total lack of windows visible from the street (there are none at street level), which I suppose somehow enhanced my parents' assessment of Unitarianism as an utterly evil doctrine, which, like all its adherents, must be shunned. They, like most other people, were on their way to hell.

Across Lake Street from the Unitarian Church, next to the library, was the more conventional and opulent limestone Congregational Church, whose members were of course also to be shunned, albeit not to the same degree; while Congregationalism was not considered directly evil in itself, merely lukewarm, but most of its members were presumably hell-bound anyway.

My best friend (I used the word loosely; he was the one I hung out with more than others, not that it was a lot, since there were too many barriers to my hanging out with anybody, and I never developed any real bonds with anyone except Norm) at Horace Mann Elementary School was Bob Kettlestrings, whose ancestor is credited with having founded Oak Park. Bob, also known to his classmates as "Kedzie", went to the Congregational Church, but only seldom. Pretty much everyone in the world was hell-bound unless they could prove otherwise, and the only truly convincing way to prove otherwise was to be among the Chosen Few at the Meeting. Besides me, there were no Meeting kids at Horace Mann during all the years I went there (except for the few years when Al and I went there concurrently), which basically meant that not a single one of my classmates had a clue about what made my parents tick and thus how I was being forced to live my life, and why I was obliged to keep my distance from all of them. Nor did my classmates realize that every last one of them was plunging headlong towards an eternity of unspeakable agony.

At work, I doubt that Dad would have shunned anybody. This suggests that Link-Belt was far better at eliciting decent moral behavior than the Meeting was. Dad was always cordial, and he almost certainly let it be known where he stood, although probably not that he believed that everyone else stood on the brink of hell. But since Grandpa was also working at Link-Belt when Dad started there, perhaps his colleagues knew what "Erisman" entailed.

The only job-related socializing I remember Dad engaging in was the one or two times my parents were invited to the home of Mr Mick, Dad's boss, somewhere in downtown Chicago. I remember once or twice when the same Mr Mick and his wife came to our house for dinner. I have no memory of how those dinners went. I was likely sent to spend the evening with my aunt and uncle in order to prevent the risk of exposure to coarse or profane language, as well as other worldly ways like smoking. I remember discovering a Bakelite ashtray tucked away in a cupboard somewhere. I figured Dad had purchased it for such occasions. I also suspect that Dad's prayer at the dinner table would have been modified beyond my youthful recognition, possibly even limited to a quick, silent version, which might have caused me to ask him uncomfortable questions about hiding lights under bushels.

One of the main reasons I didn't know Dad well was the fact that my direct, day-to-day care and upbringing was almost exclusively the domain of Mom, and she had by far the most dominant – if not dominating or domineering – personality. But the biggest reason of all was that neither Dad nor Mom ever wanted to know *me*. Their Mission was to make me a Soul for Christ, to press me into a mold, to see that I conformed to His Will in thought and deed, that I always put this unseen Lord first in every detail of my life. They never wanted to know my thoughts or desires, except to ascertain that they were developing in line with their Mission. Every utterance I might make that showed signs of deviation from the True Path was a call for correction and discipline – never a chat to find out why I had such thoughts, far less to consider their possible merits.

Dad and Mom never encouraged intellectual curiosity, reasoning, doubt or questioning. Such things were Evil in His Sight. "Man's reasoning" was regarded with the utmost contempt and abhorrence. In fact, putting "Man's" in front of anything disqualified it from all but fervent rejection. Perhaps that's why they never put "Man's" in front of any human progress they tolerated or needed; they never spoke of "Man's medicine" – not to mention Man's railways, agriculture, cars, home construction, clothing manufacture, flush toilets, etc. And the word "reasoning" (like "pleasure") was always treated with the utmost suspicion. Ours was not to reason why.

While I remember well Dad's warm smile, and his occasional chuckles, I have no memory of any out-and-out guffaws. He kept a tight rein on humor; there were no excesses. Having been raised by nearly totally humorless parents, it's easy to see where he might have picked up that tight rein or been reined into it. I distinctly remember Grandpa Erisman once rhetorically asking aloud, during a Reading Meeting, whether it could be considered proper for a True Christian to laugh, and in doing so he quoted Psalm 2:4: "He that sitteth in the heavens shall laugh: the Lord shall have them in derision." Grandpa's interpretation was that laughter was the sole privilege of the Lord.

I always dreaded going to my Oak Park grandparents' home for Sunday dinner. They were such a loveless, passionless, lifeless couple on whose laps I never sat nor was ever invited to sit, and in whose arms I was never enfolded. Grandma Erisman was never directly unkind or harsh towards me; she was just so totally bland, a two-dimensional cardboard figure in my childhood. She was a terrible cook, and to make matters worse, she always seemed to cook the things that I and my brothers liked least, time after time, never paying any attention to what we avoided. There were always Lima beans, which I hated. I loved corn, fresh corn, corn on the cob. But I hated canned corn, and that was what she almost always served, usually in a disgustingly soggy, bready, creamy casserole that made me want to *puke*. One of her two favorite meat dishes was creamed chipped beef, made from canned, thinly sliced, chemical-tasting processed beef and served with a white sauce similar to wallpaper paste. I later learned that creamed chipped beef on toast was often served in the Army, and the recruits called it SOS (for "shit on a shingle")! Her other favorite was meat loaf, with the emphasis on loaf: a mushy, bready glob that made me *gag*.

The only thing she made that I liked, relatively speaking, was her cornbread. Since honey was usually among the condiments on the table, I would take the minimum required helpings of the disgusting dishes, then pile on the cornbread and honey, and try to fill up on that. Then I claimed that I'd eaten all I could of Grandma's hateful dishes.

Was she always like that? Dad seemed to have survived his childhood in reasonably good condition. Or did the death of Dad's sister Saramae (who died at the age of 28, two years after she was married and three years before I was born) change his mother completely after Dad was an adult?

After Sunday dinner at their place during my first years in Oak Park, which of course also meant subsequent to the Bible reading and after-dinner prayers at the table, my brothers and I faced a painfully boring afternoon until it was time for Gospel Meeting. But in around 1959, it went from bad to worse. Grandpa and Dad each invested in a Wollensak tape recorder which they brought along to Bible Conferences and recorded the meetings so we could enjoy hour after hour of thrilling Sunday afternoon family gatherings, listening to reruns of these old Brothers spouting off, or just sitting there silently, or singing like crows. The only comic relief from this excruciating boredom was if Dad or Grandpa had managed to capture an occasional "*Hhhhhhhhh!!*" from Harry Hayhoe.

Dad's mildness was in evidence on the occasions when Mom assigned him the duty of spanking me. (I say me, because I have no memory of him or Mom spanking my brothers, although ass-witnesses have told me they were well and truly spanked too.) I was always relieved when she assigned Dad this role rather than assuming it herself, because her great surges of zeal could make her a real flailer. When she felt my crime exceeded her own strength, she got the hickory yard stick and whacked my ass till it was red and stinging. But I wasn't the one most traumatized by it. Mom beat one of my brothers with a hairbrush till his ass was bloody. He was six years old at the time and never understood what he'd done, nor did he ever fully overcome his aversion to her.

Dad, on the other hand, dreaded the task much more than I dreaded him having it. He didn't have the heart for it. He would get home from work, and Mom would inform him that I needed a spanking. A distressed look would appear on his face as he led me down to the basement where I was to bend over the stool at his workbench and receive whacks from his open hand on my ass until I was crying, and could be deemed penitent. It's just that Dad couldn't bring himself to deliver the kind of whacks that would make me cry (and not even Mom could deliver whacks to make me penitent), so I would help him out by faking the crying the moment he'd delivered the first feeble whack. He would immediately pause and ask if I was sorry now, so he could stop. It was clear to me that I was letting him off the hook, not vice-versa.

By the time I was approaching puberty, the entire spanking detail had devolved to Dad. I was beginning to feel that this charade was beneath our dignity, however, so one evening after Dad led me down the stairs, I broke free. He tried to chase me around and around the ping-pong table, while I cavorted in innocent impishness until he could no longer keep a straight face – and he certainly had no prospect of catching me. Panting, he finally stopped, and with a half-frustrated half-scowl-grin asked me if we could tell Mom that he'd spanked me and that I was sorry. I said sure, and that was the end of him ever trying to spank me.

Some of the disciplinary issues of my childhood were related to food that I was required to eat in spite of my distaste for it. In order to qualify for the list of mandatory foods for us kids in our household, both of my parents had to like the food in question themselves. My dad's fondness for vegetables was basically limited to peas, beans, corn and carrots. Since Dad didn't like any others, my brothers and I weren't required to eat cauliflower, beets, broccoli etc, even though Mom would often serve them when we had guests for Sunday dinner. But Dad loved oysters – which my mom hated – and about once a year he would bring a bag of them home and we would gather around in the kitchen to watch him stand at the sink, open them one by one, loosen them from the shell, squirt some lemon juice and maybe a drop of Tabasco on them, and let them slither down his throat as we made highly voluble groans of disgust. Dad just chuckled and went on enjoying them.

Unfortunately for me, I was revolted by two of the vegetables on Dad's shortlist: peas and beans. I recall one evening not being allowed to leave the table until I had eaten at least one string bean (my brief respite in the form of Ollie the Omnivore was no more). That stupid bean lay there cold on my plate for about an hour until I finally came up with the idea of tucking it between my cheek and my upper gum during a momentary lapse in parental surveillance. I claimed to have eaten it, and after showing my open mouth to prove it was gone, I was finally excused, went to the bathroom and flushed it down the toilet. I'm not sure my parents ever asked themselves whether that might be a way to get me to like beans – or to be honest. *Blind* obedience seemed far more important to them. I still don't like peas or beans to this day.

My dad, Maurice John Erisman, was born on Staten Island, New York, in October 1911. His ancestry was motley – Swiss (the source of the family name, meaning "man of honor"), English, Scottish and Dutch on his father's side. His mother was said to be half or a quarter Cherokee, although this claim has never been substantiated. Dad may have taken after her withdrawn congeniality, or maybe he supplied the congeniality part all by himself. He definitely did not take after his father – John Lockhart Erisman, my grandfather – the pope of the Oak Park Meeting, a man whose expressions of affection towards anyone, including myself, went unnoticed by me, for the possible but not proven reason that there were none.

The male Erisman lineage has been traced back to a Swiss Mennonite named Melchior Erisman, born in the 17th century (sources show dates from 1640 to 1699) in the tiny hamlet of Rued, roughly equidistant from Basel, Luzerne, and Zurich in the canton of Aargau. There are numerous variants on the spelling of "Erisman" – Ehrisman, Ehrismann, Erismann, Arisman and others – possibly because there was no standardized spelling then. And since Aargau was still a part of a district ruled by a German count (a palatinate) and didn't become part of Switzerland until 1805, did that make Melchior Swiss or German? In any case, young Melchior what's-his-name immigrated to the New World in the early 1700s; and records show he died in Lancaster County, Pennsylvania, in 1740.

As the Mennonites were pacifists, at least one of Melchior's progeny must have left the faith to serve in the Revolutionary War, a fact (?) that would one day enable Dad's aunt Anne to join the DAR (unless DAR members or my great aunt faked ancestry the way I faked bean consumption). Not until my grandfather, John Lockhart Erisman, born in Springfield, Illinois in the late 1800s, did our branch of the Erisman family tree switch to the Plymouth Brethren, the "church" of my grandma and her family.

Dad was only a few years old when the family moved from Staten Island to Oak Park, where he grew up and lived all his life, apart from the seven years that began with two in Dallas and ended with five in Glendale. While anecdotes from Mom's childhood were related in family banter on an almost daily basis, Dad rarely mentioned his childhood. (Or did he, and it just didn't register with me? I don't think so, but I could be wrong.) Did Dad feel that his childhood was not important? Or was it embarrassing? Or had he simply moved on from it? The only thing I can remember hearing about from that period in Dad's life (and I heard it more often from Mom than from Dad himself) was his occasionally having to accompany his father to retrieve my great-grandfather from Chicago's Skid Row, presumably on West Madison Street. This story was told many times, not to impress upon me anything about Dad, but about the evils of alcohol. Dad was just 10 or 12 when he had to do this. Why on earth would Grandpa give a child that age that kind of task? What did they do with Great-Grandpa once they retrieved him from Skid Row? Bring him to his own home? Did he have one? What about his wife, my paternal great-grandma? I never heard a single word about her.

I am well aware that I have a lot of the child I once was still within me in my autumn years, and still accessible, not only in the form of my memories, but in my ability or propensity to clown around, to be silly and mischievous and playful sometimes, to laugh uncontrollably as often as possible. I could see some of these traits in Mom, even in her very old age. But I never saw a trace of the child in Dad. Given the sternness of his father, was Dad ever *allowed* to be silly – to be a child even when he was one? He never mentioned any silly things he had ever done or any fun he'd had as a child. As my father,

I never saw him behave in any childlike (much less childish) way, not even the way parents and grandparents do when they see little babies and their speech immediately suffers from severe maturity regression. Perhaps my brothers remember Dad talking baby talk to me, and perhaps he did, but I have no memory of any of it. He may have shared with his father the absence of frivolity, but fortunately he seemed not to have acquired a drop of the sternness; he was warm and he was kind.

He attended a couple of courses – I think they were arranged by Link-Belt – on unexpected subjects, like semantics. One of the insights he related to us from that course was "Words don't mean, people mean." Al quickly altered this to *"words aren't mean, people are mean"* – thereby greatly enhancing the value and giving me an insight I would try to preserve for the rest of my life. Imagine being spared the futile efforts to keep one step ahead of unintentional, politically incorrect pejoratives by focusing on the *intentions* of the users and not on the words they use, and giving offendees their share of the blame for inferring verbal slights!

Another of the incredibly true sayings Dad picked up and related to us kids was *"People are funnier than anybody."* Decades later, when I told Karin about it, she felt an instant kinship with my dad, despite never having met him. Sometimes in public places, among crowds, in airports, theater lobbies, restaurants or bus terminals, observing the bizarre behavior and appearance of fellow human beings, Karin would nudge me and say, "That man over there reminds me of your dad."

Despite no formal education beyond the eighth grade, my grandfather worked his way up at Link-Belt, an industrial company on Pershing Road in Chicago that built earth-moving and excavation equipment, as well as comprehensive conveyor and materials handling systems for everything from mining industries to sugar mills. Grandpa managed to rise from office boy to draftsman and on to become a highly respected engineer, holding a couple of patents, without ever having pursued academic studies. He somewhat surprisingly encouraged his two sons to study engineering and get degrees at the Armour Institute of Technology (now part of the Illinois Institute of Technology). After graduation, Dad also got a job at Link-Belt, focusing on designing conveyor and materials handling systems. His work included developments that landed him several patents, as well as the prestigious position of Chief Engineer, and remained there after the company was taken over by FMC (in 1967) and until his death just before retiring, in 1973.

Dad was never conscripted into military service, despite the war, as Link-Belt was deeply involved in contracts for the war effort, for which his services were more urgently required. This was fortunate in more ways than one; the Meeting strongly encouraged its young men not to participate in military service, but to declare themselves conscientious objectors. Pacifists were not highly regarded by the general public, especially during World War II, but I don't think Dad saw himself as a pacifist (the term wasn't used within the Meeting). The conscientious objection was solely based on not being "of the world", and thus not participating in its wars. I never heard any Brother object to any of the wars commanded by God that the Israelites perpetrated on their neighbors, including numerous wholesale slaughters of women and children. The official Meeting standpoint was more consistent with the New Testament part of their views, but one can usually find what one needs in the Bible.

Dad's managerial position gave him a handsome salary, roughly a third of which went to the Meeting. Like all Meeting donations, it was made anonymously, causing the IRS to react when Dad claimed a tax deduction on it, since the IRS couldn't conceive of anyone donating that much to their church. Tithing was practiced by some faiths, including devout Mormons, but a *third*?! I think Dad finally convinced them it was so; he was certainly no liar and no hypocrite.

Dad grew up in the Meeting. His first real courtship-related encounter with my mom was at a Meeting event in 1932 (although he had already been a friend of her family for years), one of the annual Bible Conferences staged in my mom's home town, Des Moines. They only talked a little, but Dad was smitten by the strikingly good-looking Francys. Nearly a year went by, and as the next year's Des Moines Conference was approaching, Dad wrote to Mom to say he'd like to take her out for a soda after the first day's sessions, which he did. Many years later, Mom would write that *"I wasn't that interested – yet there was something."* (The information about my parents' ancestry, courtship, and other events prior to my own memories is taken from my mom's unpublished memoirs and her verbal stories.) Dad visited Mom in Des Moines a couple of times after that, but as he was heading for another Bible Conference in Walla Walla, Mom suggested to him to *"select a girl out there."* Dad persisted, however, in spite of not being loved, yet in the hope that he would be. One day Mom came home from work to find him visiting her mother – who did love him. *"When later he gave me his picture,"* Mom wrote, *"I tossed it to my mother who kept it on her dresser. However, when he came for the holidays, and we were skating on the ice near Union Park – Birdland Drive – he told me he loved me. My heart was stirred, but I deliberated with the proposal he tried to express. I finally told him to write what he was trying to say when he got home, and I'd think it through."* After Dad's indirect proposal to Mom on ice skates, I don't think either of them ever ice-skated again (certainly not in my lifetime).

There were a few family cultural shocks to be dealt with. My mom's Swedish background included a practice found in some parts of Sweden, called *truga* – usually related to serving food. It entails urging the guest – up to three times – to take a second helping. So when Dad came to visit his fiancée in Des Moines, Grandma Larson offered him seconds. He accepted at once. Then she offered him thirds. When he politely declined, she insisted, twice. My bewildered dad didn't want to seem impolite, and he ended up eating so much that it nearly made him ill. (Don't think for a moment that all Swedes practice *truga*; some are as stingy as stereotypical Scots....) But *truga* also meant that one should never accept an offer of a second helping the first time it is offered. So when Mom visited her new in-laws for dinner in Oak Park, she felt she should wait until the third invitation – which never came. After she had politely declined the first offer of seconds, the dishes were whisked off to the kitchen, presumably followed by my mom's still-hungry eyes.

Perhaps Dad's persistence and tenacity – not an overt or readily recognized trait in him – would somehow be passed on to me? In any case, his own version of *truga* finally paid off, and my parents were married in the basement of the Des Moines Meeting Room the next year by a local judge. They could have gotten married upstairs, but Mom insisted on the basement, for reasons unknown to me. In their motel room in nearby Ames, where they spent their wedding night, Dad was obliged to remain all night in an armchair, while Mom took a rocking chair. She was too terrified to let him near her. Her mom had even been obliged to call upon all her powers of persuasion to get Mom to go with Dad for their wedding night.

Apparently Dad took it all with equanimity, as he did with most things. When he came home from work on evenings when we would be going to

Meeting after supper (Tuesdays and Thursdays), he wouldn't put the car in the garage, but park it in front of our house. I would sometimes crouch in ambush behind the bushes near the front door, watching him somewhat wearily making his way up the front walk, then at the last second leap out in front of him, with as loud and fearsome a roar as I could muster. He would always just look up, smile, and say "*Hi, Stan!*" – as if my greeting had been routinely conversational. I couldn't ruffle him.

Dad got the hiccups one evening after Meeting. The condition continued throughout the ride home. When we arrived at our garage, behind the house, Mom, my brothers and I got out and headed for the back door, while Dad was putting the car in. Mom seemed to be in a hurry. When my brothers and I entered the kitchen, Mom was already filling a pot with cold water. She told us to get behind her and keep still. Dad arrived at the back door, started ascending the few steps up from the landing to the kitchen – and Mom threw the cold water all over him. John, Al and I howled with laughter. Dad smiled and said "*hic*".

I never, ever saw my parents fight. There were no arguments, no yelling, no raised voices, no name-calling or recriminations or tears of anger or dirty looks or frustration towards each other. It is conceivable that there might have been an occasional mild quarrel behind closed doors, but I have no reason to suspect it. They always kissed – briefly, never passionately – when Dad came home, and when he left the house. He always bought red roses for her birthday in late March and for their anniversary in early October, the number of roses being equal to the number of years for each event. Dad always bought Mom an anniversary gift as well; she duly recorded them in a little notebook. In the early years of their marriage when they had little money, the anniversary gifts were for the household – something practical that they needed, like a floor lamp. Dad and Mom usually took a short trip together in connection with their anniversary, just a couple of days or an extended weekend by car, to enjoy the autumnal colors and each other's company with no kids. As far as I remember, these were the only times they ever left us in anyone else's care. After my brothers and I left home, they took a few somewhat longer trips, like to Vermont. They both loved the autumn with its magnificent colors and cooler, crisper air.

My parents were not stingy, but they were frugal, having grown up in the Great Depression. Dad was just 18 when the Great Crash came, Mom was 16. She grew up in a home where frugality was the watchword in every little thing – but in the admirable sense of never wasting anything. Luxury was a foreign word, and a foreign world, to us. Although my parents had experienced the Depression, they seem to have been fortunate enough not to have suffered through it like many others. Dad did, after all, buy Francys Larson an engagement ring – an 0.38-carat diamond in a white-gold setting – in the spring of 1934. Note that I'm measuring the lack of extravagance in their lifestyle against middle-class American standards, which overlooks the fact that the lifestyle of Americans can be seen as extravagant by the standards of the world's vast poor population. Dad could have afforded a Cadillac; he drove a Ford, nothing but Fords, from his first car to his last. They were sufficiently modest, comfortable and dependable. They were discreet and usually forest green. He got a brand-new one about every three years. Cars were Dad's domain, and Mom didn't interfere.

Dad was discreet by nature. Although some Meeting people plastered their car bumpers with Bible stickers, Dad didn't. On the whole, he didn't shove things down anyone's throat – except for the small matter of contributing to the doctrinal force-feeding of us kids, which might well have been largely at the urging of Mom. He was a decent guy, and he probably would have been just as decent a guy had he been raised as a Muslim, a Catholic, a Hindu, or a Druid – excluding any fanatical and fundamentalist elements within those or other faiths. How would he have been as a deist? Or an atheist? I can speculate that there would then have been no compulsions, no directives, no Orders from Above, to compel him into righteous immorality and insufferability, but I can't prove that, there not being any control groups for the life of an individual human.

Dad found his niches, his habits, his cubbyholes, his Army shoes and Fords, and he stuck with them. His religion had been thrust on him as a child and became his habit too, and he never wavered from making the best of it. If he ever had any doubts, he either prevented them from fully formulating themselves as questions, or he kept all doubts and questions well to himself. The mounting payload of years of habit and blind comfort eventually excluded the possibility of his ever achieving escape velocity.

Dad was smart in the smart engineering way: figuring out mathematical problems, making calculations, keeping everything safe. There was no need for philosophical musings or skepticism regarding what he'd been taught by his father. The Bible could no more be questioned than the tables of trigonometry, where every value of sine and cosine, tangent and cotangent is neatly laid out and all you have to do is look those values up or work them out on your slide rule. Every question had an answer to satisfy Dad, even if that answer was the non-answer that "the Lord will reveal it in His time." Dad was adept at logic, that marvelous tool that shows what conclusions can validly be drawn from a given premise or set of premises. But logic is useless at testing the validity of the premises themselves, and since Dad's chief premise in life was the highly self-contradictory Bible, every word of which was the Word of God Himself and thus *had* to be true, it made logic quite useless as a tool for helping a person understand how to live and treat others. Engineering is so much safer.

When Dad wasn't engineering stuff – and to some extent even *while* he was engineering stuff – he was immersed in the Bible and the teachings of the Meeting. It wasn't just something he did; it was who he was, or at least whom he had been rigidly trained to become. Using his engineering and draftsman's skills, my dad constructed a graphic outline of the past and future of the universe, from Eternity to Eternity, in which a mere 6,000-year interval constitutes the entire history of the universe. Dad could have known better if only he had dared to expose himself to evidence, but his emotional ties to what he had been fed as a child were far too strong to allow him to look or question.

Dad could also be sentimental, and get all choked up and weepy over some of the possibly fictitious tear-jerking salvation stories in some of the Gospel tracts he left behind him with the tip at restaurants. His only real outside interest, as far as I know, was trains. In fact, Dad's great passion was running trains – Lionel trains in our basement – as well as riding real trains on our vacations.

That first (in my memory) train trip, when we moved from Glendale to Oak Park, was followed by at least half a dozen others in my youth and childhood, one-way coach versions not funded by Link-Belt. (I had one round trip on my own when I was nearly 17.) Some years after we moved to Oak Park, the three Los Angeles area Meetings joined forces to host what would become the annual Los Angeles Bible Conference, in connection with Christmas vacation time, and since my parents were interested in visiting LA for other reasons as well, Dad signed up with an agency in Chicago that arranged the delivery of cars belonging to wealthy Chicagoans spending the winter in Southern California. We would drive their Cadillacs or Continentals to the West Coast virtually free of charge, and leave them there, giving us (especially Dad) the privilege of taking the train home. The drive itself also involved trains, at least indirectly. We'd be driving along route 66, for example, and whenever stretches of road ran parallel to train tracks, Dad would do some mental calculating, then announce that "a train will be coming along here in about 8 minutes," and it did – to my mom's amusement or chagrin, and to the astonishment of my brothers and me. Dad would read the timetables of the US railroads for amusement; Mom claimed that he memorized them.

I have no memory of the model railroad setup Dad must have had at our house in Glendale (the house lacked a basement, and I don't remember a separate train room), but there was a big set-up in the house on Euclid Avenue. The stairs down to the basement ran from south to north starting at the small landing just inside the side door, ending close to the middle of the basement, although the eastern two-thirds was larger than the western third.[2] There was an open space at the base of the stairs, where a laundry basket hung in front of the gas furnace, beneath the "chute" – a small trap door in the hall upstairs. The trap door itself also served as a seat, convenient when using the wall phone above it, just outside the bathroom at the base of the stairs going up to the dormer attic. The eastern two-thirds of the basement included a ping-pong table, storage shelves, a freezer chest, and the laundry facilities. The latter consisted of a wringer washing machine, and a fairly large two-section laundry tub, made of some kind of precast concrete. Mounted between the two sections was a manual wringer, so Mom could have things soaking in one section and crank them through the wringer into the other section, to remove most of the water before hanging them up on the clothesline in the back yard or, on wintery or rainy days, on clotheslines supported by the low ceiling rafters in the eastern two-thirds of the basement. The western third was for Dad.

Parallel with the stairs, he had a small workbench, about five feet long, and a small but well-organized tool rack on the wall that separated the workbench from the stairs. Under the stairs was the dehumidifier. The rest of Dad's part of the basement was for trains, Lionel trains. At the height of their glory, they occupied a huge table he built from plywood, configured like a squared-off C, with one long side between two short ones, all three against the outer walls of the basement. (The train tables underwent several iterations over the years.) The configuration made it possible for Dad to reach every part of the setup

---

[2] See drawings of the layout of my boyhood home, Appendix 1

without having to crawl over or under anything, and to squeeze in as many feet of track as possible, with bridges and level differences.

He also designed and built a control panel that was full of toggle switches and rheostats, so he could run several different trains at the same time, and at different speeds, to open and close spurs to let faster trains by, and to make them blow their whistles. He even added smoke pellets to the steam locomotives, so that wisps of grayish white smoke would emerge from their chimneys in little whitish puffs, totally unrelated to papal selections.

Dad subscribed to *Model Railroad* and *Trains* magazines. He also subscribed to *Time*, *National Geographic* and *Reader's Digest* – he did want to stay abreast, and occasionally having women's naked breasts on display in magazines in our home was apparently OK, as long as those breasts were black, brown or red and belonged to primitive people. I read *Time* from cover to cover every week, and always studied the pictures and captions in the *National Geographic*. Dad saved every issue, as well as the maps that frequently accompanied them. In his train magazines, Dad would find and order new engines and new cars. As his interest and skill grew, he would also send away for kits, then build the cars and engines himself. He even built a few from scratch. For these he created fictitious railroad companies, based on his own initials, such as Malibu Eastern.

The layout was complex enough to require full concentration when running several trains simultaneously. If you forgot the sharp curve at the end of one of the long straight stretches, the locomotive would go plowing off the track, possibly into another train, and Dad would cringe. He loved this setup. I think the mechanics of it were what he found pleasure in. The aesthetics of Lionel would always be marred by the fact that the tracks had three disproportionately large rails, a feature prominent enough to make them hopelessly unrealistic. Dad's brother Ralph, seven years younger, had opted for the much smaller and highly realistic HO-gauge model railroad. He was considerably more meticulous than my dad, perhaps because Dad was so myopic and Ralph wasn't.

My brother Al would sometimes walk (and talk) in his sleep, and the prevailing advice was that one should never wake a sleepwalker. One night Al got up – without waking up – and went downstairs from his section of our attic dorm to my parents' bedroom, shook Dad, and mumbled something about wanting to run the trains. Dad reportedly dragged himself out of bed, put on slippers and a robe over his pajamas, led the way to the basement, and started connecting and switching on all the connections and switches it took to get the set-up operational. Just as he was finishing, and ready to get the trains rolling, Al woke up enough to say, "*It's OK, Dad, I'm awake now,*" whereupon Al returned to bed. Dad had a great deal of patience.

I've always wondered whether the appeal that trains held for Dad might not have been enhanced by his career in engineering, in view of the fact that in US English, the driver of a train is also called an engineer – and he's "in command". Or was there something in common with the materials handling that trains enable, like the systems Dad engineered for Link-Belt?

One other question will always perplex me deeply, although it didn't occur to me until much later in life. If Dad, in his engineering mode, were shown a drawing of a materials handling conveyor, and was told that it could handle a load of, say, one thousand tons per hour, I am certain that Dad would have demanded proof, would have had to see the calculations, would have insisted on pilot- and full-scale testing until he was satisfied with the veracity of such a claim and felt confident about supplying it to a customer. So how on earth could a person with his intelligence disconnect his brain to such a degree that he could swallow, at face value, the entire Bible as literal Truth, with all its preposterous claims of a creation in six days, Noah's Ark, a virgin birth, a life after death, resurrection, heaven and hell, a "merciful" god who slaughters children, all without so much as a shred (by any engineering standards on earth) of evidence? And then seek to "supply" it to his children and strangers?!

I'm not sure how much my parents' sex life improved after that decidedly non-libidinous wedding night. But they did produce three sons, and there were a couple of miscarriages in between. The doctors told my parents not to have any more children after Mom's near-death experience of giving birth to me. When I was in my teens I found some condoms in Dad's dresser drawer while my parents were off to Meeting and I was at home on my own, "studying".

Dad never gave me a single word on anything remotely related to sex education, which meant only a handful of words fewer than I got from Mom on the subject. Apparently Dad did have some astute words of advice about it for my brother John, who told me that when he, in his early 20s, was going to visit his fiancée Marj in Idaho the year before their marriage, Dad had astonished him by cautioning him with the old adage, "*A stiff prick has no conscience!*"

My parents had pretty decent singing voices, but their repertoire was almost entirely limited to hymns. There were, however, occasional exceptions.

I remember Mom often singing to me, "*Sweetest little fellow /Anybody knows/ Don't know what to call him / But he's mighty like a rose.*" My earliest memory of Dad singing to me was of the sentimental Al Jolson song "*Sonny Boy*" from 1928, which was a smash hit when Dad was in his late teens, meaning he might well have also sung it to John and Al when they were three. Anyway, I remember his clear tenor voice:

> Climb up on my knee, Sonny Boy,
> Though you're only three, Sonny Boy.
> You've no way of knowing,
> There's no way of showing
> What you mean to me, Sonny Boy.

I would have been about three or four when he sang that to me, a number of times, while we were living in Glendale. He knew the words by heart and sang them with rising emotion, often breaking up towards the end.

He sometimes called me "Yelnats" (my name backwards), which I thought was funny, and I always associated it with a special warmth from him towards me. I knew I was greatly loved, but after we moved to Oak Park, I only remember him singing hymns. Dad's parents didn't seem to be at all musical, and he deeply regretted not having learned to play the piano, or any other instrument. Mom was good at the piano, as were some of her sisters.

Dad did love a few other kinds of music, however, particularly marching-band music like that of John Philip Sousa. (Did he keep that interest below his father's radar?) The piece that got him by the throat was a trumpet-and-chorus rendition of "*The Holy City*", which, because of the chorus, I thought was entitled "*Jerusalem*", only to find out much later in life that "*Jerusalem*" was the title of England's "national hymn", with words by the mystic William Blake, based on a weird legend: since no clues as to Jesus' whereabouts for decades in His youth are stated in the Bible or anywhere else, and since the Holy Land was under Roman occupation, just like England, then Jesus *might* have spent some years in England, and since it couldn't be proved that he didn't, then obviously he did. Blake used all the tools of the oxymoronic faith-based pseudo-reasoning to prove the unprovable and refuse the reasonable notion of placing the burden of proof on annoyances like facts.

I stray again, lost sheep that I am. Dad got his first gray hairs in his early teens, and was more or less completely gray by the age of 30 (I got my first gray hairs when I was 16, after which my graying process was much slower than Dad's). Dad had nearly reached the age of 34 by the time I was born, so his gray hair, at least, wasn't my fault. He tended to be somewhat overweight, a shortcoming that I in my high-metabolic and rebellious youth could not overlook, but would exaggerate and hold against him, finding little else. I was athletic; Dad could hardly catch a ball. To an athletic kid pushing at the boundaries, Dad's lack of ball skills was damning evidence of something. In fact, I have no memory of either of my parents ever pursuing any vigorous physical activity. Even their walking was usually strolling; no running or jogging, no swimming, no sports of any kind, no hiking, no bike riding, nothing (and before I was born there was no mention of anything apart from the proposal on ice skates, and a bit of long-distance running Dad had done in high school).

I remember one balmy late-spring evening in my pre-pubertal years, as we were driving to Meeting, southbound along Oak Park Avenue, somewhere between Lake and Madison, we saw a couple of gorgeous spring-clad girls walking north on the sidewalk on the other side of the street. As we passed them, Dad's head turned involuntarily to prolong his view. Mom hissed *"Maurice!"* firmly, two shades short of a full reprimand, and he was instantly eyes front, blushing slightly. Nothing more was said. Nor did anything go unnoticed by his sons in the back seat.

Dad was, like the vast majority of people everywhere have always been, largely the product of his age, his genes and his upbringing. In the environment of the socially and politically conservative Oak Park of that time, right-wing Republican conservatism was the only show in town, and even though Meeting people didn't participate in politics, and thus didn't vote, Dad's satisfaction at the victory of Eisenhower over Stevenson, twice, was written all over his face, spilling onto mine. We never listened to the car radio, with the possible exception of the hymns on WMBI (the voice of the ultra-conservative Moody Bible Institute), apart from when the USSR invaded Hungary in 1956, and we followed every harrowing detail on the news broadcast on the way home from Meeting on Sunday, November 4th.

On any family trip (and there were many), all over the US, whenever we stopped at a diner for burgers, Dad would always leave a generous tip – together with a Gospel tract. But unlike my mom, he seldom confronted strangers with their lack of holiness, nor did he proclaim to them his heavenly destination or sainthood. He was an impeccable and careful driver, but sometimes he drove too purposefully for my mom, who had to learn to feed him salty snacks so that he would be more amenable to making pit stops on our long hauls.

From the time I was around 10, after kneeling to say my bedside prayer, climbing into bed and putting out the light, while drifting into that hazy land between sleep and consciousness, I would frequently get feelings of panic that Dad was dying, and that if I just ran and ran – flat out for miles, marathon upon sprinted marathon – I could somehow magically cure him and bring him back to health. These semi-conscious dreams were quite real to me, but I never told a soul about them before writing about them here. I think it was a way for me to somehow express to myself how much I loved and needed my dad.
I was "encouraged" to pursue the safe studies of mathematics, as my brothers did, despite my unkindled interest in them. In grades 6-8 at Horace Mann, I had the same science and math teacher (Miss Tredenick) as Al – and Dad! And in high school I had the same algebra teacher (Mr Woodruff) as John and Al – and Dad! But the pursuit of math was not for me, and I'm sure I disappointed Dad considerably when, after toiling through trigonometry in my junior year, I refused to move on to calculus in my senior year and went for art instead. (Mom could hardly back Dad on this one, her own grasp of mathematics being limited to arithmetic.) This was but one of many points of difference that had come to dominate the relationship between a loving teenager and his loving father, until that relationship bore little resemblance to a relationship at all, and all the glow of love was hidden from view by the pale cast of seemingly interminable conflicts, tensions, and a not-always-suppressed battle of wills.

Al was not allowed to engage in extra-curricular football, despite his love of the game. Perhaps his extreme near-sightedness – a problem he shared with Dad – would have denied him access to that particular sport even if my parents hadn't. Al was, however, allowed to play Little-League baseball, and then Pony League when he outgrew Little League, but since the Pony League had Sunday practice and games, Al had to be excused from them, which didn't sit too well with the coach back in the day when expressions of religious fervor seldom spilled over into everything else, except in the Meeting. But Al saw my talent in football and lobbied hard and successfully for Dad to allow me to try out for the high school team. (This was ultimately not Mom's decision.)

In my freshman year, I was so small that I only made the C-team, then was upgraded in mid-season to the B-team – thanks to my fierce competitiveness, speed, and a good pair of hands. We played on Saturdays, and Dad faithfully drove me to the games (some of which were played in the same Forest Preserve clearing where we had our Sunday School Picnic). He stood patiently on the sidelines with the few spectators (parents) who could be bothered. He took a few photos before the days of ubiquitous telephoto lenses and point-and-shoot digital, where the only possible means of identifying me was knowing the number on my jersey. In my senior year, when I fought my way to the first-string varsity team as a wide receiver (with an even shorter quarterback whose talents were mostly limited to handing off), Dad came to the games to watch me, take pictures, and enjoy the marching band at halftime.

Possibly the most tragic event of my youth – and certainly in my relationship with Dad – took place during the late summer of 1959, just before I turned 14 and started high school. One Saturday afternoon, my cousin Howie was at our place. Howie and I, as well as Norm Denton, Dave Henderson, and a couple of other slightly older Meeting boys, had just begun testing at least one limit by sneaking off to Saturday matinée movies at the Mercury Theater in Elmwood Park, at the corner of North and Harlem. On this particular Saturday, Howie was having some misgivings about these sinful acts, and was beginning to feel drawn towards "taking his place" (joining the Meeting); he probably didn't feel comfortable about opening up any new avenues of pleasure. So he and I were talking about doing something enjoyable that might also be *permitted* – a small category indeed, especially since the only approved attraction I knew of was sports, and that was nothing for Howie. But what about bowling? Was that OK? Was it a sport? Was it worldly? Who would decide? One of us – I think it was me – came up with the idea of asking our dads to join us, because then it would *have* to be OK, right? So Howie cycled home to ask his dad, while I found my dad to ask him.

He was in the garage. I said that Howie and I wanted to go bowling with him and Uncle Ralph that afternoon, would that be OK? He wrinkled his brow and asked, "*What does your mother say?*" This really irritated me; I wanted to go bowling with Dad, not Mom. But I just said no, I hadn't asked her. He said we would have to, so we went inside. "*Bowling?!*" Mom exclaimed, looking as if she'd been asked to walk a tightrope 50 feet above the ground. "*Isn't that worldly*?" No clear answer was forthcoming, not from Dad either, so she said she would have to consult her younger sister Maxine on a matter that weighty. She phoned Howard's mom, got an immediate and resoundingly final veto. That was the end of the matter. The tragedy is that it was the last time I ever asked Dad to do anything with me. I'd concluded that anything I asked him would have to be cleared by Maxine first anyway, so there was no point.

What would have happened if we'd stayed in Glendale, safely out of the suffocating presence of my grandfather and Maxine? Would Dad have been more liberal? Would Mom have been more liberal and allowed Dad to be? Would the layers of oppression that built up during our years in Oak Park never have formed? Would there have been insufficient cause for me to rebel? Could I have lived a "normal" life? These are, of course, purely hypothetical questions. We only get the one shot. There's no control group, no way of ever knowing the *what-ifs* or *might-have-beens*. But since it's clear to me that Dad was good at adapting to whatever his environment was at the time, there is some reason to think that all of our lives would have been significantly different had we stayed in Southern California.

As it was, the repression in Oak Park *did* build up, and with it the conditions that led to "the Thursday Night Massacre" – and my response to it. A state of war would soon arise between me and my parents. Once my plans were forged and the countdown had begun, my rebellion would become open, full-fledged, at times bordering on vicious. Oppression was teaching me to question, compelling me to cut myself free.

On several occasions in my early teens, when I was out with Dad on his Saturday errands, we stopped at the grocery section of Sears at Harlem and North, on the Chicago side. Oak Park was for generations completely dry, but alcohol was sold on the Chicago side, and Dad's Meeting tasks included procuring the wine for the Breaking of Bread. He always (a couple of times a year at most) bought a gallon jug of cheap Mogen David, which was kept in a cupboard in the Meeting Room basement and was used to fill the two goblets every Sunday. I never commented on this during our shopping trips, but one evening (possibly during the summer, because it was still light, and probably in 1961) when we were on our way to Meeting, I leaned forward from the back seat and asked Dad why he bought Mogen David. He seemed startled by the question and asked what I meant. I said, "*Well, when Jesus turned the water into wine at that wedding, do you really think he made rotgut!?*" Dad looked as if I'd hit him. It was one of the only times I remember his complexion changing due to anger, and being behind the wheel of a moving car might have been all that prevented him from spinning around and lashing out. But at the same time I think he knew I had a point. He answered lamely, through clenched teeth, that "it was a bitter cup", mixing up his Biblical sources to a surprising extent. Mom said nothing but turned pale.

Our biggest blowout came during one of the special meetings held in our home for the dozen or more young-ish people from the Oak Park Meeting, when those held at the Dentons were felt to be too infrequent after they cut back on hosting them in response to the cold shoulder they endured when they refused to back the change of Conference venues to Wheaton, almost resulting in Norm's dad being "silenced". Even though they weren't "officially" ostracized, nobody would speak to them. They were given a shoulder so cold that Norm told me his mom wept in the car on the way home from Meeting for a very long time. I had come to hate these gatherings – extra meetings on top of the four or five we already attended week after week, when we would sit around and sing hymns, read something from the Bible, then have a refreshment break, then go back for more cranial Novocain.

On one such occasion, when I was around 16, I cracked. During the refreshment break, a few of us young guys retreated upstairs to where my brothers and I had had our bedroom areas, but that I now had all to myself. I mostly wanted to get away so that Norm and I could update our countdown, but several other less rebellious kids followed. When my parents felt it was time for us to get back to singing the Lord's praises, Dad came (or was sent?) upstairs to summon us. I made no move to come down, so he repeated the summons, more sternly. I flatly told him *no*. The stage was set for the showdown, as clearly as in any Western. Since I'd defied him in front of others, he *had to* come after me, and he did, with a look of parental outrage on his face. I grabbed the hunting knife I'd kept on a shelf since my trapper days, waved it menacingly in his direction, my adrenalin running high. And I told him most decidedly that I was *not* coming nor could he make me. He turned pale, turned around and went downstairs, with the others following him. I felt horrible about it, but mostly because I also felt trapped: my only two choices *both* meant doing something I didn't want to do.

That incident was never discussed afterwards, but not surprisingly it exacerbated the distance between us. The only possible reference to it I ever heard from Dad was in one of our subsequent daily family Bible readings (just me and my parents by now). We'd reached I Timothy, chapter 3, which states that one of the criteria for becoming a bishop was *"one that ruleth well his own house, having his children in subjection with all gravity; (For if a man know not how to rule his own house, how shall he take care of the church of God?)."* Dad got all misty-eyed and forlornly announced, "Well, I could never be a bishop!" This was, in its own way, a puzzling thing for him to say, in view of the fact that the Meeting had no clergy at all, much less any bishops, and it wasn't even a church. The Catholics have the same problem at the other end; their bishops aren't permitted to marry, much less to have their own children (which hasn't always stopped them in any sense of the verb *having*).

But Dad continued to come to my football games and we continued to function on certain levels. After high school in '63, I worked during the summer in the Loop, and then a vacancy arose (or Dad may have helped to create it) in the purchasing department at Link-Belt, so I began working there. Sometimes I would ride with Dad to or from work, or both ways. Sometimes we would talk, sometimes not. We were balancing on a tightrope between hostility and love, and there was always tension about where we would land. I'm sure he could smell the tobacco on me after a day in the office, but perhaps he wanted and needed to attribute it to my jaded colleagues instead. We continued these occasional shared commutes throughout the winter and spring, as the countdown was coming to an end. My last day of work was May 29, 1964.

When Norm and I reached San Francisco on June 8th, I immediately wrote a strained letter to my parents. I wanted to make it clear that while I wasn't having any part of the Meeting and all the restrictions associated with it, I still loved them dearly. So we began corresponding, but it was almost always Mom who replied to my letters. I only ever got two or three letters from Dad, and some occasional lines he added to Mom's letters. When they made their first visit to San Francisco in December 1964, I was living alone in a tiny room at the back of Fred Bito's garage. By their next visit a year later, with my room a bit more livable, I'd acquired three or four pipes, which stood in a rack on my heater in the corner of the room. Mom took one look at them and burst demonstratively into tears and fled to the bathroom. Dad looked at me anxiously. I smiled and asked if he'd like me to make him a grilled cheese sandwich. He looked surprised – possibly relieved to change the subject – and said yes. Mom eventually rejoined us.

Dad visited Jeanette and me a couple of times, including once on his own, in San Francisco and and again in Vancouver. Jeanette said she loved him; he was so kind, so gentle, and she told me she saw so much of him in me, or vice-versa. I took that as a great compliment. On our way to Sweden in August '69, we stopped in Oak Park for some days to visit. Dad offered to show us some slides – Jeanette wanted to see stuff from my childhood and youth – so Dad set up the projector in the basement and showed us a lot of slides. He made sure to include everything that had me in it, for Jeanette's sake. One of the slides, from my parents' second trip to San Francisco, was half black, and I figured it was the last slide on the roll of film. Years later, when Mom offered me those slides, I discovered that Dad had taped over the half that showed my pipe collection, for my mom's sake!

At some point during the late '60s, while Dad was on assignment for Link-Belt, to work on a big materials handling project for a sugar mill in Louisiana, there was a dust explosion. Dad was not injured, but was apparently pretty shaken up, possibly having suffered shock. Sometime after that, when he went for an eye check-up, it was discovered that he'd developed diabetes, which the doctor said could have been the result of the explosion having altered his metabolism in some way. In any case, he – and Mom – embarked on a strict sugar-free diet that he adhered to faithfully for the rest of his life. He never needed insulin injections.

Although we maintained correspondence (mostly through Mom) after moving to Sweden, I would only ever see Dad once more. In May '71, my parents made a trip to Europe to see us and some other sights. They flew from Chicago to Amsterdam, where they rented a car and drove up to Malmö. During our couple of days together in Malmö, Dad and I had the only truly man-to-man (as opposed to father-son) talks we ever had. It felt good. I sensed no trace of hostility on his part (nor did I feel any towards him), even though there were some areas of residual tension due to our vastly different perspectives on life. I've often thought the tension was due to Dad's wish to shield Mom from my blatant worldliness.

One of the things we talked about was language. I guess it was quite a novelty for my monolingual dad to have a bilingual son. Although Dad (like most other Meeting people and others) knew full well, intellectually, that the Bible was not originally written in King James English, there was an almost tangible feeling that somehow it was. I pointed out that all those *thee's* and *thou's* were not reserved for the deity in Elizabethan times, but were simply the *in*formal, singular version of *you*, a fact that I'd only acquired a feeling for once I learned Swedish, a language that still had different second-person pronouns for formal and informal usage. Dad hadn't acquired that feeling, but understood its existence when I pointed it out, and was fascinated by it.

After a few days in Malmö, we drove north to see a couple of the locations where Mom's grandparents were born, before we returned to Malmö. Jeanette had to resume her Swedish secretarial studies in Furulund, so she couldn't join us when my parents and I subsequently drove down to Basel to see Bob. We first went to Bob's place in Binningen, spent a little time there, then took my parents to their hotel (the Drachen) in downtown Basel for them to get settled in. We agreed to meet for dinner a couple of hours later, so Bob and I went back to his place and had a drink or two. I suddenly became self-conscious (paranoid) about having the smell of alcohol on my breath when we met my parents again, so I ran down to the Migros grocery store and bought a pack of chlorophyll chewing gum, and started chewing about five pieces at once before we left to catch the tram downtown to meet my parents and go to dinner. As we were about to leave Bob's apartment, he said something that caused me to grin back at him and he immediately started roaring with laughter. My teeth and tongue were bright green. So I had to brush them furiously to tone it down. I don't know whether my parents noticed the slightly green teeth and slightly alcohol-laden breath of their son; at least they never said so.

On the sunny Sunday afternoon, Bob also took us all to a lovely and luxurious countryside inn in the Black Forest for a pleasant pheasant dinner. Dad expressed his sincere appreciation and gratitude to Bob. Then we had to leave for Amsterdam – so I could fly back to Copenhagen, as Mom and Dad flew back to Chicago. There, at their gate at the Schiphol airport where I would see them off, my dad and I embraced for the last time ever. But of course neither of us could have known that then.

The correspondence that followed their European trip revealed that Dad was thinking of early retirement, and so was Ralph. In fact, they decided to purchase a couple of adjoining plots of land out in the countryside, along Swedenburg Road outside Knoxville, Illinois, there to build their respective retirement homes. Mom and Dad's place would be almost directly across the road from where one of Mom's uncles lived (not Uncle Carl!), where her father's parents once lived, and where she'd spent a lot of time as a girl. We visited the house a number of times when I was a kid, because her relatives still lived there, and because it was not far from where the Nunnikhovens lived, just across the Mississippi in Burlington. It was at the old house in Knoxville that I had my first breathtaking experience of an outhouse.

In the spring of '73, with the new Knoxville homes ready for construction, Dad was going to undertake just one more project for Link-Belt before retiring. This last assignment would require a temporary move to Pittsburgh where Dad was going to start up a new engineering branch of the company. Then I got a letter in the late spring informing me that Dad had been feeling weak and had to take some tests. In June came word that he'd been diagnosed with stage-three Hodgkin's disease, but that the doctors were certain it would be treatable; after a couple of rounds of chemo in the hospital, we were told, he'd be able to continue treatment as an out-patient. I didn't understand too much about it. Mom indicated that she was concerned, but not alarmed. Going to the US was still out of the question for me – I would have faced arrest.

I asked Bob about Dad's medical condition, and he was more alarmed than Mom, but Dad was in the hospital and there was nothing I could do. I was becoming distraught and wrote him a long letter telling him how much I loved him – how much I'd always loved him, in spite of everything. I sent the letter by special delivery. It apparently arrived a few hours after he died, some four months before his 62nd birthday. Right up until minutes before his death, I was later told that his recovery had seemed imminent, and Mom thought he would be coming home (instead of "going Home") in a day or two. But something happened – perhaps some inscrutable and heartless deity misled the doctors? – and no prayers or even marathons would bring him back.

My mom's – and the Meeting's – official view was that Dad had been *"called Home to be with the Lord,"* which was supposed to be the most wonderful thing ever. So why were they hoping desperately for a cure? And if the Lord were "calling him Home", why not just send a limo instead of giving him suffering, even agony, masked only by a morphine fog? Or why not cure him?! Or is it only the advances in medical science that manage to do humane things like that? Why do people thank God when someone recovers instead of thanking the doctors? And if they do thank God, why don't they damn Him when the loved one doesn't recover? They claim, after all, that it was "His will".

I feel a certain sadness that such a decent guy as Dad should have devoted – thrown away – such a huge portion of his life to a fundamentally cruel set of superstitions, disregard for evidence, and obviation of reason – reason that Dad would have had the cranial capacity to utilize. But he seemed to lack the emotional fortitude and will to think for himself beyond what he'd been frightened into believing in his youth, which instead evolved into the comfortable, insular habit of his life. (I don't for a minute think he would have agreed with me on this....)

I would like to think that Dad passed some of his basic kindness and warmth on to me, as well as the ability (I see it as an ability, not a weakness) to be overwhelmed by the beauty of music, even though my music is often different from his. I may also have inherited his logical and analytical abilities and interest, tools I feel he could have used much more if he had liberated himself from the terrors of his indoctrination. I cannot think of any bad or undesirable traits I might have acquired from my dad – not because I don't have any, but because *he* didn't.

When Jeanette and I visited my mom in Oak Park a year after Dad's death, Ralph picked us up to go out and see Dad's grave in some cemetery way the hell out North Avenue in some place where Dad had decided to buy a burial plot for himself and Mom, a place with which neither he nor I had any associations or memories of him whatsoever. I stared at the simple bronze plate on the ground with his name and some dates and a Bible verse on it. This is *not* where I will remember him. I have never been back to that place (where Mom is now also buried) and have no intention of ever going there again. I don't believe that Dad (or Melchior) had any kind of "soul" that lives on somewhere, or that we will meet again, or that it matters. But my dad lives on in my memory, with love, for as long as I maintain the mental faculties to grasp an ungraspable word like "forever".

CHAPTER 5

The Trapper

My early years at Horace Mann elementary school were mostly free from trauma, at least from anything I would have recognized as trauma then, since I didn't know the meaning of the word. I feel quite certain that I felt secure and happy most of the time, apart from the pet problems and being constantly bombarded with frightening threats of the Wiles of the Devil and the Lake of Fire. I had no other reference points, and precious little awareness of the doctrinal pressures to which I was daily being subjected.

Although this was the heyday of Joseph McCarthy and the Red Menace, the milkman was still making his rounds in Oak Park, driving up and down the alleys in his boxy white van, carrying his wire racks of glass milk bottles to each back door and replacing empty bottles with full ones. So all was well from my little-boy perspective.

At around this time I would occasionally have dreams that I was falling, falling, falling. Once I woke up to find myself falling out of bed and landing on the floor. But more of my dreams were in an opposite and exhilarating direction: flying. They took two forms. In one, I would be standing in an open space, like the big parking lot just north of our house, repeatedly jerking my head up and down in the way I'd learned to do to swallow air so I could belch at will, except that in my dream, each downward jerk lifted me up a few more inches from the ground, higher and higher, like jacking up a car, until I was about 10 feet above the ground. Then I could just lean forward, spread my arms, and start soaring and looping everywhere, as high as I wanted to, over valleys, under bridges, across the sea. It was absolutely wonderful, and I always woke up euphoric. In the other variant, I'd be walking along the sidewalk, taking longer and longer strides, until each stride became a leap, sort of in slow motion, and ultimately I could extend my leap indefinitely and whiz along just above the ground in the world's longest long jump, one leg extended forwards, the other backwards. Both kinds of flying dreams would come back to me several times a year, well into my adulthood, even into middle age.

From the first grade, and throughout my eight years at Horace Mann (not counting the final two months of kindergarten), I walked to and from school, like all the other kids, twice a day, as no lunches were served there, nor was there a lunchroom even if I might have wanted to bring my own. These were the days when middle-class American wives with children, like my mom, were expected to be housewives, which most were, at least in Oak Park. So it was a walk home for lunch and a walk back immediately afterwards. But it would be more accurate to say I went on foot, rather than walked, since more often than not I would run or play mind-games that I was running after or from something, winning races, performing heroic deeds, sometimes stopping to examine insects or shiny scraps, interesting autumn leaves, crystals of ice, the first signs of spring, chasing robins and wrens, watching for blue jays and cardinals.

Early in second grade, we were given an assignment to write a story, my first ever; it was entitled "The wolf":

> *Once there was a wolf. He was a wild wolf. He thought he was so smart. that He tried to jump across a wide streem. but! He fell in. and there was a grate big waterfalls and he fell in! what a bad thing! But there was a seal that helped him out. then he thanked the seal. and he never thought he was so smart again. now he is a kind wolf he gives ribbits food. everyone likes him. and he likes them. one day a meen man came he kilded the wolf then he had to go to the polece and got put in jail for 100 years and that was the rest of his life. and that's all.*

Mrs Steger, my teacher in first and second grades, wrote in one of my report cards, "*He seems to be interested in art work & shows ability in that field.*" I don't recall any particular emphasis on *understanding* what we were learning, nor any encouragement to *question* what we were told. I suppose the basic building blocks had to be in place before we could start to work with them. But learning of the Pledge of Allegiance certainly fits into the category of *rote* learning – and indoctrination (the words "under God" were added when I started 4th grade).

My normal lunch fare might be cereal – Cheerios, Rice Krispies, Shredded Wheat, or Fruit Loops (John was the only one in our family who liked Wheaties, which during an extended period later in life he would eat with orange juice instead of milk). More often my lunch was peanut butter and jelly sandwiches on toast. Occasionally Mom would make grilled cheese sandwiches or my favorite: black cheese. I don't know whether the recipe was her own or not; I've never encountered it anywhere else. She put a number of slices of that orange Velveeta processed "cheese" into a hot frying pan, let them melt until they began to burn on the underside, then scraped the frying pan back and forth, and finally transferred the gooey, partially blackened cheese onto toast to make the sandwich. But I usually had some fruit as well, and a couple of glasses of milk.

At Horace Mann, we had one teacher for first and second grades, then another for third and fourth. By the time we got to fifth and sixth, our main teacher was complemented by other teachers for certain special subjects. Mrs Steger was a pleasant, matronly lady with good pedagogical skills and plenty of patience. When we got to third grade, we quickly discovered that Miss Mallon needed none of that; her looks and manner were a fair likeness of Marilyn Monroe (although I'd never heard of Marilyn Monroe then), and she knew it. In spite of puberty still being a few years away, Miss Mallon was just somebody we all wanted to snuggle up to, even the girls.

Every year before the Christmas break, Horace Mann would stage a Christmas Pageant for the parents, and the teachers would select something for their respective classes to perform on the makeshift stage erected for the occasion at one end of the school gym. I'm not sure why I was allowed to participate – perhaps I was still so safely innocent – or whether my parents attended, but I presume they did. Since many of my classmates were Jewish, the school tended to avoid overtly religious themes like Nativity scenes.

Miss Mallon selected a highly condensed version of Dickens' *A Christmas Carol*, in which I had a miniscule role. My classmate John Ozag and I were to walk slowly across the stage. One of us would ask, *"When did he die?"*, and the other would reply solemnly, *"Last night, I believe."* Those two lines (and I'm not sure which of the two was mine) would constitute my total sum of stage acting, a fact which, for some reason, didn't occur to me at the time. The important thing was that after a few rehearsals in the classroom, the big night had come.

Miss Mallon was every bit as nervous as we were, and while we were all waiting for our cue to leave the classroom and go downstairs to stand by the "backstage" door of the gym, Miss Mallon promised us that if all went well, when we got back to the classroom after our fretful hour upon the stage, we could all form a line to give her a kiss. This was heaven!

My line in the play was near the end, and when I was done I didn't go sit with the others and wait, but positioned myself to be the first to head back to the classroom, and to be first in line to kiss Miss Mallon. The classroom was darkened, lit only by the colored Christmas tree lights. There we all were, lined up, while Miss Mallon, looking more beautiful than ever, waited for us to settle down, while she took her place on a chair at the head of the class, just in front of me, the first in line. Then she smiled, nodded to me, and I came forward and placed my lips on her soft, dreamy ones until she gently moved me aside with a mildly surprised look and a smile. It was certainly nothing at all like kissing Mom, but I couldn't have explained in what way. What I *could* do was hurry to the end of the line, instead of back to my seat, and it wasn't until my lips were again on Miss Mallon's that she realized what I'd done, and with a giggling scold, she sent me to my seat, me grinning elatedly. Miss Mallon didn't return the following fall to teach us fourth grade; she'd been replaced by Mrs Shiess, although many of us would have declared *Sheiss!* if we'd known that appropriate German word to express our reaction to the fact that Miss Mallon had married Mr Shiess. And by Christmas, her bulging belly told us she wouldn't be returning for the spring term.

I was always a quick learner at school and my vocabulary was expanding. Sometimes it grew in directions that met with the disapproval of my parents. We (my brothers and I) were never given an actual list of forbidden words to unquestioningly exclude from emanation from our little mouths, but the moment we used one on that unwritten list, the reprimand was swift and harsh. Although the Bible only talks about not taking the Name of the Lord in vain, and although most of those forbidden words had nothing to do with His name, they were forbidden anyway. *Hell* and *damn* were on that list, as well as the common euphemisms for them, like *heck, darn, dang* and *drat*. *Devil* was also on the list, even though using *his* name in vain might logically seem to be desirable.

Our family's words for bodily functions had approved euphemisms. Taking a piss was "making a river"; the word *piss* was for some reason forbidden, even though it appears in the King James Bible in its literal sense. *Shit* was abominable, *crap* was borderline; the accepted term in our family was "making a BM" (as in "bowel movement"). Euphemistic expletives like *shoot, shucks* and *crud* were also borderline. Farts were called *blurps!* The only clearly acceptable expletives were *phooey* (etymology unknown and thus probably not a euphemism for anything wicked) and *rats*. Until I reached puberty, and beyond, I knew no other word for my penis than *dojigger*, which turned out to be a synonym for *dohickey, gimmick, gizmo, gadget, thingamabob, thingamajig*, and other similar words – none of which had anything at all to do with a penis. *Ass* was not OK; *rump* and *seat* were. As far as names for female genitalia were concerned, we weren't even supposed to know or think about such things, nor about fucking, not until after we were married. And if I were to use any of the forbidden vocabulary? Mom reserved for herself the right to march me to the bathroom, pry open my mouth with all necessary force and shove the bar of soap inside, twisting it around to get rid of the "filth". That happened a couple of times – the soap in my mouth, I mean; the filth is evidently still there.

We lived about six blocks from Horace Mann – three long ones and three short ones. To reach school I first went down Euclid to LeMoyne, then right for three blocks, past Oak Park Avenue and Grove until I reached Kenilworth, with its parkway divider. I turned left there, and continued on past Greenfield and Berkshire. Horace Mann occupied the block between Berkshire and Division, another main street, but one I didn't have to cross to get to and from school. (Most kids didn't take their bikes to school back then – I know I didn't; perhaps we weren't allowed to.) In the worst part of winter, the snow was sometimes so hard-packed on all the streets that I could ice skate to school (which I did a few times), except for having to hop gingerly across Oak Park Avenue, which was plowed and salted due to the bus route, its black asphalt surface standing out like a strip of dirty tape against the otherwise white ground.

Once in a great while, when snowy weather and extreme cold prevented Dad from driving to work (or sent him home early), he would drive me and/or pick me up. At six blocks away, I lived farther from school than the majority of my classmates, who regarded being picked up as a "sissy" thing, so I once ignored Dad waiting in the car for me outside school, despite my freezing feet. I hurried along up Kenilworth, pretending not to notice him. He followed along in the car, slowly, but I persisted in ignorance. He finally gave up when we reached LeMoyne and drove on home to meet me there. He looked a bit sad. I felt ashamed.

Once, after school, when there was an abundance of good packing snow, I and some classmates were throwing snowballs at passing, slow-moving cars outside the school. I had a good arm, and one high-arching shot landed squarely on the roof of a passing car. The driver, a man in his 40s, slammed on his brakes, leaped out of his still-running car, ran over to accost me (I was paralyzed), grabbed me roughly by the collar and roared at me until I wetted myself.

Another time after school, my brother Al saved my life. It was a bitterly cold day with exceptionally deep snow, and I had for some reason sat down half frozen on somebody's front steps, taken off my boots, and was sitting there with drowsiness setting in, when Al happened to come along the same way, spotted me, and got me home in the dim light of a late winter afternoon.

Apart from that, the lower grades at Horace Mann passed by fairly uneventfully. I was almost totally unaware of the outside world – the World was not the concern of pilgrims passing through it. The entire Korean War slipped by me unnoticed, except for one memory. My much-older cousin Charles stopped by our home on his way back to Detroit from Korea, where he'd been serving as a medic (he was a conscientious objector, but the role of a medic was Meeting-approved). He told us how he'd been conned out of a nice new camera he'd bought at the PX. He'd been visiting Seoul with another serviceman and was approached by a young Korean man who offered him a big wad of cash for the camera. The guy produced a roll of US dollars with a rubber band around it. He unrolled it in front of Charles, counted out a sum that was far more than Charles had paid, so Charles agreed to sell. The Korean rolled the money back up, put the rubber band back around it, handed it to Charles, took the camera, and melted into the crowd. When Charles later unrolled the wad, the only dollar bill was the one on the outside – the rest was newspaper.

When I was around 9 or 10, my elementary school librarian suggested *Call of the Wild* to me, which I devoured. By the time I also finished *White Fang*, Jack London had convinced me that I wanted to become a trapper in Alaska. I made drawings for a log cabin 100 miles or more from Fort Yukon, and I dreamed of wandering around in deep snow without freezing my feet off – something I'd never been able to do in the real world – and of layers of pelts hanging from the cabin walls behind me, Stan the trapper. My grizzled gaze swept over woods and rocks and valleys in that pristine and Arctic solitude, with my trusted husky by my side. I made detailed drawings of how my one-room log cabin would be furnished, and plans for where I would store the pelts, and how I would barter for the provisions I couldn't supply myself from what was available for free in the deep forest around me. Despite being a cute, charming little boy with a gregarious temperament, I didn't see separation from others as a problem; it had been part of the Meeting's unquestionable doctrine all my life: "Separate yourself unto Him" and "be ye not unequally yoked together with unbelievers" were oft-repeated Biblical injunctions. Mom frequently played and sang for me "*Dare to be a Daniel, dare to stand alone, dare to have a purpose true, dare to make it known.*" I never imagined that my life as a trapper would involve the company of anyone but dogs, and it made perfect sense to me; then there would be no contact with sinners either, I could stand alone and make my purpose true known to my dogs. I never made it to Alaska. Instead, I began collecting stuffed animals. My room, i.e. my corner of "the boys' room", our attic dormitory, came to be full of them.

I'd always been fascinated by animals, particularly wild ones, and a visit to Chicago's magnificent Natural History Museum was heaven enough for me. Even though all the animals there were stuffed, they looked wonderfully real. My fascination was considerably reinforced by many of the wildlife pictures in the *National Geographic*. On our car trips I always kept a sharp lookout for deer and prong-horned antelope, as well as hawks as they soared, majestic, solitary and free. But I was irrationally afraid of snakes and spiders, although not at the level of phobic panic my mom had about rats and mice. I got to ride an elephant on a visit to the St. Louis Zoo, and once when we visited the Grand Canyon on our way to the LA Conference, we saw some mule deer on the small road ahead. I demanded that Dad stop the car. I was going to feed them, and was out of the car before anyone knew what happened. The problem was that I had nothing edible on me except a pack of Charms – a kind of square version of Life Savers. The flavor was coffee – with plenty of sugar – and the deer ate them from my hand.

The sloping ceiling of our attic dorm was of matte white plasterboard. I never realized it was made of plasterboard, or what plasterboard was, until Al put a hole the size of a golf ball through it when he was practicing his swing with a driver. The end wall at the top of the stairs had three windows: one in John's section to the right, one in Al's to the left, and one in the middle, facing the stairs. By turning levers on the inside, the windows could be cranked open outwards on hinges on the sides. This enabled having open windows in the summer; the screens kept the mosquitoes out. Mosquitoes and sweltering Chicago summer heat waves tended to outweigh the joys of vacation freedom for me. Spring and fall were my favorite seasons.

John's corner, the southwest corner of the attic, was by far the narrower of the two halves of our dorm. John's quarters ran about two-thirds of the width of our house and ended with a small low door that was the entrance to the storage room. The crawl-space part of the storage room also ran behind the entire length of John's four-foot-high knotty pine wall. John's room was just wide enough to place a desk beneath the window and a bed along the low wall. The banister wall, also paneled in knotty pine, made John's section more private than Al's or mine. When John reached his late teens, he got to have a drapery from the ceiling to the banister, giving him even more privacy. It also kept the light out of my eyes when he had to study late in the evening.

In the middle of the northern part of the attic was a small bathroom – a toilet and a sink – with the entrance from my corner, which meant that I could regard it either as a privilege of easy access for myself and the ability to keep track of my brothers' goings (I didn't have a clue about their possible comings), or as a burden of occasionally having a light in my eyes in the middle of the night and hearing their grunts and farts and not having any privacy of my own. I think I always thought the privilege slightly outweighed the burden, but then Al was already off to DeKalb by the time I had my first real need for privacy in bed. There were also two windows in the north wall of the attic – one in my room and the other in the bathroom. (It was a good thing that window could be opened!)

The southern border of my half of the east half of the attic was formed by the south edge of my double bed, a dark-oak frame with flowers carved into most of the vertical surfaces. It had been our parents' bed until they got a new bedroom set when I was around eight. The space between the northern edge of my bed and the north wall formed my "room", my section where I had the stuffed animals. On the wall to the right of the bathroom door, above my chest of drawers, I had a deer head. It was kind of moth-eaten and had come from someone's attic. The antlers were covered in fuzz, so it must have either died on its own, been a victim of road-kill, or been poached out of season. I never asked, and I don't remember who was as enthusiastic to get it out of their attic as I was to put it on my wall. On the north wall to the right of the window I had the head and shoulders of a female pheasant on a wall-mounted plaque. On the same wall I had a red fox skin with thick, soft fur.

Standing on the floor was a stuffed loon that Dad's former girlfriend (before he met Mom) had in the house she shared with her old mother. The lady's name was Lottie Sanders; she was one of the only Meeting ladies – at least in the Oak Park Meeting – to wear any make-up. She'd remained a spinster, although with considerably more glamour than any of the other Meeting ladies dared to display. There were a few mostly unspoken family jokes about Mom's jealousy of Dad's having had another girlfriend, particularly one he admitted having kissed, though he certainly never got beyond first base. Perhaps he didn't try. He was no good at baseball, and besides, kids tend to find it repugnant to fantasize about the carnal interests of their parents. I have no idea how Lottie and her mother came to have a stuffed loon, but they gave it to me for my 11th birthday and I was ecstatic.

Accompanying the fox and the pheasant on my north wall was a pelt from a Rocky Mountain goat, white and soft. I bought it from a taxidermists' catalogue I discovered at the home of my neighbor friend, Johnny, who, despite being a vast year older than me, deigned to be my friend, and we had fun together. He and his older brother Bill were also collectors of stuffed animals.

The floor in my room came to be dominated by the skin of a leopard, with the head stuffed and the mouth open in an understandably outraged snarl. I got it from a classmate of Al's, whose parents were apparently glad to get it out of their attic. Mom was less enthusiastic about it than me, probably because she wasn't sure it was free of fleas, mange or other vermin, or was certifiably dead, but she didn't protest much. She apparently found my growing but extremely deceased Noah's ark to be an acceptable channel for my young energy and interest – better to devote my attention to dead animals than to unrepentant sinners. I also had a stuffed ermine on my desk. The tip of its extended tail was black, and its face, turned perpendicular to its snowy white body, showed its tiny teeth bared in a silly grin that was probably meant to be a snarl.

Johnny and I thought of becoming taxidermists (it would somehow be a sideline to my fur-trapping in Alaska), and we even sent away for a well-illustrated booklet on how it was done, information which quickly dissipated our interest. The idea of hauling home dead animals and scooping and scraping out their stinking innards (and brains?!) in the basement turned out to be no more appealing to me than it was to my parents or his, not least because Dad tended to become dizzy or faint at the sight of blood, and any talk of wounds would turn him pale and make him insist on changing the subject. I wonder how he would have handled the role of Abraham when God commanded him to murder his son Isaac...!

There was no blood and gore in the taxidermy catalogues, however, and I used to drool over the wolf skins and bear skins and lamp bases made out of deer antlers and footstools made out of elephant's feet. This was long before any kind of awareness of endangered species had appeared on my horizon, and Ernest Hemingway was still doing his macho thing, bravely posing in Africa with his big-game trophy kills.

A couple of the times when we went to the Detroit Conference, around Thanksgiving (which was also the hunting season), and stayed with my Uncle Josh and Aunt Louise, Josh would bring home some deer parts for me, from animals that local hunters had brought to him to have butchered. Although he was one of the most taciturn people I've ever met, he picked up on my interest, and supplied me with a few small antlers (too small for any respectable hunter to regard as a trophy) and some bloodied deer hooves that I didn't know what to do with. (What do bullfighters do with bulls' ears and tails, anyway?) The hooves made Mom shudder and Dad's face drain, so I guess Mom found some way for them to disappear before we returned to Illinois.

Johnny lived on Linden, one block over from us. They had creeping bentgrass – the kind used on golf greens – in their back yard, so we weren't allowed to play ball there. I don't remember where Johnny and I met, but it was probably because his older brother Bill was friends with my brother Al, and as I got to be old enough to catch and hit a baseball, and cross Oak Park Avenue on my bike, I sometimes got to join Al when he went to Greenfield Park (now renamed Lindberg Park, after a park superintendent) for an impromptu game, or to meet classmates and other friends. Bill and Johnny must have been among those "other friends", because they didn't go to Horace Mann like most of the other boys our age. They went to St. Giles. They were Catholics.

St. Giles was only about four blocks from our house, on the corner of Berkshire and Columbian. It was a huge ochre-colored sandstone complex consisting of a church, a convent, an elementary school and I don't know what-all. The bells in the tower chimed every 15 minutes throughout the daytime. At the half hour they chimed the first eight notes of the Westminster chime. At the quarter hour they chimed notes 9-12. On the hour it was the full 16, plus a gong for each hour, followed by some tune that must have been evil because it was definitely not in Dad's Meeting repertoire.

The real mystery of the place was the adjoining convent, where I was sure (thanks to my full-time influencers) that the nuns were being held against their will, probably tortured if they tried to become True Christians, and who otherwise spent their time devising ways of ensnaring people's souls, especially those of children like Johnny. Mom frequently pointed out to me that whenever they appeared outside those foreboding walls, there were always two of them, so each one could prevent the other from escaping. Every time I had to pass St. Giles, which I astutely avoided if possible, my pace and my pulse would quicken, and I would shudder in the shadow of the church's huge north sandstone edifice at what might be going on inside its evil walls. Four wild horses or horsemen couldn't have dragged me in there.

I'm not sure why my brothers and I were allowed to play with the likes of Catholics. Perhaps it was because my parents recognized the futility of isolating us more from the world than they already had. Or perhaps they were saving all the energy they could for the onslaught of puberty and girls. Or perhaps it all started when they moved back to Oak Park, and the formerly relaxed barricades hadn't yet been moved up to include Catholic children. But Oak Park, Illinois, meant two powerful influences that just weren't there in Glendale, California. One was the local Meeting. The other was that this particular Chicago suburb was extremely conservative politically, as might be expected from people anxious to keep their affluence to themselves. By doing so, the village managed to acquire a school system with an exceptionally high academic standing, which was to be expected if, for example, the science class could provide one microscope per student instead of one per class or one per school, or none at all. Oak Park had clean tree-lined streets throughout, and some tidy parks. The villagers seemed pleased with their racial mix as well. If you were black and wanted to live in Oak Park, all you had to do was be a world-class scientist. Percy Julian was the one who met that criterion back in the 1950s, after just two bombings of his Oak Park home.

I think my mom (maybe my dad too) was afraid of black people. They certainly held attitudes which, if held today would clearly and rightfully be called racist. Were they racists then? Can one apply today's standards and enlightenment to past times? I grew up in a world where, on family car trips to LA, the gas stations in Arkansas had restrooms for men, women and colored. The only second line we ever heard to "eenie, meenie, miny, moe" was "catch a nigger by the toe", and we were never given the slightest clue that it might be offensive to anyone. Were we then racist if we used it? One has to *learn* that a certain combination of phonemes can be hurtful. *Words aren't mean, people are mean!*

At least my parents had the decency to be horrified by the *Chicago Tribune's* reports of the lynchings that frequently took place in the South, and by the slavery there had been, despite slavery being condoned by the Bible, over and over. Since the Bible is alleged by its own followers to be a source of eternal, immutable, absolute Truth, the profound changes in morality that were the result of increasing civilization and knowledge must have created some real problems if one stopped to think about it. So the best approach to resolving that potential conflict was simply *not* to stop and think about it.

One evening after dinner when I was around 10 and we hadn't yet left the table, I suddenly asked anyone who was listening where babies come from. (I strongly doubted the veracity of my own theories about babies being retrieved from secret desert depots.) Since my question triggered an unexpectedly nervous parental reaction, heightened by John's and Al's too-hard-to-suppress-completely reactions – a combination of discomfort and mirth – I suspected there was something of great interest here. Mom and Dad conferred, and failing to be able or willing to give me an answer on the spot, it was decided that Mom and I would stay home from Meeting that evening, so she could enlighten me. It was almost certainly the only time in her life that she found herself being consulted in the embarrassing role of a sex expert.

Her expertise, however, was incomprehensible to me: talk of placentas and after-births, reminders that she'd almost died having me, but nothing about how the whole thing got started. Of course we'd read in the Bible many times about how some guy *"knew his wife and she conceived and bore a son, and his name was blah, blah..."*, but that didn't answer my question either; we *knew* lots of people and they didn't go around conceiving and bearing sons – or daughters – just because we *knew* them. I knew you couldn't know something unless you could conceive it, yet this was knowing first and conceiving after. But no further enlightenment was forthcoming, and I sensed Mom's great awkwardness: I simply thought she didn't know. After I presumed we'd left that topic, Mom abruptly issued a stern admonishment on what I assumed was a completely different topic: *"Don't bump your body against a girl!"* I couldn't imagine why on earth I would want to do that, especially since Mom made it clear that it was horribly sinful!

Johnny and I shared the childhood joys of baseball, baseball cards, bikes, and stuffed animals. Since he was a year older than me, I was always trying to keep up, except in baseball, where my skills easily exceeded his, thanks to Al. It was hard keeping up with Johnny's family in many ways. They had a TV, of course, so Johnny and I would spend a lot of time there on summer afternoons watching baseball games. He was a White Sox fan and I was a Cubs fan; we didn't talk about our teams that much.

Mom knew I watched baseball at Johnny's home, but she pretended I didn't, or pretended she didn't know, or managed not to mind. Except on Sundays, sports were a legitimate safety valve, although not legitimate enough for us to have our own TV. What she probably didn't allow herself to know was that between innings there would be commercials, particularly for beer (*"From the land of sky-blue wa-ha-ters, wa-ha-ters, from the land of pines, lofty balsams, comes the beer refreshing, Hamms, the beer refreshing, Hamms, mmm ..."*), cigarettes (*"You get a lot to like from a Marlboro..."*), and White Owl cigars (*"Light up your life with a White Owl..."*). I knew these things and their jingles to be sinful, but (or "so") I watched them with fascination. I was tainted. I reacted to them with a mixture of anxiety and excitement – *should we / I really be watching this?* – but Johnny didn't react at all.

We watched the Kentucky Derby and a few other big horse races. I was so caught up in the rivalry between the great jockeys Willie Shoemaker and Eddie Arcaro that it never occurred to me that horseracing might be yet another worldly, evil thing. Johnny's parents smoked and had a bar cabinet in their home. Being Catholics, they were obviously on their way to hell anyway, but they were always nice enough to me, as long as I stayed off their creeping bentgrass. So why should I react? I could see that it was possible not to, and yet I did. This was all confusing to the young boy that was me.

Johnny's living room was for special occasions only, not a place for rambunctious boys. It was sealed off from the rest of the house by French doors and there were plastic dust covers on the fine furniture. The TV was upstairs in a small den with a sofa, desk, chairs, and not much floor space left over. That was where we watched the baseball games. When we wanted to play indoors, we'd go down to their fixed-up basement, which had a large laundry room and a large open recreation room that was gradually acquiring the look of a natural history museum, as Johnny's and Bill's interest in taxidermy, and their budget to finance it, overwhelmed my own. No flimsy fox skin on *their* wall! They had a large, thick-furred timberwolf skin that you could bury your hands into to grab the coarse yet soft fur, a real wolf, just like in Jack London. I was fairly green with envy.

Johnny's family acquired several choice pieces of animalware on a vacation trip to Montana one summer, and they generously brought back a present for me: a pair of moose antlers. The two antlers were nearly the same size and roughly symmetrical. The moose had probably shed them, as they tend to do every other year. My dad kindly took them with him to the machine shop at Link-Belt to have a couple of holes drilled through each antler with a diamond drill bit so we could bolt them to a wooden plaque that Dad helped me make, so that I could hang them on my wall. Those moose antlers have followed me around ever since. They are, in fact, hanging on the wall above me as I sit and write this.

Johnny and I would ride our bikes everywhere during the couple of summers our friendship lasted. In America, riding bikes was something only kids did back then, not adults, not ever in my memory. I don't know whether my parents could or did ride bikes as kids. Anyway, one year during this time, I think it was 1956, my folks got me a special present (possibly an advance birthday present so I could use it during my summer vacation): a black Rigby racing bike with three gears. Now, at last, I could beat Johnny!

A day or two later, I cycled over to Johnny's and we set off from his home, heading down Linden to LeMoyne at full speed, me in the lead. As we rounded the corner to the right, I looked over my shoulder to see how far behind he was – and I *slammed* into the bumper of a parked car. I only suffered a few scrapes, but my beautiful new bike had a severe bend in the top tube (or crossbar) of the frame. I was horrified. I could still cycle on it, but it creaked and scraped badly and wasn't the same. A few weeks later, with the metallurgical integrity of the frame compromised, the top tube just sheared off, and the bike became useless. Dad saw how heartbroken I was. He took the bike with him to Link-Belt, where they managed to insert one end of a steel tube into one of the hollow, broken-off ends of the bike frame, then repeat the procedure at the other end (making a kind of stent). Then they welded the break, ground it down, and spray-painted it. It worked OK, but it was never the same – other parts had taken quite a hit too. I ended up replacing it with an "unbreakable" heavy steel bike with balloon tires that I could take to Greenfield Park, build up full speed while heading straight towards a big elm, leap off at the last second and watch my unbreakable bike live up to its reputation, over and over. I had a daredevil streak; I was in no way suicidal.

Johnny and Bill sometimes went to White Sox games at the old Comisky Park on the South Side. Al and I went to a few Cubs games at Wrigley Field on the North Side. White Sox fans are like the fans of any other baseball team. But Cubs fans are special: fiercely loyal to a perpetually hapless, losing cause. Coleridge's "willing suspension of disbelief" extends beyond the theater, all the way to Wrigley Field. The loser wins anyway. The Pennant will happen someday. No team can field a player like Ernie Banks and be a loser; it just doesn't happen. The ivy-covered outfield walls are the proof of anything you want to prove, a transubstantiation of mere final scores into ultimate victory. [In 2016, the Cubs finally became hapful.] The Cubs were to baseball what the Meeting was to religion, at least in my pre-pubertal mind. Johnny and Bill didn't understand these things, and I was sure they knew they didn't.

I've never quite understood what happened one day, and any connection with being a Cubs fan or one of the Chosen Few is purely conjectural, but on this particular day Johnny phoned and asked me to come over right away – there was something fantastic he wanted to show me. When I yelled to herald my arrival at the screen door on the side of their house, Johnny and Bill were home alone and called for me to come down to the basement. I arrived wide-eyed, expecting to see some fabulous new stuffed animal, a full-size panther at least, and suddenly Bill was grabbing me from behind, pinning my arms against my torso, while Johnny jerked at my pants, pulling them down around my shins. Then they both roared with mocking laughter.

I was stunned. I'd never felt betrayed or personally violated before, so I didn't recognize what it was I was feeling. My head was spinning. OK, they had "pantsed" me, a silly fad I'd heard of. But there was more: the look in their eyes. My best friend and his brother, the sort-of friend of my own brother, were consciously, maliciously trying to humiliate me. What had I done? What was the point? What was so funny about having one's pants down? I couldn't see anything funny about it, least of all the hideous scorn in their laughter, the malice.

I grabbed my trousers with my right hand and yanked them up, making a fist with my left, to be ready to fend off my antagonists, but they were too doubled up with their mocking laughter to care. I fled up the stairs, my eyes smarting with tears of outrage, but I didn't go straight home. I didn't want Mom to see me crying or to have to explain anything, so I just walked around for a while, bruised.

That was, as far as I recall, the last time I ever saw Johnny. I was prepared to forgive him, but no apology was forthcoming, so I felt doubly hurt. It just didn't make sense to me. I would revisit this scene in my mind many times, even years later, still wondering and wanting an explanation. Had I somehow subconsciously let it be known that I was one of the Chosen Few and he wasn't, or had he subconsciously picked up this attitude? In that case, it was more than my pants that needed pulling down. Or perhaps he was getting pubertal and I wasn't, making the vast age difference between us intolerable to him, and giving rise to a need to subjugate through humiliation?

I also had a stuffed alligator, about 18" long, a kind of amber color, that I'd picked up on our family trip to Florida, one of only two family trips I can remember that didn't involve a Bible Conference, and the only one where we stayed in one place for as long as a week. Along the way to Florida, and along the way home, we were able to tick off the last of the states we'd never been to, in Dad's quest to get all of us to have set foot in every one of the 48 states. The location was Delray Beach, at a beach motel also occupied by the Nunnikhoven family, meaning that my brothers spent most of their time with the similarly aged Nunnikhoven sons, John and Joe. I loved the easy access to the ocean, although my parents were anxious to keep a close watch on me, of course. That was just about love. But perhaps they should have thought more about themselves.

Mom's often panicky fear of things she wasn't in control of sometimes led her to *avoid* having to learn skills rather than simply learning them and losing the fear. So she never learned to drive, nor to swim. She had, however, bought herself an anachronistically modest bathing suit for the occasion (the only time I remember seeing either of my parents in swimsuits), and she and my dad were out in the Atlantic, at first only knee-deep. Then they ventured to waist-high, Dad holding Mom's hand the whole time. Sometimes a wave would splash a bit higher than her waist, and she would squeal with real fear. The ocean, being what it is, lacked a flat bottom, and when they stepped off the sandbar they hadn't realized they'd been walking on, the water was suddenly slightly over mom's head. It might not have been over Dad's head if Mom hadn't hit the panic button with both fists, climbing all over Dad, forcing him under. After some moments of wild thrashing, they regained enough footing to leave the water, Dad coughing and gasping, Mom looking wild-eyed back at the monstrous one-foot waves. I don't think either of them ever set foot in the ocean again.

Delray Beach also gave me my first experience of being stung by jellyfish. Early one morning Al and I went out to the beach to look for seashells and found it covered with thousands upon thousands of blue balloons, or at least that's what they looked like. As we started picking our way across the sand among them, trying to avoid them, I suddenly felt sharp pains on the soles of my bare feet, like bee stings, and realized that the source wasn't broken glass hidden in the sand, but long, thin, blue poisonous filaments extending all over the place from each of those blue balloons – Portuguese man-of-war jellyfish – not an experience I was eager to repeat.

On the trip home, we drove through the Everglades. We stopped for lunch at a souvenir shop next to a diner, and there I found my small stuffed alligator, as well as a bright yellow shirt with multi-colored borders, made by the Seminole Indians, the only tribe never to have surrendered to the White Man, according to a booklet I also bought. I was just leaving my trapper phase and beginning to discover that I wanted to be an Indian instead.

CHAPTER 6

Red Eagle

My monthly scrutiny of every picture and caption in the *National Geographic* fed my interest in animals, but it also bred my interest in the original Americans: the Indians. Everything I'd read about them pointed to their getting about the most rotten treatment in the history of mankind, as far as I knew at that time, and it upset me greatly. This feeling intensified as my pre-pubertal interest in their ways and history grew, and the more I read about them, the more I was convinced of the brutal and wanton savagery of the White Man. I began reading every book I could find about Indians, both in the library at Horace Mann and elsewhere. In 1957, one issue of *National Geographic* included an ad for the Society's hard-cover, 432-page book titled *Indians of the Americas*, which I immediately ordered. I studied it more intensely than the Bible, and certainly with greater understanding and trust.

The term *Indian* has always been problematic – a misnomer for which there is no satisfactory "nomer". For one thing, as many Americans were gradually becoming aware of the factual existence of an outside world, it became apparent that the term *Indian* is also the term for the people who come from India, the destination Columbus and other European explorers mistakenly thought they had reached on their voyages across the vast ocean and into the unknown. So you have *American Indian*. What, then, is the term for an American who has immigrated to India? Or an American Indian who has immigrated to India?

Moreover, I learned that the very name *America* came from Columbus having turned the charts of his explorations over to an Italian explorer and cartographer named Amerigo Vespucci, who was commonly and mistakenly thought to have labeled the New World with his own moniker. (It was in fact a German cartographer named Martin Waldseemüller who labelled the New World in honor of Vespucci.) Try to imagine the consequences if he'd used the last name instead: The United States of Vespucci, the song *God Bless Vespucci*, the Vespuccian Way, the House Committee on Un-Vespuccian Activities, etc. In any case, the United States of America picked up Waldseemüller's suggestion without hesitation, and its citizens came to be called *Americans*, since *United Statesians* just doesn't work, despite the protests of Latin Americans who object to Americans' usurpation of a word whose Spanish definition includes themselves, and who would prefer US residents to call themselves *North Americans* (*Norteamericanos*), but since that would also have to include Canadians and Mexicans, it would make nobody happy nor anybody the wiser about who is whom. *Native Americans*, the neologistic reference to the Indians, makes no sense either, as *native* simply means the country of birth, and that includes all whites, blacks, Asians, and Indians who happen to be born within the borders of the USA.

The problem with words is that some of them come to be used pejoratively, and then there's no defense. *Words aren't mean, people are mean!* Before the White Man came to the New World with his "Manifest Destiny", there were no Indians. There were only Arapahoe, Cherokee, Sioux, Apache, Comanche, etc – more than 500 nations, most of whom had little or no contact with each other. There were, after all, no roads, no horses, no wheels, but plenty of hostile relations. And they certainly didn't see themselves as one people or nation! The number of languages may have more or less equaled the number of those nations. I read that in many Indian languages, the word for *human being* is the same as the name of the nation, and as far as I know, none of them had a word for *Indian* – certainly not before the White Man came, bringing the distinction, in addition to bringing disease, destruction, horses, extermination – and the doctrine of Manifest Destiny.

The name for that odious, unofficial doctrine was coined by a journalist in 1845 to describe the prevailing mindset of white Americans: God Himself wanted the White Man to conquer North America, to subjugate and destroy everything and everyone who stood in their way. It absolved white men of every shred of guilt, misgivings, qualms, and shame about the Great Landgrab and the wholesale slaughter and genocide of the Indians. The view of Indians as lawful prey was captured by President Andrew Jackson in 1833 in a public speech, when he said, "*The only good Indians I ever saw were dead.*" Any similarity with the White Man's neighborly treatment of blacks was, I suppose, purely coincidental.

At about the time my interest in Indians made me want to be one, my family and I visited my mom's home town, Des Moines, also the home of Aunt Shirley, Mom's youngest sister. Her relative youthfulness was not just a question of age. She also had more quickness and girlish charm about her. And she didn't have to watch her back for Maxine.

Her husband, the dapper Nobel, "came in from the outside"; he had no Meeting background. I suspected he joined the Meeting as part of the deal to be able to wed and bed the comely, charming Shirley. Uncle Nobe served in World War II as a cryptographer, in England, and Shirley was frantic (according to Mom) most of the time he was away, fearing with some justification that he would become a victim of German bombing. She was allegedly fond of singing and playing a popular and melodramatic song of that era, "*Coming in on a wing and a prayer*", probably without realizing that the song referred specifically to the crews of bombers, fighters and other military aircraft out on missions, not land-based cryptographers.

Shirley was a fairly accomplished pianist and had a good singing voice. Nobe was a man of considerable artistic talent and potential. For many years provided for the family as the art editor of the *Better Homes and Gardens* magazine. His pencil drawings and watercolors had the photographically accurate draftsmanship of an Andrew Wyeth, although in subject matter he tended to stick to architectural and pastoral motifs, and occasionally moved even further in the direction of Norman Rockwell.

The eldest of their four children, my cousin Steve, clearly inherited the musical and artistic talents of his respective parents, which might in itself have been enough to turn him into my next hero, plus the fact that he was two and a half years my elder. But there was another reason, which I discovered on that trip to Des Moines: Steve was also interested in Indians, and could draw portraits and scenes of Indian life – with emphasis on the Indians of the Great Plains (Lakota, Cheyenne, Comanche, and others) – like nothing I'd ever seen. Steve's skills on the guitar also dazzled me. He never played hymns, but only the popular songs that my peers at school were listening to and that I had occasionally heard at Johnny's before the pantsing: Buddy Holly, the Crickets, Elvis, Ricky Nelson, and many others. To my shock, awe and envy, Nobe and Shirley didn't seem to mind at all.

The Gammell's home in Des Moines was a fairly average, fairly modest, tasteful, middle-class house on a fairly large lot that extended far enough behind the house to comprise small areas of "wild" growth that quickly became the vast wilderness of the Plains where two young Indians could scout for buffalo and enemies. Steve had already begun acquiring a collection of real stone Indian arrowheads and spearheads, and his drawings included highly detailed representations of them, embellished with the missing arrows and spears, and further adorned with feathers and beads. Steve had a small catalog from a mail-order Indian artifact company in Arkansas, from whom he had purchased a number of the flint, granite and obsidian pieces in his collection. I copied the address, sent for a catalog, and started using my allowance money to acquire some of my own. Steve and I decided to start corresponding about Indian lore. We also adopted Indian personae, for which we gave ourselves Indian names. Steve took the name Little Wolf, and I was Red Eagle. That is how we addressed our letters to each other when we began corresponding. Stephen went on to become a successful and award-winning illustrator and author of children's books. One of these, called *Where the Buffaloes Begin*, from 1981, is about a little Indian boy called Little Wolf, and is dedicated "to my friend Red Eagle". (I never heard whether that was specifically intended to refer to me.)

I was obsessed with catching up with Steve – collecting more arrowheads, making my own arrows as Steve had done, acquiring anything associated with Indians. I had three key congenital advantages over Steve in our quest to be like the Indians: one was that, unlike Steve, I allegedly had some real Indian blood in me from my father's mother's side of the family (somebody claimed it was Cherokee, but reliable evidence has never been produced); the second was that I didn't yet need glasses, whereas Steve's were bottle-bottom thick and indispensable, and we'd never seen any Indians depicted wearing glasses; and finally, I had dark brown hair, almost black, more like the Indians, while Steve's was dark blond.

But I was in complete awe of Steve's drawing talents and musical talents, as well as some aspects of his age and home environment. Steve seemed to have so much more freedom than I did, both in terms of music and in the more relaxed atmosphere of the Gammell's home, where it was possible to converse on a range of different subjects without everything winding up being about the Lord and the Meeting. Steve was definitely pubertal, while I remained in blissful ignorance of what that was all about, in spite of my little trick with Miss Mallon at the school Christmas play a few years before.

Our school librarian was delighted with my avid reading – both its quantity and its level of difficulty. But she was not happy about my self-imposed limitations on subject matter, so she told me that she wanted me to read other kinds of books too, not just about Indians. One of the Indian books I read related the story of the Sand Creek Massacre led by Colonel Chivington, in which a settlement of Cheyenne – who had signed a peace treaty with the US Government and were living tranquilly along Sand Creek doing nobody any harm – were brutally massacred by Chivington and his men. Most of the Cheyenne men had left the encampment to go hunting when the soldiers rode in and began slaughtering everything that moved, making up for the paucity of Cheyenne men by gutting all the women and children they could find (or both at once, if they happened to find pregnant women), then taking their genitalia, breasts, and other body parts as souvenirs. They dried women's breasts to make tobacco pouches. Colonel Chivington was never punished for his acts (he was a Methodist minister as a civilian), and remained proud of himself and his deeds for the rest of his life. When I read that, I nearly vomited in the library.

I managed to hold back the puke, but not my tears, so perhaps that's why the librarian wanted me to broaden my reading into other subject matter. I asked her for suggestions, and she came back with a highly heterogeneous list: classics, science fiction, humor, *The Old Man and the Sea*, even a little poetry. I read them all, with great pleasure, but I was far from done with Indians.

Once when we were visiting the Nunnikhovens in Burlington, Iowa, and my brothers were off with the two eldest boys, as usual, I was playing with the youngest, Tommy, who was a couple of years younger than me. We had little in common, not even sports, but when he showed me a small box of Indian arrowheads they possessed, I *really* coveted them, especially since the Nunnikhovens had no apparent interest in them. Tommy told me they found them in a field somewhere, and they didn't even *like* them. Such wasteful injustice could not be tolerated, so I quietly slipped a fine specimen into my pocket. Tommy didn't notice anything and gathered up the remaining ones, then put the box away.

Sitting in the back seat on our trip home to Oak Park, I couldn't resist the urge to bring my new acquisition out of my pocket and admire it. My parents caught a glimpse of it and asked me with some surprise where I'd gotten it. I tried to be evasive, but the sudden burst of crimson in my complexion gave me away. I got a hard spanking (must have been from Mom) and had to write a letter of apology, full of appropriate Biblical clichés, to the Nunnikhovens. Worst of all, I had to send that beautiful arrowhead back!

On our trips out West, where many of the older gas stations and diner stops also sold curios, I would be on the lookout for any Indian artifacts, as well as large feathers from hawks or owls. The chances of finding real eagle feathers were microscopic, but persistence eventually led me to three (I still have them).

I also found and collected a few smaller feathers of a size suitable for making my own Indian arrows, following the detailed instructions sent to Red Eagle by Little Wolf. I would cycle out to the Forest Preserves in search of straight sticks about a foot and a half long and ⅜ of an inch in diameter, bring them home, carefully remove the bark, and cut a deep notch (about ¾") for the arrowhead in one end, then a shallow notch for the bowstring in the other.

Then I would wait until Mom was preparing a pot roast. She almost always had to trim it a bit by removing sinews that would otherwise remain tough after cooking. Long sinews were precisely what I wanted. After inserting an arrowhead into the deep notch in the shaft, I would wrap a wet sinew tightly around the base of the notch, then crisscross it over the notch to hold the arrowhead firmly in place, and finally keep the end of the sinew tightly in place with some sap and a piece of tape. (The procedure is called hafting; I used sinews because I had no access to deer intestines.) After the sinew and sap dried in the sun and shrank slightly, I removed the tape. At the other end, I split a feather lengthwise and used two more pieces of sinew to secure the two trimmed halves, one on either side of the shaft.

This was my more advanced work, but I discovered that Steve had not only done likewise; he had also painted and carved Indian symbols on the shafts of his arrows, and made a war club with a stone head, as well as a feather-covered ceremonial spear. I could never catch up with him, but there was no need: he was my new hero.

My first arrows, before Steve taught me how to attach real arrowheads, were simply sharpened sticks, but I had one that was sharp enough. One evening after dinner and after the family Bible reading, I was up in "my room" playing with my Indian stuff, having changed to my beaded deerskin moccasins, when John came over and sat on my bed, 5-10 feet away from me. He began teasing me about my Indian lore. I must have been around 11, making him 19. I told him to knock it off, but he went on, and my temper started rising. He went on. I took my homemade bow down from the wall. He went on. I took up my sharp wooden arrow. He went on. I put the notch in the string. He went on. I pulled the string back, aiming in his direction. He went on. I let go: the arrow hit him in the knee. I hadn't pulled back far, and my homemade bow didn't have much *oomph*, but enough to deliver a small puncture wound and draw a drop or two of blood. "*Mom, Stan <u>shot</u> me!!*" John yelled, and Mom and Dad came charging up the stairs. John looked more astounded than afflicted, and I must have looked more hurt than he did. I think our parents instantly figured out how it had come about, and while I got a firm reprimand, John's was just as firm.

I think it was the summer just before I turned 12 when Mom and I took the train to Des Moines for a week at Aunt Shirley's. Little Wolf and Red Eagle spent a lot of time outdoors making *coups* on Comanche rocks and Arapaho flowers, walking among trees, making no sound that either of us was willing to hear, in full Indian garb, running like the wind, especially me, since I was a much faster runner than Little Wolf.

Later that day we went up to his room and he played some Everly Brothers songs on his guitar and told me about some "really neat" girl at school. He described some things he'd like to do with her. I understood neither what nor why. A day or two later we were playing in the yard for hours, crawling on our stomachs to sneak up on buffalo. After we came in, I complained of itching all over. Mom and Aunt Shirley found red spots all over my arms, neck, face, and scalp. When I removed my shirt, they were there too, and all over the rest of me. It turned out that I had a severe case of chigger bites, and the itching was increasing all the time, so it was decided that I should take a hot bath, as hot as I could stand. When that didn't provide relief, Mom and Shirley took wads of cotton and rubbed each chigger bite with ether. When they got to the bites around my neck and face, I passed out.

Steve and I continued to correspond as Little Wolf and Red Eagle. He would illuminate his letters with outstanding, inimitable (for me, anyway) sketches of Indian outfits, teepees, and new arrows he'd made. But he also wrote a few things about new popular songs he'd learned on his guitar and about some of the girls at school. The following summer, Aunt Shirley and Steve came to spend some days with us in Oak Park. Steve was closer in age to our Cousin Ed, but Ed and Steve had nothing else in common. Steve and I had Indians, and I was beginning to share his interest in popular music as well, even though (or because) I wasn't allowed to listen to it at home, but I already knew that both John and Al did. Neither John nor Al was at home that summer when Steve visited, so we had the whole attic to ourselves. It wasn't a proper environment for playing Indians, however, and our back yard was too small. Steve didn't seem to mind that we couldn't play Indians.

A day or two later, Steve and Shirley returned to Des Moines and shortly thereafter, Little Wolf stopped returning my letters. Red Eagle continued to write, imploring him to answer, but there was only silence. More time passed, perhaps a year, and finally Mom heard from Shirley that Steve had left home. I never heard any details, but he'd clearly become a renegade and turned from the Lord. I wrote him a long epistle urging him to "own his Sins", to "bow to the Lord" – all from the bank of clichés I'd now mastered without ever having stopped to think about what they meant or why things had to be expressed in archaic English. I had learned them by rote ("L M N O goldfish") with no interference from my brain. Since Steve was gone, Aunt Shirley opened my letter and shared its contents with Mom, who was delighted – and started talking to me about "taking my place"; I guess I was getting to be that age.

Seventh and eighth grades at Horace Mann meant Miss Tredenick for math and science – and my first real taste of either. She was a fearsome, formidable woman, stocky, with a commanding voice that she used to the full, turning every utterance into a command. She'd never married. Whatever youth she may have had when she was my father's math and science teacher was obviously gone, but the vinegar Dad recalled was still there. Her large classroom – her realm – stretched out from the door along the second-floor corridor to the windows at the far end of the room overlooking the playground behind the school, and was much wider than it was deep. With this configuration, nobody was ever far from Miss Tredenick's piercing gaze or her stern discipline as she paced back and forth across the front of the classroom. At the front, in addition to the desk at which she seldom sat, were various sinks and equipment needed for the science part of her teaching endeavors.

At the back of the classroom, to the left as one entered, were glass cases with shelves displaying frogs, salamanders, mice, and other animal specimens, all in formalin-filled glass jars. There were also bones, Indian (American, not South Asian) artifacts (arrowheads), and other things. Affixed to the glass doors were Miss Tredenick's special paper charts consisting of the names of all her students in the left-hand column and a list of conceivable classroom offenses across the top, creating a matrix with rows of boxes next to each pupil's name in which the offending pupil had to make a check in the column corresponding to the appropriate (or inappropriate) offense in response to a stern *"Talking in class! Check your name!"* command from the auspicious

Miss Tredenick. Those offenses included being tardy, talking when not called upon, not paying attention, passing notes, laughing, chewing gum and various other things. A certain number of checks earned the miscreant an extra session in her classroom after the ordinary school day. She thus kept us, literally and figuratively, in check.

Miss Tredenick was also ruthlessly effective in teaching us arithmetic, with frequent and dreaded quizzes on the multiplication and division tables. One of my classmates, Bob Smith, was clearly less intellectually endowed than most others his age, and his wordless, nervous giggling when Miss Tredenick asked him a question that was well beyond his ability to grasp resulted in her marching over to his seat, tapping audibly on the top of his head with her forefinger like a frustrated pianist pounding on a key that no longer interacted with a string, and declaring to the class with unbridled reproach and sneering contempt, "*Nobody home!*" Any tendency one or more of us might have harbored towards bullying poor Bob Smith for his slowness prior to such encounters with Miss Tredenick quickly vanished. He suffered enough from her bullying; he didn't need ours. And whether or not I ever had any aversion to math prior to meeting her, or any other influences that may have contributed more to my literacy than my numeracy, I suspect I might have picked up some in her classroom. But she also had good sides. And at that age, I could endear myself to practically anyone.

By the sixth grade, all the kids in my class were enrolled in extra-curricular dance classes – except me. By the seventh grade, there were monthly dances as part of gym class, for which my parents sent a written note to the school saying that "*As True Christians, we cannot permit our son…blah, blah, blah.*" So I was made the disc jockey in the days when being a disc jockey meant no more than someone who put a new record on when the previous one had finished playing.

I was beginning to feel strange buzzes when I saw pretty girls, but I didn't like what I felt because I didn't understand it, and people tend not to like what they don't understand. There was one girl in my class who was strikingly pretty, sweet, and well into puberty. Sandy Bennett was her name. At least one of her parents was French, and she had learned a little of that lovely language. She clearly liked me, but I wasn't having any of it; it was just too confusing then. One day she said softly to me, with a slight giggle, "*Je vous aime, je vous adore.*" I didn't understand a word, but she repeated it often enough for me to memorize it pretty well and ask Pearl Henderson, Dave's five-year-older sister, who was studying French at Oak Park High. Pearl first blushed and giggled a little herself, then told me it was about love: "*I think she loves you!*" For some odd reason, this infuriated my hopelessly immature self. I turned my back on Sandy completely, treated her like air, behaved like a complete jerk – and would regret it for years. I think her family must have moved away that summer; I never saw her after Horace Mann.

By my last year at Horace Mann, 1958-59, I was increasingly, noticeably, and painfully "apart" from the rest of my classmates, who were rapidly becoming pubertal, and whose common (in both senses of the word) activities – dancing, going to movies, watching TV, listening to popular music – were *all* off limits for me. My Red Eagle persona, although no longer externalized since Steve dropped off my radar, became a kind of retreat, a secret self, a way to affirm something different about me that wasn't *only* defined by the *lack* of all the other things or activities my peers took for granted.

I don't think I ever consciously strove to be different from my peers – certainly not at that age – but I was forced to. I had to figure out for myself how, without invoking the scorn of my peers on one hand, or the wrath of the Great Thought Policeman in the Sky – and my parents – on the other.

Although there were a couple of boys in my class who sneeringly referred to me as "Injun", I didn't make up for my lack of close friends by having an abundance of enemies; like Dad, I had none. I liked to joke, had good natural athletic ability, and was a fast sprinter. Despite being small, I was always among the first to be picked when the gym class was making up teams for softball or touch football.

The end of my Indian phase coincided roughly with a pre-pubertal experience that hinted at aspects of my body and its functions that were previously unknown to me. In relating this experience in *Hindsights*, I feel obliged to deviate temporarily from my dedication to total honesty, in order to maintain a shield of anonymity over those whose names have no bearing on the incidents. The names in the following account are thus fictional, although the reporting itself is as close to the truth as I am able to remember.

One summer morning, Mom and I took a train to visit Maybelline Vanderberg, an old friend of hers from the Meeting in Grand Rapids, Michigan. The Vanderbergs had a boy named Archie, three or four years older than me, so neither of us expected to have much in common. Maybelline picked us up at the station, and as soon as we arrived at their suburban home that afternoon, I noticed a prominent basketball setup on their smooth, broad concrete driveway. After a few brief introductions, Archie asked me if I liked basketball, and we were off, leaving our moms to deal with the gossip and the Meeting talk.

Archie was a lot taller than me, and a better all-around player, but I had a pretty good outside shot and was much quicker than he was, so I gave him a good workout. Archie seemed to know a lot and was very funny. He kept telling jokes, some of which included words I knew would have made Mom furious. After some sweaty hours, it was time to get cleaned up for dinner, so I followed Archie to the shower in their basement. It was spacious, with plenty of room for both of us. Archie was washing his penis, thoroughly, rapidly, and ostentatiously. It was becoming alarmingly larger than my own, and I wondered if something was wrong with him. He laughed and said he'd show me something. He lathered it up a bit more, then grasped it tightly and started moving his hand back and forth like a pump-action rifle that needed lots of pumping (is *that* why they call it "cocking"?). "Now watch this" he groaned in a strange voice, and I saw some thick pearly milky stuff shoot out. I was certain Archie had a severe medical problem, but he explained to me that the milky substance was called (in scientific terms) "gizz", assuming I'd know what that meant and what it as for. But I was dumbfounded. I *didn't* know what it was or what it was for. Nor do I remember whether he told me not to say a word about it, or whether I figured that out myself. That evening in bed, when he was sound asleep, I tried mimicking his action, but nothing happened. I fell asleep wondering what the point was, or if there might be something wrong with me.

The next day was again filled with intense basketball for me and Archie. But after a while, he began giving me lustful descriptions of a couple of the more exciting girls at his high school. I wondered what could be so interesting about that, but I didn't mind; he dropped his guard and it was suddenly much easier to dribble around him. Our day on the court was followed by another shower in the basement – and another demonstration of Archie's gizz-pumping technique. I remained puzzled.

After the family dinner, complete with prayers and Bible reading, of course, as well as Mom's endless chatter with Maybelline, everyone was off to bed. Mom and I had a train to catch the next morning. Archie and I talked for a while, first about sports, then about school, and he was again musing about the girls at his school. Suddenly he said "*Feel this!*" and carried my hand under the covers to his stiff penis. It felt weird to me. It also felt weird that he wanted me to feel it; what was I supposed to do with it? Why did it get like that – mine didn't!? *"What's it for?"* I asked. Archie told me to remove my underpants and get on my hands and knees. I did as requested, because I thought he was going to let me in on something interesting; he was older and knew a lot of stuff I didn't. Then he came around behind me and I could feel that stiff thing probing at my BM hole. It didn't feel comfortable at all, so I said (probably much louder than he expected), "*What're you doing, Archie?!*" He immediately stopped his unsuccessful efforts, and we (or at least I) fell asleep.

I never saw Archie again after Mom and I left Grand Rapids the next day. He reportedly left home a year or two later.

My puberty made an entrance at last. A few new hairs began appearing here and there on my body, and sometimes I found my cock stiff in the morning without having a clue about what or how or why. But it gave me a kind of longing urge that I couldn't put my finger on. Was there an actual bone inside a boner? And where did the bone go when the boner disappeared? Howie and I would talk about these changes, and a few times when we were at Maxine and Ralph's for Sunday dinner and spent the afternoon there until Gospel Meeting. After dinner, Howie and I would take the narrow staircase off his parents' bedroom up to the attic dormer bedroom he shared with his brother Ed to discuss and inspect the strange things that were occurring in our bodies, and the strange new urges and guilt that seemed to be associated with them. (This was before Howie "took his place".) Our only source of information was from other kids at school, not always the most reliable source, but it was not a subject our parents ever raised.

Since I was increasingly dissatisfied with Mom's non-explanation of sex that one time, and increasingly curious about the truth, I felt I had to consult other sources; I asked some guys in my class. I learned about a connection between gizz and babies. I'd never seen my own gizz, but Howie had already seen his, frequently, which was so unfair, him being two weeks and three days *younger* than me. So upstairs in his attic on 1015 Mapleton, one Lord's Day, Howie showed me his technique. We lay up there on cots, pulling away like mad, but I just couldn't get mine to work. I was painfully disappointed. The pulling part felt kind of good, and I had a sense of some new and stronger feelings building up, but maybe I was afraid of where they might lead, afraid of the unknown.

Then, about a month later, I woke up at around five in the morning in the midst of a particularly strange and pleasant dream to find my gizz all over me. I leaped out of bed, thrilled, curious, elated, wanting to shout for joy but somehow knowing I shouldn't. I hurried the few steps from my bed to the bathroom, where I cleaned myself up with toilet paper. I was so ecstatic that I willed myself back to sleep some more, perchance to dream – and had another wet one.

Although Korea passed me by, Cuba didn't. During the fall of '58, Castro's guerrilla forces were making life increasingly difficult for Battista. Civics had been added to my school curriculum, and we discussed what was going on in Cuba at least once a week. Despite the strong conservative bias of Oak Pak (with the possible exception of a few Mafia bosses), nearly everyone seemed to be eager for Castro to succeed in his bold and brave mission to oust the corrupt and increasingly embarrassing dictatorship of Fulgencio Battista. It was a country in which a few extremely wealthy fat cats, propped up by unnamed wealthy foreign interest groups like American sugar companies and plantation owners, subjugated the vast majority who were living in abject poverty. Surely this would go against American values and sentiments for the underdog?

Castro promised to make things different. But by the time he finally triumphed at the end of that year, US public opinion suddenly flipped. With Fidel now in charge, all kinds of demands were being placed by my country on how his new government should be set up "democratically" – demands that were *never* placed on the government of his dictatorial predecessor. The problem was the "C" word; not cancer, but something far worse in the McCarthy-trained ears of most Americans in the late 1950s: Communism.

Miss Tredenick knew of my great interest in her arrowhead collection (my repeatedly hanging around after the bell to gaze at it all by myself at the back of her classroom must have given her a clue), and at the end of my final year at Horace Mann, when I was again the last to leave the classroom, she came up to me by the glass case, where I was taking a final longing look, and asked me if I'd like some of those? It gave me one of those little insights that happen all too seldom in life: the realization that there can be good in people who just seem mean. Perhaps the opposite is harder to accept, since when good people do mean things, it so often involves a feeling of betrayal and disappointment. (It also tends to involve strong adherence to religions and other belief systems.) In any case, my last encounter with Miss Tredenick turned out to be the best one, and I was grateful to her.

The end of my days as Red Eagle were far from the end of the special feelings I would continue to have throughout my life about Indians and the rapacious and inhumane treatment they suffered at the hands and guns of my race and my countrymen. I have always remained proud of whatever small amount of Cherokee (?) blood I might possibly have in me, despite never finding evidence to support it (and I realize it's unlikely that the Cherokee Nation would be proud to view me as a member). I suppose one of the reasons for my strong wish to identify myself with the Indians was that they were also such outsiders, relative to mainstream America. My Indian persona, on the other hand, was an outsider's role that I had *chosen*, not one I was coerced into.

I've often wondered whether my passion for learning about the various Indian tribes might have sub-consciously contributed to my questioning the doctrines I was being force-fed. The Indians were not Christians, yet I admired them. They were essentially animists – revering alleged spirit aspects of all living things and some inanimate ones – with only vague concepts of Great Spirits who didn't seem to interfere a lot in their lives or look inside their brains. Nor did the Indians ever seem to inflict their beliefs on anyone outside their own tribes. I'd read a variety of their creation stories, and while a few tribes had an afterlife concept of Happy Hunting Grounds, I'd never heard of any equivalent of hell. I never could believe that any Indians went to hell, despite it being depressingly obvious to me that my God couldn't be bothered to care about them one little bit.

For as long as I remained in North America, I continued to look for Indian artifacts, not simply to collect material things, but through them to confirm to myself my very naïve sense of kinship, solidarity and outrage. On a couple of the camping trips Jeanette and I took in the late 60s, we visited some reservations in the Pacific Northwest. We were appalled at the conditions and obvious, severe poverty we witnessed there. We bought a number of baskets they'd made, and then felt ashamed about the pittance we'd paid for them, so we packed up several large cartons of clothing and sent them anonymously to the reservation. We wanted to spare them the bitterness they might justifiably feel in having to express gratitude for clothing to representatives of the race that had stolen far more than their clothing: their land, their livelihood, their dignity, their everything.

Even after leaving North America, I have continued to read more about the Indians, such as a deeply disturbing study called *The Earth Shall Weep* (by James Wilson). Read it and you might also weep.

CHAPTER 7

Mom at Home

Compared to the effort needed to understand and express who my dad was to me, the task of comprehending and describing my mom is many times more difficult, partly because she comprised two rather distinct and contradictory personalities, partly because Mom was alive in my life for well over twice as many years as Dad (she died during the writing of *Hindsights*, shortly after reaching the age of 101, in April 2014), plus the fact that she played a much bigger role in the day-to-day care of me during my childhood, those years being the primary focus of this chapter. The list of words that might be used to describe her in my childhood is correspondingly diverse and polarized: *one* Mom was affectionate, considerate, cheerful, fun-loving, generous, gracious and extroverted; *the other* Mom was manipulative, zealous, histrionic, rigid, neurotic, mean, judgmental and straight-laced; and *both* Moms were restless, emotional, controlling, passionate, frugal, confused, sincere, curious, impulsive, cautious, resilient, frightened and punctual. (This list is admittedly highly subjective, as is my selection of which of her many traits I think I have picked up.)

Unlike Dad, Mom talked a great deal about her childhood, her father, her schooldays and the Lord; in fact, she always talked a great deal more than Dad, except during Meeting, when she wasn't allowed to and he was. This was because she didn't have a penis and he did. The Bible tells me so, explicitly, and it is useful to bear this in mind when dealing with those who insist that the Bible is the ultimate source of *eternal* truth and morality.

Mom was proud of her full-blooded Swedish ancestry and had picked up a few words and phrases in Swedish. She cited them frequently, but most of them turned out to be "Swedish-ish", in the sense that orange (or sometimes even green) is reddish. For example, she correctly referred to her mother's mother with the Swedish word *mormor*, but she wrote it as *mörmör*, probably because she felt that since some Swedish words use diacritical marks, it would *look* more Swedish to throw in a few just about anywhere. It's just that *mörmör* means *tender-tender* (in the sense that meat can be tender).

Mom's father's parents emigrated from Sweden in the 1860s. Her father's father (*farfar* in Swedish, but *färfär* in Mom's memoirs until I corrected them), Nils Johan Larsson, was born on a moderately prosperous farm called

Vinnerstads Mellangård, a bit east-southeast of Motala, in the province of Östergötland. As he was not the eldest son in the family and thus would not inherit the farm but have to seek his fortune elsewhere, he decided to emigrate, and arrived in America as a teenager. Nils found his way to the area around Knoxville, Illinois, near the Iowa border, i.e. the Mississippi River, where other Swedes were known to have gone before. Nils eventually learned to handle English reasonably well.

His future wife, Emma Justina Jansdotter, my mom's *farmor* (not *fårmör*), emigrated from a tiny hamlet called Stensgårdshult in the province of Småland together with her blacksmith father when she was thirteen (her mother died when she was just a year old). Her name was Americanized to Emma Johnson, and she and her father eventually also settled in the area of Knoxville, where she met Nils, married, and had 11 children (one of whom died in infancy), the eldest of whom was my Grandfather, John Albert Larson (he also Americanized his surname by dropping one *s*), born in 1877. The parents and their 10 children would live to an average age of 81 years. Emma never became comfortable with the English language.

I know less about Mom's mother's parents. Her *morfar* and *mormor* were believed to have come from Sweden's southernmost province, Skåne, possibly from the town of Malmö. My great-grandfather, Andrew Carlsson (later spelled with one *s*), was a poor widower with two children when he married my great-grandmother Charlotte. Seeing no way out of their poverty, they boarded a ship bound for America, presumably in the 1870s. During the long and arduous voyage they lost both children to typhoid fever. The Carlsons eventually settled in Des Moines, where their poverty continued.

They also had 10 children, seven of whom never reached the age of 10. The youngest of the survivors was my own grandmother, Sarah Carlson. She, like my dad, died when she was 61, the year before I was born. Only one of her siblings reached a fairly advanced age; her sister Eva died at the age of 74. The other sibling to reach adulthood, Fritz, died in his 20s of alcohol poisoning. He was the last of the five or six Fritzes Charlotte had borne. The others died as infants or small children; Charlotte *really* wanted a boy named Fritz. Both Andrew and Charlotte struggled with English all their lives.

All four of my mom's grandparents belonged to the Swedish Mission Church, the venue where JA Larson met Sarah Carlson in Illinois or Iowa. They got married in Des Moines in 1904, which became their first residence together.

They were both bilingual, and were initially eager for their children to have that same opportunity. Their eldest, Edna, born in 1905, apparently learned quite a lot of Swedish, but with each new child, they began to fear (probably unnecessarily) that bilingualism might be holding their children back in school, so their interest in teaching the children Swedish waned and my mom was left with no more than the ability to count in Swedish.

Most of the Swedish words and phrases Mom thought she learned came before she was a good reader, and most of her memories of spoken Swedish were hilariously corrupted, sometimes into other Swedish words with entirely incongruous meanings. As an adult, for example, she was totally convinced that the Swedish primer her parents had given her said, *Hår år en svårt gris*. Mom recited this with excellent pronunciation – except that they were *not* the words in the real text. As I would discover many years later, the primer actually said *Här är en svart gris*. (Mom's version means *Hair year a difficult pig*, while the latter, Swedish version, means *Here is a black pig*.)

Mom's rote memory *could* be impressive, despite her pride in not being vain. At some point in her youth she committed to memory a daunting text that she would sometimes recite – at breakneck speed, yet with clear diction – to show off to us kids:

In promulgating your esoteric cogitations, or articulating your superficial sentimentalities and amicable philosophical and psychological observations, beware of platitudinous ponderosity. Let your conversational communications possess a clarified conciseness, a compact comprehensibleness, a coalescent consistency and concentrated cogency.

Eschew all conglomerations of flatulent garrulity, jejune babblement and asinine affectation. Let your extemporaneous descanting and unpremeditated expatiations have intelligibility and vivacious vivacity without rodomontade and thrasonical bombast.

Sedulously avoid all polysyllabic profundity, pompous prolixity, psittacious vacuity ventriloqual verbosity and vaniloquent vapidity. Shun all double entendres, prurient jocosity, and pestiferous profanity, obscurrent or apparent.

In other words, speak plainly, clearly, distinctly, and don't use big words.

[The above is rendered here from her handwritten notes. I have to assume that she was uninterested in the actual content, since she so frequently expressed the position that no philosophical and psychological observations should be viewed amicably, nor did she seem to make any connection to either the platitudinous ponderosity or the asinine affectation of the Meeting.]

And then she would laugh heartily. How much she understood of the individual words was unclear. Perhaps the most striking example of the incongruity between her rote memory and her otherwise straight-laced values was a little alphabet-based dialog she frequently recited to us:

A B C D goldfish?
L M N O goldfish!
O S A R goldfish.
O S I C D goldfish.

I'm sure she would have been horrified to learn what the *L* in the second line meant, so she didn't, although I'm not sure what she thought it *did* mean. On the other hand, the precedence incantation takes over meaning seems to be more the rule than the exception in many a human endeavor.

My mom was the fourth of the six Larson girls. When she was two, she also got a baby brother who only lived four months. Mom frequently told the story of her broken-hearted father riding in the horse-drawn carriage to the cemetery with the little casket on his knees, but that memory was most likely not her own. She did, however, remember the birth of her younger sisters, particularly Maxine, when Mom was nearly five. In her memoirs, she wrote that she "*claimed her there and then, and what a strong bond this created from my earliest days.*" In Maxine's early childhood, Mom was her tutor, "*...and she did whatever I told her.*" How *that* would change!

Ever since early childhood Mom suffered from claustrophobia as well as musophobia. The former was particularly visible to me in her abnormal avoidance of elevators and tunnels. Her discomfort bordered on distress when in them, especially elevators. When I went with her to the huge Marshall Field's department store in the Loop and she wanted to look at something on one of the upper floors, we would take the escalators, one floor at a time, although she wouldn't admit the real reason. If for some reason we *had* to take an elevator, she would refuse to enter a crowded one (meaning one with more than two people already in it or waiting with us, even though the elevator in question might have had a capacity for 12 or more).

Several times during my childhood, when we got on an elevator, a person already in it might politely ask where we were going, in order to press the button for our desired floor, to which Mom would reply with fire in her eyes, "*I'm going to heaven to be with the Lord! What about you?!*" I'm sure they thought she was a complete nut back in those days, and her query was met with awkward silence; it certainly was by me. If for some reason we were already on an elevator and more people got on, she would clasp her hands together, hold her arms straight out in front of her to defend her breathing space, become highly agitated, and heave a huge sigh of relief when we (or others) got off. I have no idea about the origins of this phobia.

Her fear of mice, however, may have been turned from harmless fear into a true phobia by her father. She often related a story about how her father tried to get her to come to terms with her "silly fear" when she was a little girl. Grandpa discovered that a mouse had managed to make a hole in the upholstery of the family's sofa and thought he could kill two birds with one stone by getting the mouse out of the sofa while forcing little Francys to confront her fear, and by so doing overcome it. Grandpa made her stand a few feet away and watch, despite her fearful protests, while he used one hand to maneuver the mouse closer and closer to the hole in the upholstery where his other hand was cupped and waiting to seize the little thing, thereby demonstrating to my mom how truly harmless mice were. But when the mouse reached the hole, it shot out, leaped to the floor and ran straight to where Mom was standing; it then circled her frantically before fleeing from her screams. After that, Mom would refuse to go anywhere mice might be lurking. She didn't want mouse toys, didn't want to look at mouse pictures, didn't want to hear the word *mouse*.

Becoming terrified at the sudden appearance of a large crocodile in the river in which one is swimming is a fear that is not a phobia, the latter recognizable by its irrationality and by the disproportionality of the fear to any real or present danger. In this sense, Mom could be said to have also had a third phobia, one shared with the bulk of humankind, yet strangely undocumented and unnamed. I call it *discredophobia* – the fear of ceasing to believe what one has once been rigidly trained to believe ("*dis*" as in *disbelieve*). Perhaps this phobia is undocumented for the reason that it is nearly universal, the norm, not the exception. As such, it cannot be an aberration and thus its irrationality is not exposed, much less confronted. How else can one explain the fervent clinging to ancient creeds and the abhorrence of challenges to them throughout this combative world? I inherited discredophobia from my mom; she got hers from her dad, who got his from his father, *etc, ad nauseum*.

J.A. Larson worked for some years in the shipping department at Mandelbaum's department store in Des Moines. In her memoirs, Mom claimed that he was the head of the shipping department, but she also wrote that when she had the pleasure of utilizing a new technology called the telephone, she would phone him at work and he would answer "Al Larson, 5th floor." Did the store have an unusually elevated shipping platform? Whatever his level, he must have been in a position that entitled him to some remarkable discounts, for Mom's entry in her memoirs also contains the passage:

> We girls were all known to the workers. They sent us samples and surplus merchandise and many little gifts. When they would have a "sale" they packed up enough coats for my father to bring home. That evening was a "style show" at our house.

When Mom was about 14, Mandelbaum's went out of business, an especially traumatic time for my grandma, according to Mom, perhaps because J.A. Larson would never again be officially employed in his life. Instead, he was apparently sent by the Meeting to hold "tent meetings" in Kentucky, so it seems he became a Laboring Brother, and his meager pay became paltry.

Frugality was the watchword of the Larson household. Mom describes a typical Saturday evening routine – even when Grandpa was still working at Mandelbaum's until 9 PM:

> We all had designated jobs – an early supper – and then the big round tub was brought to the kitchen. Some water was heated and added to what had been pumped in buckets. First Edna – then Louise – then Marion – then I were bathed in that same water (Maxine was too young and had been hand-bathed and put to bed earlier). Then my mother scrubbed the kitchen floor before emptying the tub out onto the plantings.

Mom not only picked up the frugality; she was also zealously generous. In her early years of elementary school, she recounted how she once lent five dollars to a desperately needy girl in her class, to be repaid in weekly installments. When to Mom's surprise the final installment was paid on time, Mom rewarded the girl by giving the entire five dollars back to her as a present. When she was in the 6th grade, the class was given an assignment to write what they would do if they won $100 – a huge sum in the early 1920s. Mom's essay was published in the *Des Moines Register*:

> Wouldn't it be nice if I had $100? I would buy my mother a new pair of shoes, she needs them so badly. I would buy Edna a skating sweater, Louise a hat, Marion a dress, Maxine a doll, and Shirley a kiddy kar. I would buy my father a silk shirt. What for myself? A five pound box of chocolates. If I had any money left I would buy mother some silverware. I would not put one penny in the bank because I fear it would be lost.

Although she wrote that the chocolates would be only for herself, her behavior suggests that she would have shared those too. She always gave eagerly and selflessly, but not extravagantly. She hated ingratitude; if she gave generously to someone who didn't thank her personally, the giving would cease. She also hated wastefulness. In another life and another time, she might have been a champion for environmentalist causes.

Piano-playing was part of the Larson household throughout Mom's childhood. The girls were encouraged to play hymns, with the whole family singing along. Edna, Marion, Francys and Shirley all became quite good pianists, albeit with self-imposed limitations on their repertoire. And Grandpa Larson would make sure his daughters sang their hymns with all due piety.

The piano would become a multi-purpose tool for Mom: it was a legitimate source of pleasure (though she wouldn't have used that word to describe it); it was a form of therapy (not that word either) for her to calm her agitation, whether from despair over the sinfulness of her children or the distress she felt when people less punctual than herself failed to meet deadlines long before those deadlines arrived; it was an alarm clock when anybody in the house was sleeping longer that she deemed seemly; and of course it was yet another instrument for immersing me and my brothers in the Word.

John learned to play the piano well at an early age, having obediently subjugated himself to Mom's strict and regimental discipline about daily practice. But he eventually learned to play some pretty good boogie-woogie; he thrilled me with it a few times when our parents were out. Al seemed to have acquired Dad's more limited musicality. I foolishly rejected the opportunities being thrust upon me to learn the piano, probably because of my early discipline issues and partly because of the unspoken distaste I had acquired for the focus on hymns. I went for the guitar instead, and got to take lessons after having assured my parents that I would learn to play hymns, even though my greatest ambition was to learn *Guitar Boogie Shuffle*.

One contradictory shortcoming from Mom's youth was her unwillingness to learn to drive. In spite of her clear need for control in just about everything else, the thought of getting behind the wheel of a car made her cringe. Her father tried to teach her once, but she managed to drive into the ditch while on a straight, flat road, probably because until she had mastered a thing, she kept the panic button close at hand at all times. Driving a car required simultaneous mastery of watching the road, considering fellow motorists and pedestrians in all directions, turning a steering wheel, pressing three different pedals in the right order and to the right degree, and shifting gears, all while breathing and sitting and listening. After that first visit to an Iowan ditch, she sat behind the wheel no more, yet never had any problem being totally dependent on Dad's driving skills – for as long as he lived.

Mom was quite the stylish dresser during her youth, with a surprisingly "worldly" look, as evidenced by several early photos. I've sometimes wondered whether her seeming fashion-consciousness in her pre-Oak Park environment would have prevailed once the fashions for women came to include pants. (I should remind British readers that I'm using US English!) But by that time she was living in Oak Park, where the Meeting, in its usual approach to anything new, would search for Biblical grounds for banning it, and since there is an Old Testament injunction against cross-dressing (Deuteronomy 22:5), pants were ruled out, and Mom never wore them, except once – when she was in her 90s. Bloomers under her dress, however, were fine, and as a girl, Mom proudly wore the ones her mother made for her.

When Mom was 13, her eldest sister Edna married Harold Krause, a stern, cold man who took Edna off to Detroit. Mom missed her deeply. Three years later she visited them and their one-year-old boy Bobby for 12 weeks. A year later her next sister Louise married Josh, another Detroit man, while on the same day Marion married Fred in California, and suddenly Mom was the eldest of the three daughters still at home. That same year, the six sisters instituted the practice of sending each of the others a two-dollar bill and a handkerchief for every birthday. The surviving sisters maintained this practice until the death of Louise in 1990.

The Monday after she graduated from high school in 1931, Mom began working at Banker's Life Insurance in Des Moines, presumably as an office clerk. She described her three years there as "not the greatest", but without elaborating on why. During this time, she reported having "*very few dates, but [I] did go with a boy from the Des Moines meeting.*" Although I never heard her mention the name of this particular boy, she left an unusually detailed account in her memoirs:

> His parents would bring me to dinner – and he would take me driving. One night when taking me to Young People's meeting, he tried to hug me, etc. I told him I would get out of the car and walk if he didn't stop. I had to do just that, and when we arrived at the meeting I was walking and he was driving slowly beside me. He took me home decently. When I wouldn't go again, he left to be a "cow-boy" in Wyoming. When he was gone a few months, I got a letter asking me to be his wife – but when he did come back he had married his pregnant girlfriend! I had no thoughts for him. [!!]

Sometime later, Maurice Erisman began to notice her, so instead of becoming a cowgirl, she eventually developed thoughts for him, became his wife, knew him, and ultimately became my mom. On marrying my dad, Francys Olivia Larson chose to drop *Olivia* from her name in order to achieve a better acronym: "*It's better to FLE[e] than to be a FOE,*" she frequently proclaimed to me.

When Mom was just six, her grandmother died, about which Mom would later write:

> It was the following months that my dear Mormor became ill, and on June 11, 1919 she sat up in bed and sang the hymn "*En morgon utan synd jag vakna får*" [the title of this Swedish hymn may be translated "I'll get to wake up one morning without sin"]. That evening she went Home to be with the Lord. My excitement over this fact [*sic*] turned to deep disappointment! When I went to the funeral, instead of being in heaven, there her cold stiff lifeless body lay in a gloomy casket. It took a long time of growing to get this sorted out.

Might the "growing" she refers to somehow be related to her high daily doses of being told how a True Christian must think and feel about everything? Given that even entertaining a thought that death was the end would have been met with a flurry and fury of accusations of wickedness, followed by total ostracism from family, friends and the only life experienced hitherto, it is not difficult to conjecture that the "sorting out" process might somehow have been influenced in a highly specific direction.

The death of any Meeting person, or any loved one who was considered "saved", was normally labeled "going home", or "being called home", or "being taken home to be with the Lord" or similar entirely unproven claims, however real the aspirations might have been. For the deaths of non-Meeting persons who might nevertheless be presumed to "know the Lord", less categorical descriptions and euphemisms were customary. Although they were not on the True Path, we felt certain, or pretty certain, or certainly hoped, they might be "with Him". About others, they had simply "passed away" or "died", usually intoned with a wrinkled brow and a slight shaking of the head. Those known to be wicked – by our definition – were now "at the Judgment Seat", a pronouncement intoned with a shudder of utter dread.

Mom's mother's death came just when my parents (as well as John and Al) were preparing to move to Dallas, a move she described as "a blow" for her. Many years later, my brother John would reveal to me something revealed to him by our Grandpa Erisman: that Grandpa had surreptitiously used his influence at Link-Belt to effect Dad's transfers – first to Dallas, then to Glendale and finally back to Oak Park – as a means of "testing" Dad's true commitment to the Lord and the Meeting.

Dallas had no Meeting, which required Dad to undertake a drive of nearly 80 miles each way to reach the nearest one, a tiny gathering in Wortham. Thanks to his steadfastness in attending, despite wartime gasoline rationing, Dad passed this test and was sent to Glendale, presumably to test his conservative Meeting position against the more liberal wing in Southern California. Having passed that test as well, Dad was "rewarded" with a transfer back to Oak Park, about which Mom would later write that she had "mixed feelings". Although it is unclear (and I think unlikely) whether Dad, Mom, or Link-Belt ever realized what Machiavellian manipulations Grandpa Erisman had been up to, it is clear (to me anyway) that Mom would have preferred to remain in Glendale.

My *mormor* died before I was born; Mom spoke relatively seldom about her own mother. But my eldest cousin Bobby, Robert, Bud – or Bob, as I later came to know him – knew her well and loved her deeply. Even though she had reluctantly joined the Meeting only after her own mother died, the change was apparently nominal. Grandma Larson had insisted to her husband that she be given a room of her own in the family dwelling, so a room in the attic was created for her "retreat", which she would frequently utilize in order to be by herself, where she could listen to the radio instead of going to Meeting with the others. When Bob went to Des Moines to visit, she would invite him to join her, and together they would relish her attic hideaway with its worldly music. Bob was nearly 15 when she died, and he mourned for the only family member with whom he would bond for many years to come.

For nearly all her life, Mom kept a diary. It wasn't the kind of diary with room for long personal musings or tales, but only the briefest of notes on what had happened each day, spiced with Biblical clichés. She was a prisoner of clichés and could hardly express herself on any emotional subject without resorting to them. Emotional subjects included any subjects in which the Lord was involved, which in her view would have encompassed almost every subject there is, including the weather, but with the possible exception of toilet paper, thank God. (*"Wipe thyself as unto the Lord"?!*) Her skills in handling Biblical clichés were honed many times daily through prayers – which were veritable strings of clichés – and Bible reading, nearly daily gatherings of the Meeting, and especially by one singular achievement: she copied the entire Bible, in longhand, a project that took her several years of diligence.

Mom's diaries always provided a swift and indisputable resolution to any discussions about when we took this or that trip, or when so-and-so last came to visit. (One day in the late 1990s, to the horror of my brothers and me, Mom deposited all her diaries in a dumpster outside her apartment building in Kirkland. This loss was only partially compensated for by her memoirs.)

She also talked (and sang) to me many times about a trip she didn't take:

You are the trip I did not take,
You are the pearls I could not buy,
You are my blue Italian lake,

You are my piece of foreign sky.[3]

She never mentioned wanting to take any foreign trips (I'm certain it was the sentimentality that moved her), but her love for me was never in question. My brothers and I have long agreed that I was always Mom's favorite, even though her sense of fairness would never have allowed her to admit it to us, and perhaps not even to herself. I don't know why this was so clear to us, much less how it had come to be that way. Was it simply because I was the youngest? Or because my impish and cavorting nature was more like the good side of her own? Or because I had been especially longed for after her third and most difficult miscarriage? Or was it because my birth had nearly killed her, and the doctor had told my parents not to have any more children? Whatever the reason, or reasons, or lack of them, many times over the years, when Mom was giving me a big hug, she would gush *"You are the son of my love!!"* I never asked her what she meant exactly, but it puzzled me. When I later let my imagination run wild, I would consider the possibility that the moment of my conception had coincided with her first and perhaps only orgasm, but realizing that one shouldn't admit such a thought about one's own mother, I banished it from my brain and never thought of it again.

The seeming bipolarity of her personality was also evidenced in how her bright, effusive affection and love could be instantly transformed into dark, roiling clouds that would take over her countenance when one of her not-always-apparent limit values had been exceeded, and the yardstick would be brought forth. Yet even when she was flailing away, she never screamed at us. Instead, she cried unto the Lord at us – and appeared to withdraw her love. In combination with unceasing reminders that deviation from how they defined Truth would lead to eternal torture, withdrawal of love was a far more effective way to manipulate us.

One game Mom and I would play when I was fairly small was called "loop de loo". She would kick off her shoes and lie down on her back on the living room floor. I would stand at her feet, and she would lean forward and grab my hands with hers, doubling up her legs so she could place the soles of her feet on my

---

3   By Anne Campbell (1888-1984) from her poem To My Child. Mom may have made up the tune she sang it to.

stomach. Then she would rock backwards onto her back, pulling me up into the air, and swinging me back and forth above her while singing

Here we go loop de loo,
Here we go loop de lie,
Here we go loop de loo,
All on a Saturday night!

I used to squeal with delight, flying through the air, and I'd beg her to do it again and again and again until she was too worn out to continue. But then moments later I might have said something, used some unknown magic word or taboo phrase, and all her love would instantly disappear from view.

Both at home and in public, whenever she chose to express her disapproval non-verbally, she would intently fix the back of her hair – the bun that she wore for most of my childhood and into her 90s. The bun-fixing would be accompanied by a highly theatrical scowl, leaving no doubt whatsoever as to her position on whatever had elicited the reaction. Even at the Bible Conferences, when I was old enough to sit among my peers instead of with my parents, I could spot her across the crowded room, leaning forward so that she could gain eye contact with me between the rows and glare at me sternly, demonstrably fixing her bun because I wasn't paying attention. Over the years, bun-fixing became a reflex action that she was hardly aware of; her bun must have been among the most fixed buns in the free world.

One Friday evening in my teens, Mom's not-so-subtle expressions of disapproval set a new record. We were hosting one of those awful Young People's Meetings at our home, and Mom insisted that everything should run exactly the way she planned it. After having us warble to the Lord one boring hymn after another for quite a while, Mom felt it was time for a short refreshment break to wet our parched throats. I, however, felt it was time to escape all the forced piety and go down to the ping-pong table in the basement.

In the kitchen, Mom confronted me as I was heading downstairs with Norm, Dave and a few others who saw no harm in it. Mom declared loudly and adamantly that it was not to be tolerated. When I nevertheless made a move in the direction of the door (from the kitchen to the basement), she immediately lay down on her back on the floor, blocking the doorway, thereby visually telling me (and the other astonished guests in the crowded kitchen) that if I wanted to go downstairs, I would have to step over her body to get there.

And yet she could be so much fun and so kind. She was always offering us "treats": little presents, little outings, little snacks. A snack was never just a snack; by calling it a treat, using the word in her special way, she always made it feel more special than a mere snack. Although she might have qualified as a chocoholic herself, she was always concerned about our health, and there was to be no overdoing anything except one. Every summer, as soon as the price of watermelon dropped to a penny a pound, we were allowed to eat as much of it as we wanted – and I always wanted a lot. I loved the taste and the juiciness of pure summer, and used my spoon to carve multiple tunnels in my large wedges. If we ran out of watermelon between the weekly rounds of grocery shopping, Mom sent me to the grocery store to bring home as much watermelon as I could carry, which was, of course, a challenge to which my competitive nature rose instantly. I once carried home two huge watermelons, totaling about 20 pounds, one under each aching arm. Grandpa Larson had been convinced that watermelon was a great purge, among its other health benefits. Mom was further convinced that watermelon was an excellent source of nutrition, despite this view being supported solely by "man's learning", medical science. For me, the taste of summer would always be the taste of sweet, ripe watermelon. (Many years later, elderflower juice would become the taste of a Swedish summer.)

Another sign of summer was the appearance of clover in our lawn. What made that bit of horticulture memorable was Mom's uncanny ability to spot four-leaf clovers. She would give me and my brothers – and whatever friends might be visiting – the task of finding a few. We would all be searching eagerly but in vain, all of us ready to give up, and Mom would come out, gaze at the little patch of clover for a couple of seconds, and then start picking one four-leaf clover after another, to our great amazement. She gloated each time she found one; she only got excited when she found a five-leaf clover.

My competitive spirit certainly came to me from Mom, although it was considerably amplified by Al along the way. Playing cards (even without gambling) was also considered evil and worldly, so of course we didn't play cards – except for Old Maid, a deck of cards in which the aces, kings, queens, jacks, and all the numbered cards were replaced with something childish like farmyard animals. The games with cute cards were nearly identical to the games with evil cards, but of course the games themselves had different names, which made them all right, even if they were played in exactly the same way. And Mom liked to *win*.

One of her favorite board games was *Sorry!*, in which the advancement of the pieces ("the men") around the board is determined by rolls of the dice (also wicked in nearly all other contexts). Landing on the same square as your opponent enables you to send him or her "home" with a totally insincere plea of "Sorry!" With a dramatic sweep of her arm, Mom would sometimes literally send her opponent's "man" flying off the board and sometimes off the table and across the floor! Mom was good at the game. She would plot carefully, her eyes flashing and blazing, to send her opponents back to the start just when they were almost home free, even if those opponents were her own small children, or later, her own small grandchildren. Then, after briefly flaunting her obvious satisfaction, she would suddenly look compassionately at her defeated rival and say, "*I'm not trying to get* you, *of course! It's just* the men!"

Mom's sense of fairness towards her three sons meant that she tended to buy things in threes ("*one for each of my three boys!*"), often disregarding differentiated needs, tastes or interests. She meant well, with the greatest love, and it would be horrendously unfair to fault her for that. It takes a remarkable lack of insight to use hindsight to judge someone's lack of foresight. (Mom liked word games too, perhaps the only trait she shared with the likes of Shakespeare and James Joyce.) Most of our clothes were purchased at Sears, primarily because the prices were lower, and maybe because the big Sears store at North and Harlem was within walking distance. They had an x-ray machine in their shoe department, enabling concerned mothers to see how well the shoes actually fit their children. Nobody knew the potential dangers of that radiation in the 50s. (Such machines were around until the 1970s.) Mom always insisted on buying shoes and other clothes a bit too big, so there would be room to grow – and thus enhance the frugality of the purchase.

She sewed nearly all her own dresses and skirts, and mended our clothing instantly. Our clothes were always comfortable and of decent quality, but we never had anything flashy. When Mom took me to Mr Weiss, the barber on North Avenue, she always told him to make sure he cut it "high in the back" – long hair was sinful for a male. (Although I realize that all artistic renderings of Jesus are purely fictitious, I find myself nevertheless influenced by the consistent portrayal of Him with long hair as an adult, and can only with difficulty imagine

Him with a buzz cut.) Dad gave Mom whatever money she needed for the shopping and other household expenses (he took care of the big bills himself). I'm sure he'd have given her whatever additional amount she might have asked for, but Mom saw it as her wifely duty, and her duty "before the Lord", to be thrifty. And she was – while retaining her generosity.

Mom had little respect for snobbish behavior or attitudes, except for the Meeting's underlying holiness one-upmanship, which neither she nor they chose to recognize as a variant of snobbery. She regarded with a certain amount of suspicion women who were well-dressed and nicely made up. If they expressed views or put on airs that could be interpreted as snobbish, she would label them "cookie ladies" and meet their snobbery with withering disdain. She tended to have an extremely black-and-white worldview, good versus evil, no nuances or relativism, please.

At least some of her fairness (and love of "treats") towards us kids must have been inherited from her father. Just about every time there was a large family get-together, which most frequently took place in connection with the Des Moines Bible Conferences during the three-day Memorial Day weekend in late May, Grandpa Larson would have all his grandchildren line up, side by side, according to age, laughing in his jolly but firm way as we sorted ourselves out. We were bursting with excitement, because we knew what was coming. First he would reach into his suit pocket and take out a small cloth bag tied with a drawstring. Then, starting with the eldest and moving along the row to the youngest, he would hand each grandchild a penny. Then he would take out a new bag and repeat the procedure with a nickel. Then a dime. Then a quarter. Then a half dollar. And finally, the great moment: a real silver dollar for each grandchild present. He had apparently done things like this for his daughters as well when they were children. No wonder my mom doted on him. And at one of those Des Moines gatherings, the treat was far beyond anyone's expectations. He'd made a small wooden "suitcase" for each of the small grandchildren, suitable for use as toy boxes. On the lid, he'd used a wood-burning tool to write each child's name decoratively, accompanied by a wood-burnt drawing of a train, the template provided by Uncle Nobe.

As a child, I liked to climb trees and was pretty good at it. One summer day, I think it was just before I turned eight, I was shinnying up the elm tree out by the street in front of our house. I successfully reached the first branch, about seven feet above the grass, stood on it, and looked up to see how to get up to the next branch. It was a foot or two higher up and looked OK (I failed to notice that it bore no leaves), so I stretched one foot up onto it and prepared to hoist myself up to stand on it (all the while grasping the trunk), but when I lifted my other foot off the first branch, throwing the whole of my weight onto the higher one, it broke, and I went tumbling to the ground. A couple of neighbors, who were out watering the flower beds in front of their houses, looked up in alarm, but I just stood up, brushed myself off, smiled and bowed slightly all around me. With feigned nonchalance I then headed casually up the walk to our front door, where Mom was waiting with a concerned look on her face.

    I entered the house, closed the door behind me – and let out a horrible wail. Mom didn't know what to do. She looked for bleeding, but there was only a slight scratch. No swelling. No signs of bruising. Yet I was in great pain. She decided that the best thing would be her universal cure: a hot bath. After a long soak, the pain in my lower arm had not subsided at all, and there now appeared to be some swelling. I don't know whether she consulted Dad or Maxine or a doctor, but she eventually got me to Oak Park's West Suburban Hospital on Austin, where they x-rayed my arm. The doctor told her "Lady, you can't soak away a broken wrist!" Mom always claimed to be so ashamed of herself for doing what any normal parent would have done under the circumstances, but she told the story often, and with a smile that over the years extended to a chuckle.

    The following winter, she and I were walking to Maxine's. It was pretty cold, and there was new snow on the concrete sidewalks. It was perfect for taking a running start and sliding for many yards, as Mom walked along LeMoyne. When we crossed Ridgeland after about nine blocks, we had only one more short block to Harvey, then a dogleg onto Mapleton after one block, then less than a block to 1015, and Mom thought it was time for me to settle down (visiting Maxine was obviously somber business). But the thrill of the snow was too irresistible, and I took off along the sidewalk on Harvey. This incurred Mom's wrath, and she took a hard swat at me as I went sailing past her. She must have hit me at a strange angle (or I was rolling with the punch), because I felt almost nothing but an extra push through my heavily padded winter clothing; she, on the other hand, broke her wrist. Then she felt deeply ashamed to tell the doctor she'd broken it trying to swat her little boy.

    Another visit to the doctor was the result of my having been playing around in the lot next door, probably when the foundation of the DeLeo's house was under construction. I was balancing along a pile of planks on the ground and didn't notice a long nail sticking straight up through the plank I was walking on, until that nail was also sticking up through the sole of my sneaker and deep into the sole of my foot, filling my sneaker with blood and me with pain and panic as I went hobbling and squishing in to Mom. I had heard about the risk of *lockjaw* from rusty nails. I was so afraid of it that I sat there holding my mouth open with both hands until Mom explained that tetanus didn't set in quite that fast, and she took me to the doctor's for a shot. (I wanted to be sure that if my jaw did lock, it would be in the open position so I could eat.)

When I was eight, Mom's sister Edna died. Mom wrote this entry in her memoirs:

Dear Edna's diabetes was such a bad kind and the Lord took her Home Feb 14, 1959. It was a great loss to us, but the beginning of real joy for her.[4]

Edna's eldest son, Robert, was serving as a pathologist in the US Army in Europe at the time, and was sent home for the funeral, but missed it, arriving only in time for the burial at the gravesite where he was immediately set upon by Aunt Shirley, who began castigating him for having "turned away from the Lord" and causing his mother grief. Mom went to the funeral on her own. At this point, I'd only met my cousin Robert once, in Des Moines, when I was three and he was 20; I had no memory of the encounter, but it would turn out that he did.

Mom was always a mother hen to us boys. One summer, John and a bunch of other Meeting boys took off together in two cars bound for the Meeting's Otter Lake Bible camp (about three hours' drive north of Toronto) for two weeks. Mom was not worried much about what John might get up to there, but she was anxious about the 650-mile homeward journey, which they intended to do in one stretch from Ontario. Mom and I stayed up half the night with a large bag of licorice to keep us company, until I got sick as a dog and threw it all up, temporarily realigning the focus of her anxiety. (Many decades would pass before I could stand the taste of licorice again; Pernod helped.)

She was always supportive of our schoolwork, as long as the subject was

---

4   Sic[k]

safely non-controversial. She made sure that we always "applied ourselves" and got good grades. I suppose she and Dad presumed that we were all fairly gifted, because their expectations were very high. Mom played hands-on. She drilled me on my addition, subtraction, multiplication and division tables until I got them right, and then right again, and then right again. In eighth grade, when we had to learn the chemical symbols for the elements, she drilled me on them as well, providing associative memory aids. Since the symbol for mercury is Hg, she told me to think of how the mercury looked on the dentist's tray when he was mixing the amalgam for fillings, explaining that mercury was that shiny, slithery liquid metal you couldn't grab or hug. "You can't *hug* it, you try to *hug* it, but you can't *hug* it!" she declaimed dramatically. And mercury became Hg in my mind forever.

The fact that our many long multi-day cross-country car trips never became boring – at least not in my memory – was largely thanks to Mom's actively encouraging my brothers and me to invent games based on observations of the places we were traveling through. We counted cows, horses and sheep; we used the letters on the license plates of other cars to make words; we read the Burma Shave signs diligently; we kept a sharp lookout for deer and other wild animals; and we (especially me, I think), strained our eyes eagerly towards the western horizon to catch the first glimpse of the snow-capped Rockies.

There was a lot of freedom in those games; there were no "answers" or clear goals, and, because we could modify the rules to make any game more interesting for the environment in question, our imaginations were stimulated. There were no mind-numbing games invented by others, involving killing, zapping or obliterating endless opponents.

We read Chicago's largest newspaper, the *Tribune,* at home every day except Lord's Day. Oak Park had its own local rag, every Thursday morning, called the *Oak Leaves,* to which we subscribed, and for which first John, then Al, then I had a paper route that stretched from Kenilworth in the west to the western half of Fair Oaks in the east, and from North Avenue to Greenfield, with our home about halfway along the east-west axis. Dad and Mom encouraged us to supplement our modest allowances by earning a little money ourselves, and the paper route was a good way to start. I took over the route from Al fairly early (I think it was in 1956 or 1957), as Al was occupied with his role as sports editor on the staff of the *Trapeze,* the high school's newspaper.

The *Oak Leaves* was published in tabloid format, and some issues could be pretty thick, especially with all the ads in the issues preceding Christmas. The procedure was that the newly printed papers would be deposited at around 3:00 AM in three or four bundles on the sidewalk in front of the gas station on our side of Oak Park Avenue, just south of the corner of North Avenue, early every Thursday morning. I would get up at 4:45 AM (or sometimes a little earlier if there was a lot of snow), dress, and go down to the kitchen where Mom would make sure I got a quick bite before I headed out into the winter darkness or the beautiful and tranquil dawn, depending on the time of year.

On my way to retrieve the bundles, I'd pick up the garden cart from the garage, then enter the alley behind the house, walk the short distance to the drop-off point, load the bundles into the garden cart, and start walking down Oak Park Avenue until I got to LeMoyne, stopping to take papers up to nearly every porch on both sides of that block along the way. Nearly every household subscribed, so I only had to remember the few that didn't. Then I'd park the garden cart at the corner, and take a number of papers corresponding to the number of subscribers in the block between LeMoyne and Greenfield, lay them over my arm and go down one side of Oak Park Avenue, then back up the other side. When I returned, I'd take the garden cart along LeMoyne over to Grove, park it, and head north with one set of papers, then south with another, etc. When I'd completed Kenilworth as well, I'd head back to Euclid, roughly the halfway point.

We weren't allowed to roll the papers up with rubber bands and throw them onto the porches, or there would be complaints to the newspaper office, resulting in a call and a stern reprimand. We had no plastic bags to protect the papers from the rain either, so if the paper was too thick to insert through the mailbox slot in or beside the doors and it was also raining, it took some creativity to find ways to avoid complaints of wet papers.

During cold winters, I'd stop off at home to warm up, and Mom was always waiting for me with a cup of hot chocolate, with marshmallows melting on top for extra energy and because she knew I liked it that way. Then I'd complete the route, and when I got to the last street, Fair Oaks, I first delivered to the southern block, then wheeled the garden cart up the northern block to North Avenue, where I'd deliver to the subscribers all along the way back west. These were mostly tenants of commercial buildings – real estate agencies, insurance offices, small stores of various kinds, medical practices, my barber shop, etc. One special feature of the cold mornings was that when I got home, having become frozen again, Mom would give me money to scamper across to the bakery on the Chicago side, next to the pet store, and get some freshly baked almond crescents (croissants filled with almond paste) for her and me, with more hot chocolate – a real treat!

Having the paper route entailed another chore: collecting the subscription fee once every two months. This meant first cycling down to the newspaper office at 100 S. Kenilworth, meeting the grumpy circulation manager and getting a special kind of small, thick, brick-shaped, dual-ringed loose-leaf binder, about 4 x 8", with red, rigid canvas-clad cardboard covers housing a number of cards equal to the number of subscribers on my route. I then had two weeks to go from house to house and collect the cash for two months' worth of subscription fees. I think the fee was around 60 cents a month, of which only a small part would be mine, but the big deal was that many of these affluent subscribers would hand me two dollars and tell me to keep the change. And at Christmas, they might hand me an extra five dollars, and maybe also some candy. Christmas tips were where the money was.

But I didn't visit every household. Some cards were marked "PA" – paid in advance – no tips to be had there, except a few times when I "mistakenly" rang the doorbell of a PA subscriber just before Christmas, then apologized in my endearing way for my mistake, and sometimes got a tip anyway, if the Christmas spirit was upon them. But there would always be subscribers who were never at home when I came to call. If I was unable to catch them by the end of the two weeks allotted for collection, I would have to return the binder with a few cards marked "NH" for "nobody home", which made the grumpy manager even grumpier.

One day Mr Grumpy announced that all paper boys were being given a new task: one Sunday a month, we would have to distribute a thin "shopper" – a free flyer in newspaper format consisting only of advertisements – to all households, not just the *Oak Leaves* subscribers. Three bundles of them would be delivered to the same street corner as the *Oak Leaves*, but these shoppers first had to be individually rolled up and fitted with rubber bands. It was, however, OK to just throw them onto each porch. And the extra pay? There would be none, but we would get to keep our jobs. And they would graciously supply the rubber bands. (There was no union....)

I was unhappy about this development, muttering at them under my breath and cursing them in my mind. Mom sympathized with me, and said she would help me roll them up, so I began bringing these bundles home unpleasantly early on the designated Sunday mornings, and Mom and I would sit in the living room (Dad sometimes joined us), rolling up the kind of advertising rags that people usually deposit directly in the garbage without reading. After a few months of this, I got the idea of depositing one of the bundles directly in a dumpster permanently parked behind the gas station on my way home from picking them up. Mom didn't seem to mind or notice there being fewer, or maybe a combination of the two. I saw to it that every neighbor of ours in all directions got their damn shopper, just in case the subject came up in the fleeting contact Mom might have with any of them. After another few months, I also deposited about half of the rolled-up shoppers in the same dumpster.

Mom was always eager to help me in practical ways – with my newspaper route, my schoolwork, all the little treats – and it must have rubbed off, because I tended to reciprocate. For some strange reason, I enjoyed doing the dishes, as well as doing kitchen chores like slicing, peeling, rinsing, wiping, sweeping and scouring. (I didn't relent and start using a dishwasher – rather reluctantly – until 2007.)

I started taking guitar lessons at the Modern Music Center on the north side of North Avenue, in the second block east of Austin, in June 1959, the summer before I started high school. Folk music had not yet fully entered the national music scene – nor my consciousness – back then. Whether or not that would have influenced me at that point is moot; the Crickets, Buddy Holly, Jerry Lee Lewis, Elvis, and many other rock-and-rollers were my entire and surreptitious interest. An electric guitar was thus what I was after. The problem was that I wasn't the only one who associated electric guitars with worldly music; so did all three of my parents. Consequently, I had to be pretty convincing that I was aiming to learn to play hymns, that an acoustic guitar would be drowned out if I tried to accompany Mom playing hymns on the piano, and that a solid-body electric guitar would enable me to practice without disturbing anyone, since the sound wouldn't carry unless it was plugged in and the volume turned up. (Two years later, I could practice *Blue Hawaii* without Mom recognizing that I wasn't playing a hymn.) I persevered.

The Modern Music Center was a 14½-block walk straight down North Avenue, a real B-movie establishment run by a most unlikely couple. The principal owner was a short, wizened, unspectacular Italian in his 70s, who smoked constantly and not only thought he was still a big-band leader (which he had been), but also a big-time big-band leader (which he never was). The other owner was his vulgarly flamboyant wife, probably 20 years his junior, seemingly twice as tall, who appeared to think she could disguise her long-faded talents as a singer in the aforesaid band with the thickness of the makeup she applied somewhat randomly all over her face to fill the deep furrows resulting from too many years of excessive sunbathing in a futile effort to cling to the last vestiges of what might once have been a touch of glamour. This mask continued up to – and partly into – the hairline of her highly unnatural, maroonish, heavily sprayed coiffure that looked to me like it might have benefitted from an annual washing. She competed fiercely with her husband for the smoker-of-the-year title. He was the guitar teacher, she ran the rest.

Mom went with me to sign up for lessons and quickly turned pale. I think she was so flabbergasted at the sight and manner of the proprietors, and so utterly bowled over by the innumerable and vehement objections she might have raised, any one of which might have brought a swift and final veto to the whole idea of my taking guitar lessons at all, let alone at the Modern Music Center, that she just allowed her jaw to drop, her brow to crease, and concentrated on not fainting while she paid for my first six months of lessons. (Fortunately, the moment gave her no opportunity to consult Maxine.) I selected and paid for my plain, solid-body electric guitar and amplifier with my savings from *Oak Leaves* tip money.

Behind the somewhat shabby storefront of the Modern Music Center, with its guitar-filled picture window, the premises comprised glass cases bursting with guitars, as well as a few other instruments and accessories, along the entire wall to the left. To the right were two small rooms behind walls with glass on the upper half. These were the cubicles for the lessons. There were well-filled ashtrays scattered everywhere in the store. And there was a small office at the back.

It was kind of boring at first, learning how to breathe in that small smoky room, how to hold the guitar and the pick, and how to play scales and the most basic chords. But soon I got my first book of actual songs. I didn't recognize any of them, but my parents certainly seemed to. Most of them were my teacher's favorites from his days as a dance band leader in the 30s and 40s – songs like *Tenderly, Sentimental Journey, Lullaby of Broadway, Paper Moon* – songs that my parents were reluctant to let on that they were familiar with, and unhappy about me learning. I wasn't that happy about them either; I wanted rock and roll, particularly from the late 50s.

But by spring of 1961, I was nearly 16 and things had improved. I bought a new and beautiful Gibson guitar, and the teacher was organizing a recital where all his students would play for their parents. The crowning number on the recital playlist was none other than *Guitar Boogie Shuffle*, which I had to practice a *lot*. My parents hated it. On the day of the recital, my teacher asked me to ride with him in his huge white Cadillac to the concert location: an old theater – another trial for Mom and Dad. He needed to fill his car with things for the concert and needed my help to carry them. He seemed too nervous to drive, and was certainly too short. (His wife, who usually did the driving, was otherwise occupied.) He could barely see out the windshield and probably not out the rear window at all. I think he looked *through* the steering wheel rather than *over* it. The recital was fun – my parents hated that too – and that August, my guitar lessons stopped after pressure from my parents and the prospect of again trying out for the football team.

I have to say, with hindsight, that I had a largely secure and happy pre-pubertal childhood. Mom showered me with love and affection, nearly all the time. Dad clearly loved me very much as well. Apart from a few incidents where Mom's own insecurity overwhelmed her into drastic actions such as those that led to the demise of my pets, my world was harmonious, and I didn't suffer from its insularity (I'd never known anything else) *until* my approaching puberty began to upset the balance in ways that Mom was ill prepared to handle.

She always meant well – more than well; the very best. But because her own childhood indoctrination had "taken", however much it may have warped whatever inherent ability she might have had to think critically, she truly believed in heaven and hell as actual places of eternal bliss and torment respectively, and she literally and fervently believed that a totally good god created and deployed the latter.

Part of what she'd been force-fed to believe in was the inherently sinful nature of every human being, that going to hell is the default setting that has to be corrected and atoned for, that unless her own little children were truly saved, they too would burn in hell forever, in accordance with the arrangements also created by her loving God. What an awful burden to bear!

Who am I to judge anyone for things having gone awry when the intentions had been so loving and so good? And yet I cannot help wondering what she'd have been like had she been free from all her superstitions and had channeled all that theatrical energy and fundamental goodness and fairness unfiltered into her family and the world around her. What if her faith had not taught her – commanded her! – to administer harsh corporal punishment to her children, or to treat so many people with disdain and contempt, all those unrepentant sinners on their way to hell? What if her righteous zeal had broken free of its yoke, unequal or otherwise, and worked for the happiness of the many in this life instead of the glory of the few in an illusory next one?

She did, however, manage to salvage a warm and fun-loving side of her personality from her dark, righteous, fanatical side. It took many years of great tension in our relationship for me to identify this dichotomy, a discovery I doubt she ever made herself. Once I came to recognize it, when it emerged so clearly to me under highly traumatic circumstances in the late 1970s and I could act accordingly, Mom and I gradually found a common and solid ground of love for each other that would always remain.

During my adolescence, however, this insight was invisible. Mom found nothing more positive to write about me in her memoirs for this period than *"Stan was a real help in the kitchen."*

CHAPTER 8

Crumbling

Leaving Horace Mann behind in June 1959 was probably much more of a milestone for me than I realized at the time, amid all the other profound changes going on, like John and Al being away from home most of the time; like my growing interest in girls without seeing any way of doing anything about what I didn't yet quite understand what I wanted to do; like my persistent disillusionment over the disappearance of Steve (including Little Wolf and Red Eagle); like my growing thrill in doing forbidden things, especially going to movies; like the prospect of starting at Oak Park and River Forest High School, with all that would mean in terms of new friends (or acquaintances or at least classmates), new teachers, a new and vastly larger school (more than 2600 students), the prospect of playing real football with uniforms, helmets, shoulder pads and everything; and like my growing and still mostly subconscious resistance to the Meeting and all its seemingly limitless anachronisms and prohibitions. The entire edifice of my childhood was crumbling and I didn't know it yet.

That summer Howie already began having misgivings about going with me, Norm and Dave to movies anymore, after just a few times. (My classmates had no interest in going to Saturday matinees, and besides, they wouldn't have understood the need to sneak, or not to breathe a word about it to anyone who might let something slip to my parents.) Howie also began talking about "taking his place". Since I was his elder (by 17 days), I think he saw it as a matter of protocol that I should be given the opportunity to take my place before he took his, a kind of right of first refusal. My disinterest, however, was as keen as Howie's interest, yet he felt uncomfortable about by-passing me. He hinted at it with increasing frequency and fervor, while I felt uncomfortable about formally joining the ranks of a group whose foremost (in my mind) feature was repression. My family was one thing; I was willy-nilly a member of that. But the Meeting? The spiritual home of Grandpa Erisman, Matilda Johnson, Richard Evans and Harry Hayhoe? The appeal underwhelmed me.

Late that summer, Howie was at our house one day and attempted to bully me about it, which was kind of weird. Although we were roughly the same height, I was a great deal stronger, quicker and more agile. After I repeatedly dismissed his nagging, his irritation with me grew to the point where he started swinging his fists at me. His totally ineffectual pugilistic skills caused me no more harm than if his fists hitting my body had been flies, but even flies eventually provoke, and finally, growing tired of warding off his nagging and flailing, I turned in irritation and let him have a single blow to the body, a roundhouse to the solar plexus. I hadn't been aiming for it – I was just avoiding his head – but he buckled, fell to his knees, the wind knocked out of him, wheezing "*You bastard!*" several times while I backed away wishing it hadn't come to that. It was the only time in my entire life I've hit a person in anger; when the class bullies at Horace Mann challenged me to meet them after school to "settle" some silly argument, I would always tell them that if I didn't make it on time, they could start without me. I could run faster than any of them; macho has never been my thing.

When I reached Oak Park High, Dad expected me to choose a full program of math, not only the obligatory algebra and geometry (plane and solid), but also advanced algebra, trigonometry and calculus. Dad's expectations may have been reinforced by his own predilections and the successes of my brothers in these subjects. We were told that Oak Park High had an exalted academic standing among America's high schools, and my parents' admonitions to "apply" myself basically meant that I had to get A's. B's were grudgingly acceptable, but generated little praise, C's were a real problem, D's were downright sinful, and F's were unthinkable. The math curriculum I was facing was thus no easy task for one with my inappropriate aptitude and confounding lack of interest.

I always walked to and from Oak Park High, some 15 blocks away, which was a lot farther from my home than Horace Mann, but there was a lunch room with a cafeteria where they sold subsidized milk, Twinkies and Snowballs, as well as hot lunches for those who hadn't brought a lunch bag from home (as I usually did), so I only had one round trip to and from school each day. Initially I walked 10 of those blocks together with Bob Kettlestrings, the nearest thing to a friend I'd had at Horace Mann. But we weren't in the same homeroom, nor did we have any classes together, nor did he play football, so we were drifting in different directions.

One day on our way home, we were discussing female anatomy, more specifically the configuration of female genitalia, and he declared, with the full and assertive certainty of unfounded faith, that girls had a single unbroken orifice for their urethra, vagina and anus, a U-shaped vertical slit between their legs. I told him that according to a book I had read, this was not the case. Sex education being what it wasn't, we were literally speaking different languages; I used the Latinate anatomical terms from my textbook source, Bob used the Anglo-Saxon words he'd picked up from our classmates. He insisted that his sources were superior; besides, he had a sister and I didn't, so there. I insisted that there were separate orifices. He jeered. And so we proceeded, making claims and counter-claims without evidence, up East Avenue to Division and on over to Euclid, our usual meeting and parting point, but that particular parting turned out to be our last; Bob couldn't handle my questioning the veracity of his claim (which was contrary to Compton's Encyclopedia). I somehow harbored doubts that he'd engaged in a detailed discussion with his sister on the subject, much less that he'd conducted a gynecological examination of her. He never spoke to me again, ever.

That first semester at Oak Park High was largely unremarkable, except that as a freshman I was suddenly among the youngest, rather than the eldest, at the school. By this time most of the student body, even most of the freshmen, were well into puberty, which tended to show most prominently in the girls' bodies and the boys' eyes.

Our Spanish teacher wanted the class to use the Spanish equivalents of our first names, which worked fine for all the Marias and Josés, but Stanislao seemed too far-fetched even for him (he was American), so he dubbed me Pancho instead.

Schoolwork was easy enough for me, provided the teacher had the slightest skills as an educator. Mr Storey, our biology teacher, didn't; he was more concerned about classroom discipline than about imparting any actual knowledge to stimulate our intellectual curiosity or to capture our attention. Moreover, he seemed convinced that the only education we needed about reproduction should be limited to post-conception frogs. When I got a 'D' for my first half-term grade, my parents hit the ceiling, demanding that I spend much more time studying. I quickly learned how to do what was needed to raise that to a 'B': no need to study more, just more effectively. But I also learned that my parents' urgings that I spend more time studying could free me from going with them to Thursday night Prayer Meetings and, later, even the Tuesday night Reading Meetings. As long as I got the grades to show for it, they were content that I was applying myself. After I made the "honor roll" in the second semester of my freshman year, I was literally home free.

After Bob Kettlestrings started taking a different route, I soon noticed that another freshman in one of my classes, Roger W, also walked my same way home. He lived on Columbian, near the corner of Thomas, in a pseudo-Frank Lloyd Wright house that I passed every day anyway, so we started walking to school together most of the time. I usually walked home alone during the football season, since I had practice after school. Roger was pencil-thin, taller than me, with narrow, almost Asian eyes and a perpetual sneer. He was also much more a "man of the world" – both in the popular sense and in my parents' sense of the World – than anyone from Horace Mann, which basically meant anyone I knew in my peer group. His parents didn't seem to practice any religion (they might have been nominal Catholics or Lutherans for all I knew), which put them far from our small-minority end of the spectrum. Roger had a vocabulary that I quickly associated with bars of soap, for some reason. Anyone who earned his disdain (which he granted liberally) was dubbed a "pimp", which he pronounced by squeezing out the vowel into something like *m'ylmp*.

Roger was allowed to do all kinds of things I could only dream of, and his emergence into full-blown puberty was accompanied by greater and greater feats during our high school years, including smoking, drinking (the latter became his over-indulgent weekend routine during our senior year) and sex – all-the-way sex – with Nancy W, a pretty classmate of ours. She had an extremely cute younger sister, Sue, who flirted shamelessly with me, which became agonizingly frustrating, since she clearly wanted me to take her out, but there was no way I could. I somehow realized that inviting her to sneak with me to a Saturday afternoon matinee at the Mercury Theater wouldn't count in her mind as taking her out. Roger asked me if I wasn't interested, probably the result of Sue having asked Nancy to ask him to ask me, and I tried to explain why I couldn't to Roger, which didn't seem to make any sense to him at all, I'm sure. I can hardly imagine what he then told Nancy and what she told Sue, but the result was that Sue stopped flirting with me, and I simply tried to bottle up my feelings.

One day, far in the future, I would find it difficult to understand why so many people would claim that Bill Clinton had lied about not having sex with Monica Lewinsky; to me and all my peers (and I presume all my contemporaries) at that time, having sex meant "going all the way," having intercourse, coitus, screwing, fucking. Anything less was petting or heavy petting, but not "having sex". Did they all forget?!

During my freshman year I was also frustrated by my size (about 5'7" and 145 lbs), especially since my shortcomings in that department initially relegated me to the C team in freshman football, despite my Jim Brown spirit. I could gain yards, but I simply couldn't gain pounds. I was pretty strong, in a wiry sort of way, and could already overpower both of my brothers, at least one at a time, when we occasionally horsed around. And yet I was so skinny. I could suck in my stomach to make a huge "bowl" out of my abdomen, such that I could probably have worn a fair-size watermelon under my shirt without appearing to have a pot belly, an ability that I would retain well into my early 20s (when I also put it to use). Although I was promoted to the B team halfway through the season, I decided not to go out for sophomore football the next year, to the great disappointment of Al and the relief of my parents.

For my first high school math course in algebra, I again had a teacher who had also been my brothers' and my dad's, but I knew at once that Mr Woodruff was no Miss Tredenick. He was a gentle gentleman with white hair, a soft voice and a great deal of patience. My first algebra course was no problem either, except for Mr Woodruff's mild and not-entirely-suppressed disappointment that I wasn't anything like the math whiz my brother Al had been a few years before. One of the pleasures of my sophomore year, however, was leaving algebra behind after the first semester and moving into geometry – first plane, then solid – and without even realizing it, getting my first taste of symbolic logic. Those geometry courses were probably the only math courses I ever loved. I don't even remember who my teachers were or whether there were any exceptionally pretty girls in my classes – the two usual criteria for my enjoyment of high school courses.

History class bored me to tears, and I was frequently reprimanded for clowning around and talking in class to the girls sitting beside or behind me. I was a good enough student, and could always charm my way out of any real trouble, but one day, the teacher got so tired of reprimanding me for talking to the girls that he made me sit by myself. The classroom was quite a bit larger than required for the number of students in that particular class, so our teacher seated all of us in the rows farthest from the door and closest to the windows, while the three rows of desks closest to the door remained empty. The blackboard and teacher's desk were along the wall to the right on entering the room. He made me move to the row closest to the door and farthest away from the rest of the class, all the way at the front, where he could keep an eye on me. I quickly discovered that with no seat in front of me, I could easily and silently slide my desk (the desk and seat formed a single unit of furniture) to another position without getting up. While the teacher was busy writing on the blackboard, with his back to the class, I began inching closer and closer to him, until he suddenly turned around – or looked straight down – to find me directly beneath him, gazing upwards at him with a look of impish and adoring innocence on my face, as if I were hanging on his every word, while I feasted on the appreciative and audible sniggers of my classmates. My teacher, however, was not amused. He ordered me to report to the dean immediately.

I sauntered out of the classroom, went along the corridor and down one flight of stairs to the boys' lavatory, where I sat and read until the bell rang. When we had history class again a couple of days later, I resumed my usual seat near the door as if nothing had happened. And I behaved myself. After class, he took me aside and demanded to know whether I'd been to see the dean. I told him that I'd gone to the lavatory instead and was sorry that I'd behaved disrespectfully towards him. He stared at me for a couple of seconds, then said he hoped I meant that, and let me go.

By the time I was in my junior or senior year, there was some whispering making the rounds in the school corridors about a new freshman girl, because she was the daughter of Sam Giancana, the head of the Chicago Mafia, who had replaced Tony Accardo, the first Chicago Mafia boss to retire with his heart still beating. The Giancana girl looked plain, like many other girls – unlike Tony Accardo's stunning daughter, who attended Oak Park High with my brother John, and who was deservedly voted "most beautiful girl" in the graduating class.

Dad would sometimes take us for a drive to ogle the opulent, gated, 24-room Accardo home in River Forest. My parents guessed that our next-door neighbor to the north (whose home was built on my ducks' pond), Mr DeLeo, did odd jobs for the Mob. He was a small man with a worried look on his face at all times, and seemed to have no employment (his hugely obese wife was a pharmacist who ostensibly supported the family). They had a very pretty, totally off-limits daughter a year or two younger than me. Once in a while, we would see Mr DeLeo standing around in front of his house for half an hour or so, as if waiting for something. Then a well-filled car (usually a Cadillac containing three or four burly men in suits) would pull up, and Mr DeLeo would walk briskly over to it and either receive or deliver a manila envelope. Then the car would pull away. After some years, a small new building went up just north of the DeLeo home, on North Avenue, part of which housed a hot dog diner, owned and operated by Mr DeLeo. We guessed that the diner business was a reward for services rendered, and was now the front for all envelope transfers.

The rush of pubertal hormones in me coincided with my first real exposures to all the gorgeous girls and women in movie after movie, Saturday after Saturday. My desire to become an Indian gave way to a new career choice: I wanted to be an actor. So did Norm. We had no idea how we would make it happen, but somehow we would go to Hollywood together and be "discovered" and become big stars, and get away from all our depressingly repressive oppression. Going to the Saturday double-feature matinees at the Mercury was pretty much routine for us now. Norm would run straight south on 73rd and I would run straight west along the alley just south of North Avenue, and we would meet in the lobby just in time for the start of the first movie. No other kids seemed to get such a thrill out of just going to see a movie – any movie – on a Saturday afternoon, nor could they understand our enthusiasm. We saw westerns and horror movies, musicals and farces, dramas, romances and epics. We would become heartsick, terrified, thrilled, outraged, inspired – and horny for one beautiful new actress after another. And then we would run home, making sure we were sweaty and out of breath enough to make it convincing that we'd spent the afternoon playing ball at Greenfield Park. Even at the Detroit Conferences, which Norm didn't attend, I would sometimes sneak off with Dave Henderson to a movie at a theater we'd discovered just three or four blocks away. It was here Dave and I saw a really moving picture, *Splendour in the Grass*, with Warren Beatty and the most beautiful actress of them all, Natalie Wood. It was so overwhelmingly romantic and tragic that I could hardly handle it, and of course I had to look up the source of the title – four lines nearly hidden in Wordsworth's *Intimations of Immortality*, quoted in the film:

> Though nothing can bring back the hour
> Of splendour in the grass, of glory in the flower;
> We will grieve not, rather find
> Strength in what remains behind.

Another of those movies that made a particularly strong impression on me on multiple levels was *Inherit the Wind*, based on the true story of the Scopes "Monkey Trial", with the wise Spencer Tracy and the bombastic Fredrik March (who reminded me of my Grandpa Larson). The Reverend, played by Claude Akins, certainly reminded me of quite a few of the Brothers, despite the Meeting having no official clergy. Many movies I'd seen made me feel things I'd never felt before; this one made me think things I'd never thought before, things I didn't think I was allowed to think or even could think.

There were other movies that made me think that capital punishment might not be right after all (Grandpa Erisman was a staunch supporter of it), or that the Civil War and the Emancipation Proclamation had not achieved liberty and justice for all, nor made the color of a person's skin an irrelevant criterion for the worth of a fellow member of the human race (*To Kill a Mockingbird* was particularly influential in 1962).

I was, in fact, being introduced to a whole new set of morals, morals whose morality was rooted in what enables humans to live together in harmony, not morals based on the often inscrutable commands of some mysterious Thought Policeman in the Sky. It gave me glimpses into areas that were sharply at odds with what I'd been immersed in, yet they appealed strongly to an unknown, non-Meeting view that made so much more sense, that was so much more defensible intellectually, a view that was also humane. The new morals seemed to have something to do with what I spontaneously felt – in my heart, my mind, and my gut – to be *good*, not simply what one had to do to placate Him.

If He was all-good, all-wise and all-powerful, and had created the universe (including every last thing within it), why was there all this misery, pain, sorrow, injustice, horror? Why would He create people to be innately sinful and then demand them not to be? Why would He give me a brain that insisted on making sense of things, and then act in ways that made no sense at all? Why did He create the Devil and Hell? How could He know every detail of the future and then do nothing about its horrors? After all, He made all the rules!

Many of these challenges to the worldview of my childhood were indirect, coming from an accumulated sprinkling of insights into "normal" homes like Johnny's and Roger's, homes that seemed harmonious enough without the constant neurotic threat of displeasing someone or incurring His wrath, homes where people went about the business of living and seemed none the worse for it. The notion of the "wilderness wide" simply didn't fit the experiences I was both witnessing and having. Other insights into this alleged wilderness came from books, especially where normal lives were not the focus, but merely the framework in which the plots transpired, and had been transpiring for centuries. The gripping tale of *David Copperfield* unfolded without Divine intervention, the Forsyte family's saga progressed through generations of prosperity and adversity without any of them ever once going to Meeting or doing much invoking of heavenly Powers.

The only movie I'd seen that focused directly on such matters, apart from *Inherit the Wind*, was *Elmer Gantry*, a powerful satire of the hypocrisy that reigned within the sort of tent meeting movements that my own Grandpa Larson engaged in. The coercive nature of religious fervor found in both movies (and my own experience) served as an eye-opener to me – and an external perspective on what I'd been immersed in all my life, the somewhat subtler coercion to which I'd been subjected. The floodgates of awareness were being nudged open.

Ever so slowly, I was becoming conscious of a constant, terrifying threat of withdrawal of love and affection from those I loved for any failure on my part to display sufficient piety, reverence and obedience to His unknowable will, to feel deep and mortal guilt for any of the natural impulses that in a sane world would be part of the natural learning process of the trial and error of growing up, and that in a sane family would at worst be labeled naughtiness rather than wickedness, to totally curb any signs of sexuality, and to think correctly (when what was being demanded of me had more to do with *not* thinking, and nothing to do with any correctness that could or should be proved).

I *know* that my parents loved me. But I also know they sincerely felt obliged to make their love *appear* contingent on my subservience to their ethereal search for His will and His total control of our lives. They didn't always succeed; their real, human love often showed through. What didn't show through was the logic in their constant ranting about how God loved everybody, yet most people were destined (even *pre*destined!) for eternal torture. It seems we defined the word "love" somewhat differently.

Still, I didn't want to – didn't dare to – entertain these thoughts more than fleetingly. I didn't allow them to move in or even stay for dinner. They were far too scary, thanks to all the conditioning and indoctrination that required the complete subjugation of my thoughts to God's will.

By now I was in my mid-teens without having joined the Meeting ("asked for my place at The Lord's Table"), but I still hadn't yet consciously and explicitly ruled it out, despite aspiring to be a movie actor. However, the cracks in the wall my parents had attempted to build (to keep the World out and me sealed inside) were multiple and growing rapidly. It wouldn't take much to make that crumbling wall come tumbling down.

CHAPTER 9

The Thursday Night Massacre

One Thursday afternoon in 1960, in the fall of my sophomore year – probably not more than a month after my 15th birthday – Mom was cleaning Al's room, inside his desk, inside the envelopes that were inside the desk drawer. There she found, in a letter written to Al by some co-ed, a presumably joking P.S. ("presumably joking" because it seems likely that anyone who knew Al would have known about at least some of the many restrictions placed on him by our parents) with the admonition *"Don't get too drunk this weekend!"*

On reading these words, Mom immediately went downstairs to the phone to call Dad at work. She was most likely ashen and highly agitated. I understood that Dad would immediately phone the dean at NIU and order him to locate Al in whatever classroom he might happen to be at that moment, and instruct Al to take the next train to Oak Park, where Dad would be waiting for him at the Lake Street station. When I got home from school that afternoon (no football practice that year), Dad and Al had not yet arrived, but Mom, still ashen, told me they would soon be home and I was to go up to my room and remain there. No other information about what or why was given to Al, but it was clearly of extraordinary import.

(Some years before, when John was in his freshman year at Northwestern and commuting to Evanston, Dad discovered that in the English course John was obliged to take despite being an engineering major, the required reading list included Salinger's *Catcher in the Rye*. Dad wrote a stern letter to the dean to protest the necessity of John's being exposed to "such filth". I don't know the outcome of that protest.)

Thursdays were normally Prayer Meeting days, but this was no normal Thursday. It turned out to be one of the most pivotal, seminal, watershed experiences in my life – and, as I see it, in the life of my brother Al. Dad was on his way home from work, having left early. Al was taking the train home from DeKalb – in mid-week! – and Dad was picking him up at the Lake Street station. Mom told me nothing about what would happen after that. And the less I was told, the curiouser I grew.

First I must describe the setting – the scene of the crime – in our relatively (to Oak Park) small, compact house.⁵

The small entrance alcove inside the front door of our house opened onto a small, grayish-blue living room, with light beige wall-to-wall carpeting, a three-seat sofa to the right, a piano along the far wall, a small bookcase in dark oak, a dark oak coffee table, and a dark oak bench near the front door. To the left, the living room opened onto a dining alcove filled by a large dark oak table and six matching dark oak chairs, a dark oak linen cabinet, and a china cabinet. The dark oak furniture was part of a complete set of living room, dining room and bedroom furniture my parents started buying when they were newly married and furnishing their first apartment, and followed them on all their subsequent moves, including to their first house on Taylor Street.

The living room also contained an easy chair, as well as a couple of captain's chairs with round wooden frames that formed the backs and armrests. Draped over the sofa and at least one of the chairs were pretty afghans that Mom had crocheted, mostly in muted greens, but occasionally in a bright rainbow of colors. The wall decorations comprised various framed Scripture texts, a kitschy Enstrom painting of an old man with a loaf of bread, praying (the man, not the bread, was doing that), as well as an intriguing impressionist painting by Kay Scott, depicting a leafy residential street. They bought the painting when we lived in Glendale.

To the left of the piano was a narrow vertical niche housing a pendulum wall clock with Westminster chimes. Straight ahead, the far end of the room to the left of the clock opened into a small hallway, with the open kitchen doorway first on the left-hand side (there was also a swinging door to the kitchen from the dining alcove), just before the stairway, also on the left. On the right-hand side of the hallway, there was a small "broom closet" for the vacuum cleaner and the hickory yardstick, as well as other cleaning and cleansing aids. Level with the stairway was another alcove with the entrance to the bathroom. In the alcove itself there was a niche for the wall-mounted telephone (Village eight-o-nine-one-five), and beneath it was a flat seat (where Mom would sit during her daily long calls with Maxine, Euclid six-six-o-six-two) that was the lid of a laundry chute, where dirty clothes would land in a bushel basket that hung beneath it on chains, close to the basement laundry facilities. The hallway beyond this alcove and stairway entrance extended only far enough

---

5   See drawings of the layout of my boyhood home, Appendix 1

to accommodate the door to the den, on the left, and the door to my parents' bedroom, straight ahead.

In the small bluish-gray den we had another sofa, a couple of chairs, a desk and a cabinet for the hi-fi that my brother John built from Heathkits. He'd painstakingly soldered every circuit and connection, and mounted every transistor and a wide and baffling (to me) variety of other tiny components, until he achieved a well-functioning amplifier, pre-amplifier, and tuner on which to listen to WMBI (and sometimes baseball). But when Mom and Dad were at Meeting, and I'd been "obliged" to stay home and "study", I listened to Buddy Holly and the Crickets, Ricky Nelson, Elvis, and many others. John's stereo also included a record player on which to listen to more hymns and Dad's marching bands, with few other exceptions.

At the top of the staircase was a bookshelf beneath the window, containing a number of Meeting-approved Scriptural interpretations and stories by various Meeting authors, all purchased at the Bible Truth Publishers. But there was also something else, my personal gold mine: the *Compton Encyclopedia*, 1951 edition, my well-illustrated source of seemingly infinite pleasure and fascination as I was growing up. I could pull out a volume at random and lie on the floor for hours, studying the cutaway drawings of the human body, or volcanoes and vertebrates, China and cheetahs, mangos and mongooses. It seemed to me to be the only source of information in our home library that wasn't specifically designed to make me feel guilty about something. The 15 volumes were bound in black leather, with a dark green band in the upper part of the spine of each that provided information about what part of the alphabet the subjects in that particular volume covered.

The area to the right at the top of the stairs was originally John's section of the open-dorm furnished attic that we three brothers shared until first John, then Al, then I, grew up and moved away. The ceiling above the stairway was of normal height at the flattened peak, then sloped down along both sides to waist-high walls along the two long-sides of the attic. When our parents decided to replace their dark-oak bedroom furniture with a lighter (and less squeaky?) set, they offered to move the double bed upstairs to replace one of the single beds, if any of us wanted it. It wouldn't fit on John's side, and Al didn't want the bother of making a double bed, but I was eager to have the extra space, so it became mine. John's section was partly walled off by a waist-high, pine-panel-covered banister around all three sides of the stairwell. Whenever we wanted to say something to someone downstairs, or listen to anything interesting going on down there, we could and would lean over this banister. From that position, the acoustics were quite favorable for picking up whatever talk was going on downstairs.

John started studying engineering at Northwestern in the fall of '55. He began his exodus from our home in the fall of '57, when I turned 12 and he turned 20, and he was finally allowed to live on campus instead of undertaking the two-hour daily commute to Evanston, having satisfactorily proved (to our parents) his maintained piety (what they didn't know didn't hurt them). He was in a co-op program, alternating quarters with studies at Northwestern and work for International Harvester (where our Uncle Ralph also worked). IH underwrote much of the cost, while assuring John his first job as a full-fledged mechanical engineer upon graduation in June '60, the same month he married the lovely and demure Marjorie Klassen (who, being a Meeting girl, needed little other approval from our parents) from Aberdeen, Idaho, where they got married in the backyard of the farmhouse on her parents' potato farm, and completed John's departure from 1231 North Euclid. John and Marj moved to an apartment in Berwyn, just south of Oak Park, and listened to music that had little to do with hymns or WMBI.

Al began his exodus in the fall of '58. John's apparently good example at Northwestern sufficed to embolden my parents to permit Al to attend Northern Illinois University in DeKalb, 57 miles due west of Oak Park, right from his freshman year, provided he would come home for the weekends to attend Meeting. On John's final departure from our parental home, Al took over John's section of the attic for his weekend visits, abandoning his former corner, immediately to the left from the top of the stairs. I remained in the farthest corner from the top of the stairs. My section also contained the entrance to the upstairs bathroom, which had only a toilet and a sink. But with both John and Al mostly gone, I had the entire attic to myself throughout my high school years and until I left home in June 1964, apart from one lodger that last spring.

Our parents were control freaks, to put it mildly, a trait they probably shared with just about everyone in the Meeting (and passed on to us kids, in varying degrees), since living on this planet means living in the World, that "wilderness wide". We were often told – we had it drummed into us – that we were *in* the world, but not *of* the world, we were pilgrims passing through, our home is in Heaven, our dwelling is a camp. They truly believed this, or at least they truly *believed* that they truly believed it. (If our home in Oak Park was a camp, then I'm a flying turtle.) Perhaps one had to be a control freak to be in the Meeting; they were constantly mindful and watchful of every little trick the Devil might be up to. The important thing was their attitude towards the outside world: keeping it outside, dissociating themselves from it, not participating in it politically, not partaking in its pleasures and pastimes, and making every effort to keep social ties outside the Chosen Few to a bare minimum. If a thing was deemed "worldly" it was invariably also deemed sinful and should obviously be avoided. Nicely appointed homes and possible stock portfolios were apparently exempted from this rejection of everything worldly. And I never heard of a Meeting person who had to fear lacking the basic necessities of life.

During my childhood, the eight-year difference between me and John played a major role in keeping our paths and interests from overlapping or even intersecting frequently. Al was my role model, my big hero, my closest friend. He was my coach in all the big sports – football, basketball and baseball – and he seemed to think I had a lot of talent, which he was eager to help me develop, probably even more eager than I was to develop it. We could hardly look at each other without one or both of us grabbing a ball. Al would train my pitching arm hour after hour in the alley behind our house, squatting there with his catcher's mitt, urging me to throw harder, harder, jeering at me every time I failed to throw a strike, and whooping his approval every time I did. In the back yard we'd throw fly balls to each other, requiring us to crash into our brick wall in order to make the catch, and mockingly deriding each other with cries of "*Wall shy!*" if we backed off and let the ball bounce off the wall. If I failed to catch a ball, it resulted in Al's wild imitation of a sportscaster: "*He drops the ball!!! One run is scoring, two runs are scoring, three runs are scoring, four runs are scoring, five runs are...*" and then we'd both burst out laughing.

Al took me to a number of Cubs games at Wrigley Field and I was dumbfounded by the majesty of a Major League ball park, the ivy-covered outfield wall, the roar of the crowd and all that came with it. Al always insisted that we get there early in order to watch batting practice too, and he was always trying (and sometimes succeeding) to get players' autographs. On one occasion, we were down behind the Cubs' dugout during batting practice, trying to catch the attention of the players. The great Ernie Banks was there. If Al or I had any baseball idol, Ernie was it. We were calling to him, pleading for him to give us an autograph, but Ernie just stood there staring out across the field, concentrating, paying no attention to us, possibly pretending we weren't there. I finally called upon my most entreating boyish tones and implored *"C'mon Ernie, you were a kid once too?!"* The congenial Ernie broke into a wry smile, slowly ambled over to me, and gave me his autograph. Al was so proud of me.

Our parents didn't object to our interest in sports, as long as it wasn't on Sundays (the Lord's Day). Al and I ignored that restriction several times and went to the park to play catch anyway. One sunny early autumn Sunday afternoon, we had to go to greater lengths than usual to circumvent the restriction. Our football was unfortunately upstairs, as we'd forgotten to put it in Al's car the evening before. There was no way we could sneak it down the stairs and out to the garage unseen, so Al removed the screen from his window while I went downstairs and out the kitchen door to the small porch along the side of our house, right below his upstairs window. Al dropped the ball into my waiting grasp and I quickly deposited it in his car. Then we got our parents' permission to take a little drive that beautiful Sunday afternoon.

Mom and Dad probably had no idea that John had been going to movies, enjoying jazz, testing beer, laughing at dirty jokes, reading *Playboy* and other deliriously wicked acts while at Northwestern. Nor did they know that Al frequently attended the movies, and made out with non-Meeting girls. (I doubt my parents would have approved of the making-out part, even with Meeting girls, if any willing ones were to be found.)

I knew about a lot of the exciting things my brothers were up to, and in the summer of '59, as I was about to start high school, I and a couple of Meeting friends snuck off to the Mercury Theater. I saw my first movie ever: the sappy musical *Bells Are Ringing*, with Judy Holliday, with whom I immediately fell in love, of course.

Al had already established himself as a math whizz in high school, and he channeled his great interest in sports to become the sports editor of *Trapeze*, the weekly Oak Park High paper. He was a highly congenial, outgoing guy who even throughout high school cultivated a number of relatively close friendships outside the Meeting, somehow without drawing fire or ire from our parents.

Al's big hero during his early teens was our cousin Wallace Labenne from Detroit, a smooth, suave, sophisticated-looking guy with the panache and style of a young, would-be Hugh Hefner. We didn't meet the Detroit side of the family often; the only given occasion was around Thanksgiving, in connection with the Bible Conference staged by the Detroit Meeting at a union hall they were able to rent for the annual event. My mom's two eldest sisters lived in Detroit. One was Edna, who had a bad case of diabetes and who in my memory always looked emaciated and gaunt. She was the eldest of the six Larson girls, and was married to Harold Krause, a man who could have given my grandpa Erisman a run for his money in any competition involving humorlessness, sternness and self-appointed piety, but Harold never achieved any major role in the Detroit Meeting (unlike my grandpa's papal status in Oak Park), as there were already too many "big guns" in Detroit. Edna died of nephritis in 1959.

I have no memory of ever visiting Harold and Edna's home; at least I'm fairly certain I never spent a night there. Their son Robert (17 years older than me) was unknown to me in my youth, and was already out of the picture (he was only mentioned rarely, and then with shudders) by the time I became aware of his existence. We never talked about him, except my mom's rare references to "poor Robert", or more often "poor Edna", who was even poorer because of poor Robert's apostate ways. Their other son, the affable Charles, a couple of years younger than Robert, was somebody we mostly met at Bible Conferences, although he and his family did stop by our place in Oak Park once or twice.

My mom's other elder sister in Detroit was Louise, Edna's polar opposite in terms of appearance and temperament. She was mountain of a woman, jovial, weary and warm. She was married to Josh Labenne, a butcher who had his own small neighborhood meat and grocery store, and whom we seldom saw because the store was where he spent nearly all his time, at least after fathering five children: the Bible-thumping Larry, Mr Cool Wallace, the weird Donald (think Liberace without the piano), the radiant Edna Lou, and the sensual Karen.

We always stayed at the Labenne's cavernous home when we came to the Detroit Conference. That was where Al met and came to worship Wallace, trying to be in His Presence as much as possible (when Al wasn't making out with Edna Lou), and to absorb Wallace's manner, even though Al's own temperament and style made that all but impossible. Wallace had married a breathtakingly elegant girl named Shirley, a tall, shapely blonde with the looks and deportment of a model. But some things happened in the months and years around that time that were only spoken in whispers and out of my earshot. The upshot, anyway, was that one of the top dogs in the Detroit Meeting, Mr Sheldrake, had orchestrated the excommunication of Wallace from the Meeting – Wallace was "put away from The Lord's Table", damned. Al was horrified, angry, devastated. His hero was lost to him. Al never said so to me directly, but he left little doubt in my mind about what he would like to do with Mr Sheldrake.

Al was extremely competitive in everything. We couldn't walk from point A to point B without Al saying *"I'll race you!"* – at least until he no longer had a chance to beat me in any short sprint. Longer distances were another matter. I was always a flat-out sprinter from the start, a burst of top speed; I could never pace myself. Al could, and did, and always beat me in footraces over the longer hauls. And he imbued me with his competitiveness; it has taken me decades of conscious effort to tone down those impulses, which I still try hard to control since I don't like feeling like the person I feel I become when I become competitive. Perhaps it's unfair to blame Al for any of that, since Mom was also extremely competitive. She channeled a lot of it into *Sorry!* You played her at your peril.

Al taught me not to be wall-shy, which would come to serve me well in football, but the fantasy could have cost me my life many times. In my teens it had become my welcomed chore to fetch the *Chicago Tribune* at the northwestern corner of Oak Park and North avenues, on the Chicago side, as soon as the papers reached the drugstore there, at around 6 PM. I usually went about 10 or 15 minutes ahead of time, ostensibly to be there in case the *Trib* arrived early (and my parents were understanding about arriving early for things), but the real reason was to give myself time to check out the latest *Playboy* in the drugstore's magazine rack. I had no idea that the magazine sometimes also ran some pretty interesting articles.

I could have *walked* to the corner of North and Oak Park and waited for the traffic lights, the four-lane traffic on North Avenue being pretty fast and furious at that hour, but as I left the house, less than a hundred yards – the length of a football field – from the busy street, I became the great Jim Brown, first dodging, spinning and weaving among the parked cars and concrete blocks in the Prince Castle parking lot, then hitting full stride as I reached the edge of the pavement of North Avenue in mid-block. My idea of a successful run was not to have to stop, but to head right into the traffic while twisting and swerving my way across the street. Honks and tire screeches were the roar of the crowd.

And it's another touchdown for Jim Brown!

Anyway, Al was my hero in a much more direct and active way than Wallace had ever been his, and Al didn't become less so when he headed for DeKalb that fall to major in mathematics and minor in journalism. Apparently my parents' good experience of allowing John to live on campus enabled Al to live on the DeKalb campus right from the start of his freshman year. Al immediately joined the university newspaper staff as a sports reporter, and covered the football, wrestling and basketball games, which conveniently prevented him from coming home on Fridays, since most of the basketball games were on Friday evenings and the football games were on Saturday afternoons. A couple of times I was given permission to take the train out on a Friday evening and spend the night in Al's dorm room, go to football or basketball games with him, and a couple of wrestling tournaments. I watched Al in action covering the games, interviewing the players and chatting with pretty co-eds and cheerleaders, despite the fact that the girls were not part of his official assignment as an intrepid reporter. I knew that he had tried both smoking and beer – what a guy!

One Friday evening, Al had a special treat in store for me: tickets to a concert with Errol Garner, the brilliant and incessantly grunting jazz pianist. I was thrilled beyond anything I'd ever experienced, and Al had made it happen. I wonder whether our parents might have permitted me to visit Al those times in DeKalb in the hope that my presence would help to prevent him from engaging in any mischief he might otherwise be tempted to commit when no family or Meeting member was around? But by the fall of 1960, the primary source of our parents' anxiety and the chief target of their disciplinary and constabulary efforts had become me, not Al, and had been heading in that direction for well over a year. Where I was increasingly either confrontational or evasive, and seldom gave in, Al was acquiescent. Where I was bold and flamboyant, Al was submissive. That made my parents' discovery of Al's wicked ways on that portentous Thursday all the more shocking and alarming.

I'd already begun struggling under the yoke of prohibitions, most noticeably when all my classmates in 6th grade at Horace Mann starting taking dancing lessons. I alone did not participate. I had a note from home telling the school that I was not allowed to dance. At first, I was the envy of the pre-pubertal 11-year-old boys who didn't want to dance with creepy girls anyway. But by the following year, when hormones had begun to awaken, that envy disappeared

– or switched directions. I no longer liked being the only one who couldn't. *All I wanted at that age was to do what everyone else was doing!* Mom's attempts to encourage or console me consisted of reminding me to be like the Prophet Daniel, to stand alone, resisting all those against him in Babylon. That was *not at all* the advice I was looking for, but it turned out to be pretty good later in life, for reasons unintended by Mom.

Another painful prohibition was our lack of a TV. All the other kids had them by now, and were always talking about their favorite programs, in effect banning me from the comments and conversations. Sometimes I would walk home from Horace Mann with Joel Meltz, who lived only a block away from us, and watch some of the late afternoon programs in his basement on LeMoyne Parkway before hurrying the last block home. But after my repeated parentally-ordered refusals, I never got any more party invitations, and nobody would have wanted to come to mine even if we'd had one for non-Meeting kids. I was becoming an unwilling loner, and I began to rebel. Mom and Dad seemed only to see my mischief growing into revolt, and nothing of their role in it. The more restrictive they became, the more I found to do in secret, and the wilder my deportment became.

Yet another main reason why the focus of our parents had been on me was my withheld request, my firm refusal to ask for my place at The Lord's Table. I hadn't explicitly said no, since a request to take my place wouldn't be considered sincere if it didn't come from my own wish to do so; but I had none, so it didn't. Both John and Al had succumbed to the group pressure in their early teens, but I resisted. I had seen what a creep it made of Howie and others, and I had no interest in it at all. I dared to be a Daniel. I wanted to play my guitar (not hymns!), look cool and dream of being with beautiful, affectionate girls. If those girls happened to be gorgeous actresses like Natalie Wood, I was not going to hold them accountable for their excessive beauty – or their failure to have joined the Meeting.

When Dad brought Al home from the Lake Street station that fateful Thursday, they and Mom went into the den and closed the door. I'd been sternly instructed to remain in my room upstairs, but of course I was leaning over the banister as far as I could without risking a fall on my head. They went down on their knees (all six of them); I recognized the shuffling sounds, quickly followed by the first of many heart-rending entreaties to the One Above. I was above, all right, leaning over the bannister, soaking up nearly every word with increasing horror as the realization of what was unfolding down there began to dawn on me.

First it was Dad, entreating and beseeching the Lord to work in the heart of their dear boy as he plunged headlong away from Righteousness and Truth, and to lead him back into *Thy* Light. This went on for about ten minutes. Then it was Mom's turn, with all the histrionics and fervor she could muster – and she could muster a lot – weeping and wailing and gnashing her teeth before the Lord to protect her beloved son from the wicked ways he had so foolishly chosen, and to lead him to repent of the evil he hath done and all the displeasure in *Thy* Sight. It was Mom's high drama for about 20 minutes. Then it was Al's turn to confess – out loud, of course – his grave guilt, his sorrowful sinfulness, his wayward wickedness, his fearful foolishness, his wrongful wretchedness, his woeful worm-of-the-dustiness.

Al managed to keep it up, tearfully and agonizingly, for quite a few minutes before coming to the end of his prayer, perhaps hoping he'd said enough to atone for his monumental sin. But it was *not* enough. It was time for another round from Dad, then Mom, then Al again, then Dad again, then Mom again, then Al again. On and on. Al's will and spirit was being destroyed before my ears, under the roof of the only place I knew as home. I was starting to feel physically ill. I realized for the first time what brainwashing was. There and then I solemnly and firmly resolved something to myself: *this will never, ever happen to me.*

When Al finally emerged from the den with my parents, he was not the same person. In my view, he never has been since. His spirit had been massacred. The light had gone out of his eyes. Carefree mirth and sparkle had been replaced by a heavy load of seriousness and a nearly total and abrupt rejection of the frivolities that belong to a healthy growing-up experience. He looked prepared to shake Mr Sheldrake's hand. He avoided my eyes. Perhaps one shouldn't expect the joys and sense of freedom experienced by many a young man in his undergraduate college days to remain intact when marriage, kids, and career come to dominate. I've seen that *gradual* transition take place in one acquaintance after another, even in people outside the Meeting. But never before or since have I witnessed it in a single dramatic stroke, during one late afternoon and evening. I've never seen the joy ripped away, the freedom pummeled and broken, the way it happened to Al.

As I saw it, Al's spirit was massacred that Thursday night. And the hard outer shell of my naiveté was irreparably cracked. My eyes were being pried open. My parents had allowed the teachings and tales of an ancient book written by a collection of superstitious desert nomads to overcome their innate goodness to effect the psychological destruction of the person my beloved brother had been to me.

Our parents were both loving people, Dad's love being calm and kind, Mom's more intense and overt. Both obviously cared about the well-being of us children, about providing shelter and nutrition, about education (at least in approved fields), about politeness and courtesy, about warmth and security. But there were always strings attached. Outside the insular confines of the Meeting, things like love, kinship, friendship and safety could be withdrawn, held back, cut off, rescinded, revoked. Outside the Meeting was a great abyss, an unknown, the wilderness wide. My parents had painted a frightening and false picture of where freedom was leading, and Al had become terrified of rebelling. I, on the other hand, saw the frightening thing they were doing and became terrified of *not* choosing freedom.

Dad and Mom were probably pretty sure they had succeeded – at least for the moment – in a job they sincerely believed it was their obligation and holy duty to perform, but they seemed not to be sure whether they had truly done enough to lay the ax to the root of the tree, whether Al's will and willfulness had been forever severed, and whether he would be restored to the fold with the rest of the sheep. As a result, they continued to keep a close watch over him in the weeks and months to come. There was to be no more staying or straying on campus for weekends – and no more visits from me out there; the risk was now that I might be further corrupted by that worldly atmosphere. I also began to be afraid that once it was time for me to go to college, there would be absolutely no possibility of my living on campus. Even though they hadn't raised the subject, I strongly suspected that their funding of my further education would depend on my finding a nearby college or university to which I could commute daily while continuing to live at home under their watchful eyes. My sense of panic was palpable. Was I trapped?

With Al having briefly drawn the spotlight onto himself and thus off me, and with my mounting desperation to find an escape route, I began to identify and consider my options. Before the Thursday Night Massacre, my parents had been aiming the artillery of their righteous fervor at me. Now Al had just drawn their entire attack back onto himself with a fake up the middle, and it was Jim Brown's chance to take off with the ball around left end and score. I was already a half-fledged, metaphor-mixing rebel. Sneaking off to the movies had become a passion, my new sport. Norm and I were now meeting up at the Mercury Theater for the double feature nearly every Saturday afternoon, claiming to be off to the park to play ball, but instead drooling over one cute actress after the other, with both of us now dreaming of little else than becoming actors.

Norm was a good-looking boy with wavy, blondish hair, about my height and build. He always had a real gift for talking his way into or out of any situation, and he had a much more relaxed temperament than mine. He also had double-jointed thumbs and could bend his outermost thumb joints 90 degrees backwards like a seven – without pressing against anything. He apparently had a few neighbor friends and school friends, and he probably wasn't as much of a loner by temperament as I'd become. Until puberty, I didn't spend much time with Norm. His interests were probably more similar to mine than Howie's were, but that wasn't saying much.

Our parents didn't seem to be on the same wavelength in a lot of ways, and we rarely visited each other's homes, apart from all those extra hymn sings and meetings. I think my parents regarded the Dentons as socially inferior to themselves, although they would have denied it emphatically. Norm's parents had come into the Meeting from the *outside*; they'd basically been non-religious until Norm's aunt (Dave Henderson's mother) recruited them into the Meeting when Norm was a little boy. Norm's Mom, Elinor, whose temperament was similar to my mom's, immediately latched onto it with full fervor (as new converts often do), while Norm's dad more or less went along for the ride, although he did his best to accommodate Elinor's wishes. My brother John "dated" Norm's sister Margo for a year or so.

But apart from having found the Mercury Theater to be an excellent halfway-point between our homes, Norm had his after-school activities – often more matinees at a theater at Grand and Harlem during my football season (it was closer to his home), or hockey after school at a park close to him – and I had mine. I played basketball in the alley behind our garage, usually alone after Al was off to college.

When I related to Norm what had happened to Al on that fateful Thursday evening, and about my feelings of desperation to escape, Norm immediately responded to and shared those feelings. We agreed that we simply would *not* let this happen to either of us. We also knew, or felt, that neither of us might be able to manage to escape on our own. But together we could make it; we'd have the critical mass: the Two Musketeers, one for both and both for one. We made a pact that we would leave home, together, once and for all, best friends. But how and when? We had no idea what an extraordinary amount of determination and solidarity such a move would require, but there was going to be no turning back.

In spite of my occasional dare-devil antics, I had a practical streak a mile wide, and was afraid of devising any escape plan that might entail the risk of any Prodigal Son shit. Foremost among the practical things to consider was finishing high school. And since Norm was a year behind me, a mere freshman, I decided I would work for a year after my own high school graduation, as much as I could, and save as much as I could in order to acquire a nest egg, some seed capital that Norm and I could fall back on if we were unable to find jobs right away or anything like that. (More than four decades later, I would be saddened to discover that I apparently never succeeded in conveying this purpose with sufficient clarity to Norm; he'd assumed I was building up that nest egg for myself alone.)

As our resolution to pursue this new path grew and developed over the months to come, it gradually began turning into specific plans. In June of 1961, Norm found out that Elmwood Park High School graduations were typically held on the first Friday in June. Using the perpetual calendar I found in Compton's, we were able to figure out the exact date that Norm would graduate: Friday, June 5th, 1964. We decided unanimously that we would leave the next day: June 6th, D-Day! I then calculated how far off that was – more than 1000 days at the time – and that became the starting figure for the countdown Norm and I would now begin. We weren't quite sure where we'd go, but since we were both so enamored of movies, and had already begun dreaming of becoming actors, Hollywood seemed like the obvious first-choice destination.

The only trouble was that Norm, at 17 in June 1964, would be underage, by any legal standards. At 18, I *might* be able to make the move without parental consent (although I wasn't sure), but Norm would definitely not be, and parental consent or even reluctant acceptance seemed at that point no more likely to be forthcoming than a nude sock hop in the Meeting Room. We needed to do some more thinking, and while we were working on it, Norm and I started wearing our rebellion more and more openly. We would "hang out" in front of the Meeting Room on Sundays, before, between and after meetings, updating the countdown and looking as insolent, impudent and intimidating as possible – nothing that anyone could put a finger on, apart from our upturned collars, but it was there.

Sometime after the Thursday Night Massacre, my parents discovered that Al had been dating one NIU girl in particular: a journalism major and fellow member of the newspaper and yearbook staff, and their attention instantly shifted back to him. *What was her name?* Nancy Schuler, from Garden Prairie, near Rockford. *Did she know the Lord?* Al wasn't sure. *What church did she go to?* Some mainstream Protestant church, although kind of seldom. Upon extracting this information from Al, my parents instructed him to inform Nancy that if she wanted any further relationship with him, she would have to come to Meeting and take the Lord as her Savior. Otherwise, say goodbye to Al. So Nancy began coming to Meeting on Sundays and was getting a lot of private coaching from Dad and Mom – and from "the new Al".

Al and I had little contact and no shared secrets any longer. Our former informal camaraderie, full of humor and pushing the limits, was all but gone. Al's new focus on solemnity and piety reminded me of Howie – and was totally foreign to the relationship we'd had. And John and Marj were leaving for Southern California. It was not the best-ever time of my life.

One Sunday after the Breaking of Bread, with Nancy in tow at the Meeting Room, Al came looking for me and found me and Norm with our upturned collars on Clem Dear's sidewalk, which ran parallel with the ivy-covered western wall of the Bible Truth Publishers. Al was boiling with rage, glaring at me. Norm withdrew a step or two. I stood my ground. When Al reached me, he hissed, "*If you ever offend Nancy so that she won't come to Meeting with me, I'll never speak to you again!!*" My brother Al, whom I probably loved more than any other human being at that time, was clearly gone, massacred, replaced by this shell that only looked a lot like him.

Loneliness suddenly became tangible. My parents' bans on nearly every form of social activity outside the Meeting, in addition to the *de facto* elimination of common ground with my peers, had always been the only world I knew, apart from the glimpses of freedom Norm and I were catching, and the resulting bond that was forming between us. I was "secure" at home (in the way that a prisoner is secure in a solitary confinement cell in a maximum-security prison), provided I obeyed, but obedient action was not enough; my thoughts were also under scrutiny and constant threat. Home was where I had been loved, but all too often I was now being made to feel that my parents' love was to a significant extent contingent on my conformity to Will of the Lord. Only Al had made me feel that his love for me had been unconditional. I no longer felt that.

Al's behavior – towards everyone I could see, and most definitely towards me – had indeed changed radically, overnight. He had become tense and distant. Jocularity on my part was met with icy rejection. If I asked him about a movie, he threw up a wall of sanctimoniousness between us. Everything turned solemn; smiles were scarce, anxiety abounded. Trying to get him to talk about what was going on inside him was like trying to milk an owl. Trying to tell him what was going on inside me was worse. He would hardly speak to me, much less listen; he seemed too busy trying to reinvent himself to conform to the demands of our parents and their version of a Lord. I had never before seen a person change so radically or so quickly (nor have I personally witnessed another case like it since then). That's how it felt to me, and how it felt to me was what altered the course of my life. Many years later, when I told Al what a huge impact the Thursday Night Massacre had had on my life, he claimed at first to have no memory of it, then claimed that I had got it wrong; his perspective is somewhat different from mine....

The profound *outward* change in Al, as I perceived it, was not permanent, however. He didn't remain solemn, although he had become more so than before. His anxiety became less obvious. He soon returned to being one of the most amiable, socially adjusted people around, anywhere. But he was no longer free to explore, free to question. He had become a victim of discredophobia. And like so many people of considerable intellect who for emotional reasons do not dare to question the first premises of their beliefs, he became an apologist – the apologists' apologist – with arguments always starting from sacred premises that are off-limits to doubt.

The impact of the Thursday Night Massacre on me – and on Al, in my perception – was huge. Prior to that night, I'd already experienced being the primary focus of my parents' concerted efforts to mold every aspect of my being, forcibly (psychologically speaking) holding me under water (metaphorically speaking) until my own will and thoughts could no longer breathe – all nicely couched in and condoned by their firm belief that drowning me was following His will, and was thus for my Eternal Good. Now their more urgent need to focus on Al gave me the chance to get my head above water again, to gasp in a few breaths of the air of freedom and see where I *didn't* want to go. It would take much longer for me to figure out where I *did* want to go.

Nancy was officially "saved" in January 1962, but it took another half a year before she was deemed sufficiently groomed to "take her place" in the Meeting. A month later, on August 25th, 1962, seven years to the day before Jeanette and I would arrive in Sweden, with Nancy safely saved and her place duly taken at the Lord's Table, Al and Nancy got married in Nancy's home town, and I was Al's best man. But my hero was long gone, and I would only ever see glimpses of him again.

CHAPTER 10

The Countdown

By the end of my sophomore year, I had grown a little taller, a little stronger, and a little bolder, so I decided I would again try out for the football team at the start of my junior year. I figured I'd at least have a pretty good shot at making the junior-varsity team, which I did, keeping my position as a wide receiver, although it was called "split end" in those days. I was quick and had played enough touch football and catch with Al to have acquired a pair of hands that tended not to drop even badly thrown passes, which helped. (Al threw good passes except when he was purposely trying to train me to catch bad ones – to give everything – which I willingly did. Al claimed that if I could touch it, I ought to catch it even if I had to dive – that was his standard for me.)

But no matter how much I wanted to be part of the team, not just a split end out there to one side, I could never belong to the group; I would never be one of them. It was never by choice, but because I wasn't allowed to go out with my teammates, nor share any camaraderie, which would have been seen by my parents as an "unequal yoke", and by this time I'd been branded as the kid who never hung out or went out with anyone anywhere, ever. Perhaps they thought I didn't want to, which seemed to me a ridiculous conclusion to draw, and which nobody would have drawn if they knew what lay behind it. But nobody ever wanted to know why, or even listen to me if I wanted to explain, although it's unlikely I could have made my situation comprehensible to them. It wasn't that I was bullied by my classmates in any way, nor was I actively frozen out. Off the playing field, I was simply irrelevant to the social lives of everyone else, which I suppose was a fair enough way to view me, if views were based on effects rather than causes. There was, however, a great deal of implicit superiority of the varsity players over the junior varsity. And I was still a junior and still small, after all.

In the fall, my math curriculum moved onwards from geometry, which I'd enjoyed greatly, to Mr Woodruff's advanced algebra, which I endured. But by the spring semester, with the Thursday Night Massacre behind me and the countdown to freedom already ticking, an entirely new situation was emerging. By the time Mom and Dad felt confident that Al's waywardness was truly and finally broken, and they turned back to me to give me the full force of their oppressive attention, Jim Brown had already mentally broken free down the sideline, and was heading for the end zone. Soon just about everything my parents wanted me to do or not to do became that which I wanted not to do or to do, respectively. Dad wanted me to keep studying math. But I had already pumped all I could out of my waning interest in that subject, particularly since taking math courses was at the expense of taking art courses, which I did want to do. Dad could see no point in that, and "firmly guided" me to voluntarily sign up for trigonometry in the spring; I was gagging. But our trig teacher was one of the assistant football coaches for my team, so I knew him from the rigors of football practice. He was OK, but it didn't help; I loathed trig. There might have been some influence from the fact that the art classes had much prettier girls than the trig class, even though I wasn't allowed to date anyone anyway. I only managed a C. By this time, the war I was having on so many other fronts with my parents was raging and blazing, and I felt hog-tied in my struggle against restrictions at every turn.

Meanwhile, in Elmwood Park, Norm's rebellion was escalating in pace with mine, but his parents seemed to make no connection to the Thursday Night Massacre. Perhaps they knew nothing about Al's fate. However, since they did feel quite certain that Norm' rebellion involved me, Norm's mom Eleanor briefly forbade Norm from associating with me, even at the Meeting Room. But Norm argued his case to his parents, and he argued it forcefully and well: the ban on outside, unequally yoked friendships was already cruel enough, he implored; it would be impossible for him to observe a ban on the one Meeting person (despite my failure to join) he loved and wanted for a friend. Norm's dad was obliged to agree, and he lifted the brief ban, despite Norm's mom remaining convinced that I was a bad influence on Norm.

My parents would certainly have proffered the contrary view – that Norm was the instigator of *my* rebellion – and perhaps they thought that two rebels united would be stronger in their rebellion than if they were separated. They would have been right. Coincidentally, both my parents and Norm's somehow forgot to consider that our pleas to stay home from Meeting on Tuesday and Thursday evenings "to study" just might involve the use of the telephone. As a result, nearly every one of those evenings involved an hour-long phone call between Oak Park and Elmwood Park, during which Norm and I would discuss, suggest, weigh, mold, forge and reinforce the strategies for effecting our escape.

Thus the amount of contact we had, and the time to work out and discuss our plans in the greatest detail, was far greater than any of our parents presumably suspected. And each time Norm and I spoke, we updated our countdown.

Somewhere within this timeframe, Norm and I went with our respective parents to a two-day Bible Conference in the small town of Lawrenceville in downstate Illinois, probably organized by the Buchanans. The town's dismal movie theater had no matinees to duck out to during Reading Meeting, but Norm and I were determined to find something else to do, anything else. Richard Macy from Bloomington was also at the Conference, and on the first day he took us for a ride in his car, far from the mind-numbing Reading Meeting, across the border into Indiana, where we drove as far as Vincennes (only around 10 miles away), playing rock & roll on the radio full blast and singing our hearts out. If we missed more than a Reading Meeting, *we* weren't going to cry about it.

It took a lot of persuasion on my part to get Richard to join us again that night in sneaking out of the dormitory or whatever quarters the Gathered Saints were housed in during that Conference. We managed to escape at 2 AM, but there was *nothing* to do in Lawrenceville at 2 AM. Richard Evans (*"Oh, the gluddy!"*) spotted us leaving, and of course told our parents, but we were past caring. The next day, we again persuaded Richard Macy to join us, or rather to let us join him to a destination of our choice; he was the one with the car. Richard was tall and gangly, a sweet guy who was bemused and somewhat awed by his two relatively city-smart and openly rebellious companions. Unfortunately, Richard had a severe case of acne that tended to jeopardize his chances with girls.

Lawrenceville's sole worldly social offering consisted of a diner with a pinball machine. We hadn't been there long before a couple of cute girls entered and quickly became interested in finding out who these three out-of-town boys were, particularly Norm and me. They joined us in our booth, and we started chatting. Playing real tough guys, we told them knowingly that we were from Chicago. Mutual attraction was rising. Norm and I began searching for an angle whereby we might exploit it. I felt a little bad that Richard had become a fifth wheel, so I started praising Richard's unbelievable talents on the piano, and if we could only get the use of one, we could *rock and roll!* As it happened, one of the girls had a piano at home, and as it also happened, her parents were away for the weekend, so maybe we could all go there? This was *exactly* what Norm and

I had been hoping for. We all piled into Richard's car, four of us crowded into the back seat. Richard, alone in the front, was understandably a little hesitant to be a mere chauffeur, but he acquiesced, perhaps out of curiosity, or not to be seen as a killjoy.

Once we reached the one girl's house, Richard delivered on his Jerry Lee Lewis imitation and the girls were thrilled and giggly. One of them was using her eyebrows as semaphores to send me the kind of messages I urgently wanted to get. But no sooner had we started necking (perhaps Norm and the other girl were doing likewise, I lost track) than Richard started getting cold feet and wanted to leave – and wanted Norm and me to leave with him. The girls couldn't understand what was going on. We didn't exactly feel like telling them that we were in town for a Bible Conference, so I tried making up a story about some mysterious Chicago business we had.

On the way back to Oak Park, my parents were furious with me for my disappearances from the Conference, but I was beyond their command. I no longer had any privileges that could be revoked – everything I wanted to do had been forbidden long ago – so I just slouched sullenly in the back seat and tried to sleep through their clichés and rantings. They thought they still had a trump card (what's that in Old Maid?), but they weren't ready to play it yet. That would come when it was time for me to apply for university, in the beginning of my senior year.

My parents must have been in denial, reluctant to entertain the idea that I would go so far as to leave home, probably convinced that with my consistent honor-roll academic performance I would certainly end up choosing to continue my schooling at a local university – their non-negotiable criterion for financing my further education. Norm's parents knew roughly what we were planning by the time Norm was 16, and announced to Norm that since he was underage, they had the legal right to have him returned – a right they were fully determined to exercise. So, Norm and I thought, what if we were to tell our parents that we were going to New York instead, then go to Hollywood anyway, in order to get them to send the pursuing police in the wrong direction?

We played with that idea briefly, for lack of a better one, until one day I had an errand at the Post Office, and the rack of literature from the US Naval Recruiting office caught my eye. I discovered that a guy could enlist in the Navy – without parental consent! – from the age of 17. Although the Navy wasn't

Hollywood, that would only be a question of time. The main thing was that if Norm and I enlisted right after he finished high school, when he'd be 17 and I'd be 18, our parents would be unable to stop us. The fact that our parents felt it was our duty to be conscientious objectors only sweetened the deal for us not to be. Norm and I were thrilled that we'd found a way to be home free – or *leave* home free – so we began leaving Navy pamphlets lying around ostentatiously on our desks at home, hoping to provoke parental reactions. I even wrote "Navy" in large letters with a marker on the off-white lampshade on the desk in my room.

Nobody said anything about it for several months, possibly because by this time they had begun to realize that any position they argued for was the one we were least likely to adopt. Eventually, the implications must have dawned on Norm's dad: If they tried to stop us from leaving home, we would join the Navy, which meant that *we would be beyond their control for a minimum period of three years*. If, on the other hand, they didn't try to stop us, there was always a chance, for which they would pray fervently, that we would soon become destitute and come crawling back begging for forgiveness within a few weeks or months, like true Prodigal Sons, voluntarily taking upon ourselves the yoke of the Meeting, and forsaking all our dreams of freedom. So Norm's parents told him that although they were deeply saddened or staunchly furious (whichever worked best) with our plans, they would not stand in our way, but would allow us to pursue our willful, headstrong and sinful march along the road to perdition. Of all of our parents, Norm's Dad offered by far the least resistance to our plans. While he didn't support them in any way, he tended not to react emotionally, or at least not *only* emotionally. Norm's mom was the dramatic one in the Denton household, much like my mom was in mine.

In early 1959, when the Oak Park Meeting decided to change the venue of their Bible Conference from Concordia to Wheaton, Mrs Denton was vehemently opposed, presumably on grounds that it no longer looked like the mere rental of premises, but could be seen as an alliance with the fundamentalist Wheaton Bible College – an unequal yoke. Even though Wheaton's fundamentalists were technically Believers too, they weren't *sufficiently* aligned with the Truth, according to Eleanor; hence the protest. At a Brothers' Meeting to decide the issue, Norm's dad cast the sole vote against the move to Wheaton, and thus against Grandpa Erisman, whose immediate ire he roused. The decision was followed obediently by everyone else. For their dissent, the Denton were made to feel the chill of Meeting ostracism. Nearly all my family's already sparse social interaction with them ceased. But this did not prevent the Dentons from boycotting the Wheaton Conferences, thereby only exacerbating their outcast position.

Not long after this tense atmosphere had arisen, Norm's dad was taken ill with hepatitis, as well as serious kidney problems, and had to be hospitalized for quite a long time. As a result, Norm's mom was for a time focused on her husband's health and not on Norm's plans with me. While Norm's dad was in the hospital, his uncle A.C. Brown (he only used his initials, that's how big a Meeting bigshot he was!) from Southern California came to see him, and informed him that his illness was God's punishment for being "stiff-necked". A.C. apparently had some kind of direct line to Heaven (or to Grandpa Erisman), and managed flagrantly to disregard Jesus' repeated injunctions to comfort the sick, not distress them. In any case, although disciplinary measures against the Dentons were being considered, no formal action was taken, possibly because God's direct and loving intervention was felt to suffice as punishment.

In early 1961, I replaced my first solid-body guitar with a vermillion specimen of Gibson perfection, a thin hollow-body model that would enable me to hear myself practice while unplugged. Even the hard-shell, crimson-velvet-lined case was a thing of amazing beauty to me. I paid for it with my own Oak Leaves earnings, complemented by winter snow-shoveling jobs and summer lawn-mowing jobs, and I treated it with the greatest reverence and passion. It was on this guitar that I learned to play *Guitar Boogie Shuffle*, but not long after the fateful recital, and in the face of my increasing rebellion, my parents would no longer foot the bill for lessons, a cost which I could not afford to defray myself. I was never particularly adept at the guitar, but playing gave me a kind of solace, possibly akin to what different kinds of music did for my parents, in their way, and with their different versions of solace.

In the summer of 1962, just before I began my senior year at Oak Park High, I took a train trip to spend a week or so with John and Marj in Southern California. They were living in an apartment in La Habra, and their 10-month-old son Brian was not only crawling but was able to stand on his own two feet, albeit holding on tightly to whatever was at hand. If music was playing, he would stand holding onto a table or chair, bend his knees slightly, and rock up and down, in time with the music.

I think my parents must have let me go on this trip in desperation about their inability to curb my rebellion (this was nearly two years after the Thursday Night Massacre), perhaps hoping that John would somehow have a dampening effect on me. Mom and Dad probably didn't know how eager John and Marj had also been to get away from the smothering influence of the Oak Park Meeting, and that as soon as John had fulfilled his contractual obligations to International Harvester for subsidizing his studies, he began looking for jobs in Southern California. I was interested in seeing my brother and his little family, but perhaps more in being close to (and maybe visiting) Hollywood.

Among the innumerable things I didn't understand that summer was that a distance of 30 miles in Greater Los Angeles was nothing like 30 miles in Greater Chicago. Metropolis-wide public transportation was non-existent in Greater LA. Walking even part of the way, along streets and roads without sidewalks, was unthinkable. Hitchhiking, apart from the present and potential dangers, was bound to be an exercise in patience that I didn't have, even if I had known where I was going, or even less what I would do if I ever got there. I had convinced myself that I could just stand on a Hollywood street corner until some producer came up to me and asked me if I wanted more money than I'd ever imagined to act with sensual girls more beautiful than any I'd ever seen....

John had no interest in driving me there, perhaps because he didn't want to risk our parents finding out, or perhaps simply because he was saner than I was. But I was not to be dissuaded. I simply left the apartment one morning and set off down the road on foot, looking for bus stops that weren't there, walking and walking, dodging honking cars, getting dustier and more discouraged all the time. I didn't even have a map. By the time I'd finally had enough frustration, and made my way back to John and Marj's apartment, Marj was half-crazy with worry and John was furious with me for making her that way. I knew I'd been an idiot.

Marj was a terrific cook, who totally redefined "home cooking" for John's taste (and mine). I was convinced she could do anything with food, and she seemed to like challenges. Lemon meringue pie was a staple at our home in Oak Park, but I'd always wondered whether other citrus fruits would work just as well, a suggestion Mom had dismissed outright. But I persuaded Marj to try making a tangerine meringue pie (fabulous), a lime meringue pie (exquisite) and a grapefruit meringue pie (interesting, tangy and tasty). I brought my guitar with me, and John and I jammed a little, he playing the 5-string banjo or the piano (he excelled at both). I don't think I heard any hymns at their place that summer, but I did hear a lot of jazz (Herbie Mann, Dave Brubeck, Don Shirley) and folk music (Peter, Paul & Mary, the Kingston Trio, Burl Ives). John had little interest in rock & roll, but that was OK – at least it wasn't hymns. We did get our ears filled with hymns when we all went to Meeting on the Sunday – a meeting that was a lot more relaxed than the one in Oak Park, but still....

One day we all went to Newport Beach, and the waves were perfect for some exciting body surfing, which I loved. I was out there paddling around, waiting for the perfect wave, and as one approached at last, I turned towards the shore to catch it just right, swimming like mad, and glancing back over my shoulder. I knew this was going to be a thrilling ride, but at the last second, right in the crest of the wave, I spotted – too late – a jellyfish as big as a family-size pizza. Its toxic tentacles lashed across my mouth, like multiple wasp stings. When I came back to the others on the beach, I was in a lot of pain, and my lips were already beginning to swell up. We tried rinsing with pure water, salt water, whatever lotions we could find, all without relief. Back at the apartment we tried more lotions, baking powder, creams and ointments, also moist aspirin tablets, to no avail.

The next morning the pain and swelling were still considerable, even if somewhat reduced, and I had welts that looked and felt like multiple cold sores. That evening we'd been invited to visit one of Marj's older cousins, the former Edie Giesbrecht, who had lived in Oak Park and worked at the BTP, and was long thought to be headed for spinsterhood when she suddenly married Keith Sartorius, of whom I'd never heard.

On our arrival at the Sartorius home, Edie had some special kind of ointment ready to deal with my pain, and it gave me great relief. I was full of gratitude, like the fabled lion that got a thorn removed from its paw. Keith was highly extroverted; I guessed he was in sales. Quite possibly the gratitude I felt made me more receptive than I otherwise might have been when he started telling me about all the secret plots and Communist conspiracies that were threatening the very existence of America, and something called the Protocols of the Elders of Zion, a secret society bent on taking over the world. He had many books on the subject, books that he gave me and encouraged me to read. I was in the early stages of casting aside one form of fanaticism, and was totally unprepared to be confronted, seduced and duped into embracing another – replacing John Nelson Darby with John Birch.

Keith was eager to meet me the next day as well, and it was mutual. I wanted to find out more. But he was smart enough to balance his messages with other fun stuff, so he took me on my first-ever experience of snorkeling, at Santa Monica beach, where I had my first view of the amazing underwater world of starfishes and sea urchins, while simultaneously trying not to ingest too much saltwater, since the technique of snorkeling was new to me and the mask he lent me leaked.

Having heard of my passion for Hollywood, Keith even drove me there, to the sacred corner of Hollywood and Vine. But that particular intersection was about as dull and tacky as any in the world, and I couldn't see any signs of movie producers standing there holding contracts with my name on them, just waiting for me to sign, so they could start sending those truckloads of money to my door, and busloads of gorgeous starlets to my bed. I was beginning to have second thoughts about this whole Hollywood business. Still, it would be nice and fun and all that, if it worked out, but maybe hanging out at Hollywood and Vine or Sunset Boulevard wasn't the way to go, maybe it had been done before, maybe all the lampposts were already taken.

One thing seemed pretty sure: Norm and I would not have a budget that would allow us the expense of a car, and being without a car in LA would be like being without a camel in the Sahara. Norm and I would have to talk about this.

The week in Southern California had been transformational in many ways, few of which I recognized at the time. I was, however, pretty clear about the doubts that had been planted in my mind about the feasibility of moving to the LA area. But I swallowed Keith Sartorius's bait concerning extreme right-wing politics. And my exposure to John's musical tastes had a great impact on my own. A year earlier, I would never have suspected that I could find it easier to relate to my eldest brother John than to Al, nor that John would have simply abandoned so many of the trappings of life within the Oak Park Meeting, not only without any apparent adverse effects, but clearly with beneficial effects on multiple levels. Apart from my pathetic attempt to walk 30 miles to Hollywood, John didn't berate me for my wicked ways, didn't browbeat me for the insufficiency of my righteousness, and didn't castigate me for the paucity of my Meeting clichés.

Even the train ride home was a milestone of sorts for me. I had a small stateroom, all to myself (I think my parents paid for that in order to try to minimize the risk of unequal yoking during the trip), but I spent the first leg

– starting in LA in the afternoon, and throughout the first night – up in the observation dome that was in the same car as my stateroom. I brought my red Gibson up there with me, but with its thin body, the unamplified resonance was hardly enough for even me to hear what I was playing above the din of the train. It was nevertheless enough to get me the attention of a pretty girl my age. She had a classical guitar with her and was en route with her family from her home in Santa Barbara to a dude ranch in Colorado. Her classical guitar had a lovely mellow sound, and she plucked the strings with her fingers; I'd only ever used a pick. She played and sang ballads and folk songs, which I'd only just been introduced to during the past week; my Elvis and rock & roll were nothing for her. *The Banks of the Ohio* was her top song. We spent the entire night first talking, then necking in the observation car, but she declined to join me and my hormones for some unequal yoking in my stateroom. She was definitely out for a thrill, but not *that* much of a thrill. She was playing it safe, and I wasn't the pushy type.

It wasn't until morning – an hour or two before she had to get off the train and when her parents had joined us in the observation car – that she surprisingly picked that moment to raise the stakes. She and I were sharing a blanket, spread loosely over both of us, all the way up to our necks, with our arms and hands and legs under it, and she had no objections at all to my caressing her between her legs, farther and farther up, all the way up, as we sat there nonchalantly chatting with her parents. By the time they all got off to go to her dude ranch, she had turned my head (my neck was probably double-jointed at that age); and she had destroyed my love of rock & roll, causing me to make one of the most moronic decisions of my life: to trade in my beautiful Gibson on a fairly cheap nylon-string acoustic guitar. The old man at the Modern Music Center was only too happy to offer me a deal: an even trade, with him getting a guitar worth perhaps 20 times more than the one I got. That trip to Southern California should have taught me that I might be a bit too impressionable, too gullible, too outer-directed, but at that point, anything non-Meeting was all I needed and all I was looking for – or all I was capable of seeing.

As I was about to enter my senior year, Dad finally relented and permitted me to abandon further studies in higher mathematics (perhaps he saw the risk of dragging down my grade-point average) and instead take a course in art. (I wouldn't, however, have been allowed to take drama or try out for any of the school plays.) I wanted to go to UCLA (which I told my parents) to study drama (which I didn't tell them). But UCLA was out of the question anyway. They hadn't allowed John or Al to study so far from home, and look what problems they'd had with Al when he was only as far away as DeKalb (and look at how much trouble I was causing them now, even in high school)! No, they would now play what they presumed to be their trump card, the one I suspected: they would cover all my college expenses (as they had for my brothers), but *only* on condition that I went to a nearby university, one to which I could commute daily; in other words, one I could attend while still living at home and remaining under their watchful eyes, suffocating restrictions, and high-pressure thumbs. I said nothing. They thought they had me. But I had a countdown running.

The twice-daily football practice sessions that would determine who made the cut, first for varsity and then for first string, began in early August. I was prepared to go for broke. The practice field was a block north of the stadium and had a new, waist-high chain link fence on three sides. The fence on the north side was still under construction; there were just the steel posts and a heavy-gauge steel wire slung low between them.

The first week of practice was largely devoted to hard workouts in full gear, which meant a tee shirt, shoulder pads, a frayed practice jersey, jock strap (we supplied our own), kidney pads, knee pads, pants, socks, cleats (also our own) and a helmet, all in the sweltering Midwestern heat, doing pushups, situps, jumping jacks, knee bends, wind sprints and whatever other forms of torture the coaches could dream up. After nearly three hours of this, we hit the showers, shoved our sweat-drenched clothes into our lockers, and cycled home for lunch. Then it was time for the afternoon practice session. First we had to face pulling on the now-ice-cold, clammy, soaking wet tee shirts that reeked of ammonia. They had to be forcibly drawn down over our not-yet-sweaty-again torsos. Then we suffered about three more hours of making them even wetter.

Those who returned after that first week began other drills that were more directly related to football, like running an obstacle course consisting of car tires lying flat on the ground, requiring short, high steps to avoid tripping, yet at maximum speed. Then we faced off to block and tackle each other. Our head coach was a wiry elderly man named Orin Noth, whose physiognomy and lack of humor reminded me a lot of Grandpa Erisman. Although he was far from a big man himself, he seemed to be skeptical that anyone of my slender build and short stature could have much to do with his varsity football team. I was determined to prove him wrong; I had already demonstrated my speed in some of the wind sprints.

Late in our second week of practice, we progressed to scrimmages, where one side donned red vests over their jerseys to distinguish them from the vestless side. My side was on offense, starting from the southern end of the practice field, and I was to run a pattern 10 yards up the left sideline, then cut sharply to the middle, where hopefully the quarterback would spot me. My cut fooled my defender and I got a couple of steps ahead of him, as the safety started to close in. When I caught the pass – the best pass our quarterback would throw me all season – with two defenders in hot pursuit, I was *not* going to be tackled. Looking over my shoulder, I could see that I was gaining on them. Then I hit the low-slung steel wire (marking the future fence) right across my shin. I somersaulted twice into the neighboring yard, still hanging onto the ball (*no wall-shyness here, Al!*). The pain was excruciating, but Jimmy Brown doesn't show things like that. I couldn't walk, however, and Orin Noth himself came over to have a look. I had somehow managed to acquire a wire-thick notch in my shin, that was swelling rapidly, but nothing was broken. I grinned and pointed out that I still had the ball and had scored. Orin Noth could not completely hide his smile before wordlessly walking away. I hadn't broken any bones. And I made the cut for the varsity team.

Our final practice week came just before the first week of school, which would be followed by our first game. This was when the first-string team was going to be selected. It was all scrimmages, apart from the usual vigorous callisthenic warm-ups. We had running plays, passing plays, goal-line stands, numerous formations. Some of these sessions also involved me playing defense – outside linebacker. Despite my size. I refused to be daunted by huge blockers determined to plow me out of the way, or by fullbacks nearly twice my size aiming simply to run me over; I hung on till they went down. Although there was no way I would ever make first string as a linebacker, catching the ball was what I loved most anyway. So on offense, I was always in the role of split end, except when we were practicing goal line stands, and split ends became tight ones in Orin Noth's world, not a role anyone expected a boy of my size to handle.

The guy I had to beat for the first-string spot at left end was George Tye, a six-foot-four junior, well over 200 flab-free pounds, which meant he was at least half a foot taller and some 60 pounds above my weight class. In one of our final sessions, we were practicing goal-line stands, including a play where the left end was to run a glance-in pattern (later known as a *slant*), get a pass almost immediately after the snap, and bull his way into the end zone. George was big on the bull part, but kept dropping the ball, so I was sent in to give it a try. The ball was snapped, the quarterback stood up and fired a pass at me as I shot beyond the linemen. I caught it and was immediately hit from behind, from the front, and from both sides, but I hung onto the ball and refused to go down. My legs were churning, and while the defenders were wrestling me around, I was churning backwards, my helmet was ripped off, my jersey torn half off, my nose bashed and bleeding, and I still wouldn't go down. After I crossed the goal line, the coach blew the whistle, the defenders moved away, and I was standing there with the ball clenched in my arms, blood all down the front of my tee shirt, grinning. I made first string.

We had two quarterbacks that season. They mostly took turns making handoffs, and only occasionally throwing the ball, because they were not much good at it. I never dropped a pass all season, but they never threw me a pass that was possible to catch without making a flying leap parallel with the ground to get a hand on it. I never once had an opportunity to run with the ball.

Instead of calculus during the autumn of 1962, I took a general art course: a little art history, an introduction to the whole new worlds (for me) of Van Gogh and Picasso, some rudimentary principles concerning a number of -isms, experiments with various techniques like woodcutting, etching and lithography, charcoal drawings and water colors. We also visited the Chicago Art Institute and its fabulous collection of Impressionists. We didn't go into actual oil painting that semester – I signed up for a separate painting course during the spring term – but I began to dabble at home with a cheap set of oils on canvas-coated slabs of hardboard that were available at department stores. I think Dad found it incomprehensible that I could prefer that kind of thing to calculus, but he didn't complain to me, and Mom could perhaps see the potential for creating edifying motifs like our oil of the old man praying thankfully over a loaf of bread, or perhaps decorations to supplement the framed scripture quotations on our walls at home. Depictions of Biblical figures would not have been allowed. That would be too close to graven images, and that was the idolatry that the Roman Catholics practiced, and we all (at least within the Meeting) *knew* that the Catholic Church is the Beast of Revelation, the epitome of evil, and wicked corruption of the Truth. But painting flowers was fine.

Some far-away country called Vietnam (one word or two?) was receiving increasing mention in the newspapers, although it seemed to have no real relevance to anything going on in our lives in America. I, along with most of my classmates, had no idea where it was. But it did involve fighting Communists, and since Keith had taught me to hate the Commies, I felt there might be a future opportunity to go there and kill some. The right-wing fire that he ignited was continuing to blaze, and even books that in no way aimed to promote a right-wing agenda could be used in evidence against my better judgment. I whizzed through Sinclair Lewis's *It Can't Happen Here*, somehow convinced that this only proved how real and imminent the danger of a Communist takeover of the US was. I even managed to interpret Upton Sinclair's *The Jungle* as adding to the validity of right-wing arguments. Had I been even a little bit more observant and reflective, I might already then have suspected, if not realized, that if you've already committed to believing what you're trying to prove, you'll admit no impediment to proving it, nor tolerate any evidence to the contrary. The applications of this principle are nearly limitless.

After the Navy scare, and once Norm and I were allowed to see each other again, most of our serious conversations about our future plans were still limited to those Tuesday and Thursday evening phone calls, especially in the fall of 1962, when my Saturday afternoon football games ruled out our usual meetings at the Mercury Theater. Ever since my trip to LA that summer, we'd been wondering how to deal with the practical problems that life in LA would impose. Then I came up with the idea of San Francisco instead. After all, it was still in California, which was about as far away as we could get (the notion of moving to another country was literally foreign to us). The big advantage of San Francisco was that it was supposed to be one of the better major cities in the country for getting around in by public transportation, so the unaffordability of a car would no longer be an insurmountable problem. Neither of us knew anything at all about San Francisco (I may have been there on a family weekend trip once while we were living in Glendale, but I had no memory of it), so we tried to read up on it and ask anyone we knew who had been there. It sounded like the perfect place: by the ocean, beautiful, compact, a temperate climate, easy to reach the mountains – and no Meeting apart from one in Oakland, as if that mattered. We spent most of the autumn weighing all the pros and cons we could come up with and decided that, for the time being at least, San Francisco would be at the top of our list.

During that autumn semester, all Oak Park High seniors were expected to apply for college. A number of homeroom hours were set aside for this purpose; application forms were distributed, and the homeroom teachers were on hand to provide advice and assistance. My homeroom teacher, Mr Carroll Anderson, was an English teacher whose somewhat unusual first name might have reflected parental fondness for rabbit holes and looking glasses. He was proud of me for regularly making the honor roll, and later the National Honor Society, and was looking forward to helping me with my applications. Would it be Yale? Princeton? When I told him I wouldn't be applying to any university yet, he was aghast. I tried to explain that I wanted to study art or acting at UCLA, but that my parents wouldn't allow me to study away from home. An unconditional condition for their financing my college education was that I pick a school to which I could commute daily, and I was not about to go on living at home because I was suffocating, which I tried to explain to Mr Anderson in a way that might make some sense to an outsider.

Although he said he understood my plight, he couldn't let it go. "With your academic record, you can go anywhere," he pleaded. "You can get a scholarship!" I pointed out that a good academic record was only one of the criteria for scholarship funding. The other was financial need, and since that need would not be based on *my* income, but on my dad's healthy income as the chief engineer at Link-Belt, I would be disqualified. I was caught in the middle. I would have to work, save money, and *then* resume studying. Mr Anderson was skeptical. "*Once you've gotten used to having your own income, you'll get comfortable and won't want to give it up,*" he claimed. "*You'll never go back to school!*" I insisted I would. He insisted I wouldn't.

When Mom and Dad began to realize that their trump card was trumped – that I had no intention of going to a university in the Chicago area, and that I would sooner forego college completely than remain at home – they tried to sweeten the deal by offering to buy me a brand-new Ford Falcon to commute with, but I wasn't to be bought. They had no idea how desperate I was to get away, how repulsive the restrictions of the Meeting had become to me, how strong my urge for freedom to think and learn had grown. And because they so staunchly clung to the creed I was fighting so hard to free myself from, they had no idea how much I loved them. Nor, probably, did I.

I went to Hollywood one more time, after my brief viewing with Keith Sartorius. It was during the LA Conference in '62, when I was just 17. I was staying with the Woehl family (old Meeting friends of my parents), and their son Tommy (a year or two older than me) took me to Hollywood the evening before the Conference began, probably to stop me nagging about it. We went to a café on Sunset Boulevard; I was sure that this was the place to get discovered. If not discovered, at least laid. Tommy was both horrified and intrigued. This wasn't exactly the kind of thing he expected to hear from the grandson of a couple of PB patriarchs.

In order to make myself as discoverable as possible, I took off the glasses I'd started wearing the year before, primarily for driving. Of course my nearsightedness was a bit of a handicap, but a couple of dames sitting across the room in the dark café looked all the better for it. I motioned to them to join us. Tommy winced (he had 20-20 vision). As they were sitting down at our table, now within my focal range, I realized that they had probably spent quite a decade or two trying to get discovered, and I had no wish to be the one to do it. Tommy and I left as soon as they sat down, and they probably wondered why the hell we wanted them to have our table instead of theirs.

Although I walked to school most of the time with Roger, I made no lasting friendships throughout high school. I was gregarious and outgoing, and people responded favorably to that, but I was never allowed to join my classmates for any evening or weekend activities. My football teammates were largely hidden behind blustery, macho facades, and I must have failed the advanced swaggering exams (I never got past sauntering). The only football teammate who talked to me like a friend was John Erickson, who was also in my homeroom class. John was about the right size for playing split end, but played offensive center instead, a position for which he was also theoretically far too small, but he played it well anyway. He was extremely myopic and played without his glasses, but playing the inside line didn't seem to pose a vision problem. He and his twin brother Jim were of Finnish extraction and lived at the southern end of Oak Park. Both were friendly, and regularly amused me with their coarse language and raunchy jokes, some of which were so raunchy that they used them to shock and disgust a couple of squeamish guys at our lunch table in the cafeteria, causing the squeamish ones to abandon some of their food, particularly their desserts, for Jim and John to take over. Otherwise I was pretty much an involuntary loner, and becoming well used to it.

After the introductory art course in the fall, I was eager to begin a course in painting in the spring. My enthusiasm was not dampened by the knowledge that one of the girls in my fall art course would also be there. The art class studios had their own wing on the second floor, with windows to the north overlooking Erie Street. Our teacher, Miss Robinson, was a slightly bohemian-looking lady in her late 50s (at least that's the way I remember her, bearing in mind that when I was 17, people were starting to get ancient when they were 25).

We began with a brief introduction to some of the practical stuff: how to stretch and prime a canvas, a few mixing techniques, as well as the use of palette knives and different kinds of brushes. Miss Robinson introduced us to what various painters had done. I had made several more genuine visits on my own to the Chicago Art Institute (not just those that were a pretext for Dave Henderson and me to go to the Loop and cram at least three movies into one Saturday afternoon, usually including a foreign movie, such as Ingmar Bergman's *Silence*, the first time I ever saw on-screen nipples or heard the Swedish language spoken by Swedes), with its dazzling collection of Impressionists, but Miss Robinson didn't want to be overbearing by influencing what and how we would paint; that was to come from us.

We took to the easels and were given complete freedom to create what we wanted. I'd been fascinated with some of the aspects of Cubism – overlapping planes, the use of a limited color palette – but I also had some notions of my own, as well as one from Seurat: creating recognizable objects from seemingly random shapes. Our classroom was filled with a variety of objects for our use if we felt inclined to do a still life. I chose a guitar (since I played a little) and a wine bottle (since I wanted to try). I would call my first painting *Guitar and Bottle*.[6]

I strategically placed my easel next to Linda's. She was the girl I'd had my eye on, the one I wanted to impress, i.e. the one who inspired me, and while we painted we also talked and got to know each other. One of the best things about painting class was that talking was allowed, as long as we worked and kept our voices down.

Linda lived on Clinton Place, just two streets west of Harlem on the River Forest side, and just north of the corner of Greenfield, so we could walk the

---

6   Painting #1 (see Appendix 2)

same way home together – a mere 14-block detour for me. By the time the snow was gone, I'd gotten to know her better, and the feelings of spring were not entirely meteorological. I suggested that we walk together, and she agreed without hesitation. (She may have wondered why I hadn't asked her out long ago.)

I walked with her as far as the corner of Greenfield and Marion, the southwestern-most corner of Greenfield Park, my old sporting haunt and cinematic alibi. Once the weather started turning warmer and flowers and leaves were starting to burst forth, we would sit for a while on a bench there before parting, talking about anything and everything. We spontaneously began creating small "sculptures" on the ground, using sticks and pebbles we found lying close by. The next day we would look to see if they were intact, and would be thrilled if they were or rebuild them if they weren't. And with all the force of spring behind us, we finally began to kiss. Once we'd broken the ice, we went to that bench with that main purpose.

I was floating on clouds. Linda must have been wondering why I *still* didn't ask her out. I had to do something! The school was putting on a concert one Friday evening in April. A week or two before, I announced to my parents that I was going – with Roger – but of course I took Linda. A week or so later there was another concert, possibly in early May, and I again announced I was going. I agreed with Linda that I would meet her at Oak Park High; she had the use of her parents' car that evening. (This was back in the day when high school students were not allowed to drive to school, and few had cars of their own, even if their parents could afford them. But driving to extra-curricular activities was acceptable.) The concert itself was amazing: a jazz trio led by Oak Park High's only Latino student, Oscar Cabrera, on the piano, together with a string bassist and a drummer, playing laid-back Herbie Mann-style stuff.

After the concert, Linda said she wanted to show me the Oak Park Country Club, which was not in Oak Park at all, but in River Grove, so she drove me out there. Her parents were charter members – her dad owned some sort of industrial company in Chicago. Linda explained that three weeks later the country club was putting on a square dance for members and their guests, and she wanted me to be her date. I tried to explain that my parents would never allow it, but it seemed she didn't want to hear any excuses, and she probably found mine too ridiculous, too bizarre, so she just assumed I was making much ado about nothing. *No problem, you'll come*, she said.

When we got out to the country club after that jazz concert, it was dark and shuttered. It wasn't the season yet, Linda explained, but she had a key to the big main gate, so in we drove, all by ourselves, and strolled around by the covered pool in the dark. She kept waiting for me to make a move, but I had so little experience and so little confidence. The idea of dates had always made me think of palm trees. But after a while we suddenly found ourselves standing there kissing, and then I think she realized I might not need further lessons or further encouragement to go further, and she said it was time to go. When she drove me home, she first stopped and parked around the corner on LeMoyne, at the corner of Euclid, opposite Joel Meltz's home, and we necked in the dark for a while. Again, I was so timid that she had to take charge and literally carry my hand to her breast. I exploded with delirious joy. But then, lest I might again wish to go still further, she indicated that it was time to go, and she pulled up in front of our house, gave me a final kiss, and drove off.

Mom was lurking in ambush. I had lipstick smeared all around my mouth and a bleary, joyous expression on my face, like I had been to heaven and back. Mom's expression was more like I had been to hell and was still there. She demanded to know what girl I had been out with, and threatened to phone the school and make a scene if I refused to tell, so I eventually caved.

When I met Linda in art class the following Monday, I was sure Mom would have caused some trouble already, but Linda gave no indication of any such thing. She was warm and friendly, and jokingly reminded me of our upcoming date for the square dance less than three weeks later. I chuckled nervously, and tried again to tell her that I meant what I said about it being impossible, but she just laughed it off. We continued walking home from school together and making out on "our" bench in Greenfield Park.

She told me that her parents would be out that Friday evening, so perhaps I could come over? I was prepared to do almost anything to make that happen, and when Friday came, I announced to my parents my intention to take a long walk that evening and go shopping at Weibolt's department store on the Forest Park corner of Lake and Harlem. I was well aware that a visit to Linda's home would only entail a slight detour. I didn't ask for permission, I just left, and made a beeline for Clinton, where Linda was waiting to greet me. We immediately went down to their expensively furnished basement recreation room, where we listened to some music, talked, caressed and necked. For once, Linda was as nervous about *her* parents coming home to find her entertaining a boy as I was about my parents finding out anything at all, so she said I couldn't stay long. But it was long enough to make me soar. I left her place, floating on updrafts of infatuation, came to Greenfield, turned the corner, and started walking towards Harlem, debating with myself about whether I should hurry down Harlem to Weibolt's or just hurry home. At that moment I sensed a car slowly crawling along behind me. It was my parents. I'd been caught red-handed. I stopped walking, but all I could feel was betrayal as they ordered me into the car and began ranting. They'd obviously done their homework, and had worked out my every move. Some parents might have been happy that their child had found someone special, but all they could see was an unequal yoke with Linda, and all I could feel was an unequal yoke between my parents and me.

Mom would soon be up to even dirtier tricks, but I didn't discover them until more than a week later, when I came to art class and Linda wouldn't speak to me or look at me. I insisted relentlessly that she tell me what the matter was, but she only accused me of having stood her up for the square dance on Saturday. But the truth was worse than that, as I would later get Mom to admit. Mom had phoned Linda's mother and explained to her that *"We're real Christians, and we don't engage in the wickedness of the world, nor do we share the company of those who are not born again, so please keep your daughter away from our son!"* Linda's mother may have fainted, or hit the ceiling, or burst out laughing, or threatened to sue. I have no idea. But regardless of how she reacted, she clearly conveyed to Linda the message that I was by no means the right sort of boy for her.

Linda was angry with me and offended. I was heartbroken and furious with Mom. All I could do was keep visiting that corner of Greenfield Park every day, alone, repairing or creating new little sculptures of sticks and stones on my own, hoping to catch a glimpse of Linda – which I never did – and remind myself that there were fewer than 400 days left on the countdown. (Many years later, I found out from her that she'd never seen me as more than an amusing flirtation.)

My painting was now finished, as were those of my classmates (Linda had painted a harlequin), and they went on display in the big, bright corridor outside the big school cafeteria, for all to see. Mr Anderson told me how good he thought mine was, and when he continued harping on what a rotten shame it was that I wouldn't be going to college – "*You'll be the only one in your graduating class who's not!*" – I got an idea. "*You like my painting in the corridor, right?*" I asked. He nodded. "*Would you like to buy it?*" He looked astonished and immediately asked how much. "*It'll cost you 25 dollars,*" I said, and waited to see his reaction, which was instantly and enthusiastically affirmative. "*But,*" I quickly added, "*don't pay me now!*" He looked puzzled. "*You can take the painting at the end of the semester, but don't pay me for it until you get a photostat copy of my university registration. Then you can send me the money.*"

Mr Anderson looked pleased and relieved. I think he finally understood my tenacity, but still not my desperation. In either case, he no longer had to nag. I brought the painting home and Mom's reaction was one of distress: "*Is that what your life is – broken music and a bottle of wine?*" That was her only comment. (I had not yet even had my first sip of wine, nor had I said anything about what the bottle might have contained, and my guitar was intact and I didn't play *that* bad.) I gave my painting to Carroll Anderson shortly before the last day of school.

With only a couple of weeks to go before graduation, I was in a softball game (no gloves) one day in gym class. I was playing first base, and the batter hit a grounder to short, which the shortstop fielded and fired to me, but his throw was high. When I stretched for it while trying to keep my foot on the bag, the ball hit the extended tip of my right ring finger head-on, smashing the outermost finger joint into a glorious compound fracture. I had to go to the hospital to have it set, then back again the week before graduation to have it re-broken and set again.

Nearly all 700 or so kids in my graduating class would be going to the graduation ball, except me (and Howie, who had absolutely no desire to go anyway). Linda's date was Bob Kettlestrings, of all people. Charming. After the graduation ceremony, Howie and I found ourselves totally separated from all other classmates at my home on Euclid, together with his parents, drinking soda pop and eating cake. Maybe there were also Rice Krispie squares and Hawaiian Punch. No girls in sight. Whoopee. My ring finger was in a splint; it should have been the middle one. And Mom and Dad's graduation present to me was another new Bible. Hallelujah.

CHAPTER 11

The Final Year

The Bible Truth Publishers frequently used the printing services of Gregg-Moore, a small offset lithography company on South Wacker Drive in the Loop. Clem Dear told me that they were looking for someone to work in the shipping department, and since I was looking for a job right after high school, I went down to the Loop for an interview on the Monday after graduation. The premises were aging, dark and dirty, and I was hired on the spot. The main part of my minimum-wage job was boring: wrapping parcels and filling cartons with printed leaflets, flyers, tracts, booklets and other printed matter, then labelling and loading the parcels and cartons onto pallets, then taking the pallets to the shipping platform by means of a hand-powered forklift, which was a new device for me. No girls worked there, and the other guys were middle-aged. I don't know whether they had been told that the new kid was going to be from that client with all the religious stuff, but they seemed to look at me with some suspicion for the first day or two, then quickly found I was not much different from any other kid my age, possibly because I was trying so hard not to be different.

Three others, including my boss, worked in the shipping department. My skinny boss looked like he might have been a recovering alcoholic, with his strained, wrinkled and constantly anxious face, his pants pulled halfway up to his chest, and the legs correspondingly elevated partway up his shins. A cigarette dangled perpetually from one corner of his mouth in such a way that his eyes seemed always to be wincing from the smoke he himself was producing.

The production staff included a few press operators, one of whom was a huge, barrel-chested man who reminded me of an XXL version of Ralph Buchanan. He explained to me that if a speck of dust was left on the plate, the result would be a tiny white spot on the paper where no ink could be applied. He seemed to be deadly serious when he insisted that the technical trade term for such defects was *assholes*. I have never found anything to support his claim, but I think there might be a good deal to support the hypothesis that those guys had a lot of fun with a gullible young man like me. Even the cutters, who operated huge cutting machines with razor-sharp guillotine-like blades for trimming the edges of entire reams of paper after printing, enjoyed my reactions when they held up their hands in my direction. I had previously naively assumed that all human hands had five fingers, even if you made your living operating a machine like that.

The fun part of my job was my role as a courier all around the Loop and a bit up on the North Side. Gregg-Moore clients often wanted to see some printed samples or galley proofs before giving the go-ahead for a full-scale production run. Over the course of the summer of '63, I must have taken large envelopes and small parcels up and down every single street and into most of the office buildings, from the Prudential Building to a number of landmark buildings along the river: the brand-new corncob Marina Towers, the voluminous Merchandise Mart, the white Wrigley Building, and the auspicious Tribune Tower, and even once to an address on West Madison Street just west of the River – a slum area then known as Skid Row.

Dad took us to the top of the Prudential Building when it was fairly new in around 1956. Its 41 floors made it Chicago's tallest at that time. We were told that the elevator was one of the first high-speed elevators in the world, but it looked much too exciting for Mom, who stayed below. The even-taller 65-storey Marina Towers, both residential and commercial, were not yet complete when I delivered my first parcel to a brand-new tenant. When he opened the door to receive my parcel, I craned my head eagerly to get a glimpse beyond him into the pie-slice apartments and out to the skyline. I was a diligent worker, and if I happened to dawdle for a minute to inspect some new building or gaze at the river, I had the speed and condition to bolt off and make up the time. I was curious, not lazy.

To get to work, I usually cycled down Oak Park Avenue to the Lake Street L where I left my bike, took the L to the Loop, got off at Clark, and walked a block or two to Gregg-Moore. About halfway along the L ride, the train passed a tool-and-die company, which I easily deduced was the one owned by Linda's father, a reminder I probably didn't need five days a week that summer, which was one of tangled and trying emotions for me. With school out, and all my former classmates college-bound, I felt more isolated than ever, not because I'd ever had any close friends among my classmates, but because I'd at least had daily contact and some of the trappings of a social atmosphere all around me.

Gregg-Moore was a lonely, grimy, noisy place, where each person worked pretty much on his own and where I had few things in common to discuss with anyone on the breaks. The best I could hope for was that the L ride in the morning would be so crowded that the other strap-hangers might include a pretty girl or two who wouldn't mind that the lurching of the train and the jostling of the other passengers would occasionally lead to us bumping our bodies into each other. Mom's lesson was at last making sense, but more in the breach (or breeches) than in the observance.

This was the summer of my discontent, my year of treading water while I waited for Norm to graduate. I was saving as much money as I could even though I now had to pay a little rent to my parents. I was trying to finalize plans with Norm to reduce our level of chaos while wrestling with my restless hormones and a strong urge to paint. I continued to be caught up in right-wing political writings. And I was trying to love my parents and get their love without feeling it was always contingent upon – always coming back to – whether I lived up to their warped and warping creeds, which I couldn't and wouldn't.

Having graduated, I no longer had any homework, but I continued excusing myself from participation in the Tuesday and Thursday evening sessions of the Meeting. Three sessions on Sunday were more than enough for me, and I made it wordlessly clear that this was not negotiable.

My final year in Oak Park, following my graduation, came during an eventful period in the world on many levels as well, beginning with the murder of the black civil-rights activist Medgar Evers. Martin Luther King's *"I have a dream"* speech came in August; Nelson Mandela went on trial; Alcatraz closed before Norm and I got there; Stan Musial retired; the ZIP code was introduced; the Beatles, Rolling Stones and Bob Dylan all had breakthroughs; Kennedy was assassinated; Vietnam was no longer only the name of some obscure faraway country, but now also the name of a waxing, vexing war; Jim Brown set a new NFL record; smoking was officially linked to cancer; and the Great Society was launched.

I would paint seven more paintings during that last year at home, four during the fall of '63, and three during the early spring of '64. The first of these seven – *The City*[7] – was done in a totally different style from *Guitar and Bottle*, by now residing in the Anderson home. My trips to and from the Loop, observing and thinking about the lines of the roads and tracks crisscrossing the flat Chicago landscape, lines temporarily drawn on land that had existed for hundreds of

---

7   Painting #2 (see Appendix 2)

millions of years, Bishop Ussher notwithstanding, while generating smoke, grime and slop. I envisaged rather clearly what I would paint before I started; not exactly, not in every stroke, but close enough.

The Nolans were a family who came to Meeting on a somewhat irregular basis, almost exclusively on Sundays. Mr Nolan was an old friend of Norm's dad's and owned a jewelry shop on the corner of Grand and Harlem, in which the Mafia had taken some interest, and had even kindly offered to protect. Mr and Mrs Nolan had two children: a boy, Vince, about John's age; and a daughter, Mary, older than me and younger than Al. Vince didn't look at all like he fit in, and in fact during my early teens he stopped coming to Meeting altogether. I was told that he'd started doing errands for the Chicago Mafia.

At some point, I think it was around 1959, Mrs Nolan died, and everyone felt so sorry for Mr Nolan, even though his Meeting attendance was infrequent. He occasionally took trips to Florida. Then one Sunday a few years later, when I was a senior in high school, Mr Nolan brought his new wife to Meeting. The new Mrs Nolan was from Florida, had been married before, and had two children with her: Mary Lou and a sibling, about whom I remember nothing at all, because Norm and I were so bowled over by Mary Lou, a tall, shapely brunette our age, with a coy and slightly frightened look in her dark doe eyes. She looked like she could have been a model. (In fact she did once model bras for the Sears or JC Penny's catalog.)

At last, Norm and I had a real reason to come to Meeting, on Sundays at least. But Norm had more self-confidence than me, and managed to find some way to meet Mary Lou outside the Meeting. Perhaps his parents, who were close to the Nolans (mine were not), not only approved but encouraged the romance as a way to get Norm to forget the countdown. Not long after Mary Lou appeared on our horizon, the Mafia bombed Mr Nolan's jewelry store for the second time, and he shut it down and moved his family to Florida. The Dentons went on vacation to visit them there, possibly at Christmas 1962 (when I was with my family at the LA Conference for the last time), or in early '63. Norm came home all bleary-eyed, but his interest in Mary Lou seemed to be quickly overshadowed by one or more girls at school once he got home.

A neighbor of the Dentons in Elmwood Park, Gladys Holt, had begun coming to Meeting some years before, together with her son Lloyd, whom everyone called Butch. Mr Holt never came to Meeting; he was a non-believer –

an alleged alcoholic and atheist (but we never used that latter horrifying word). Butch was a jovial kind of guy with curly light-blond hair, a couple of years older than me, always thoughtful and friendly. He had a lot more freedom than Norm and I did, maybe because his father wouldn't allow it any other way. When his father died, Butch was heartbroken for a long time. I never knew Butch to have had a date, something that was hard enough at the Meeting, without the further disadvantages of his fairly coarse and fleshy facial features, and more body weight than he should have had.

The few halfway-attractive Meeting girls his age had no interest in him, and by the time he was past high school, nearly all the older ones were married, unless they were exceptionally homely, like Stearly. She was a doctor (psychiatry) who for some reason had moved to the Oak Park area to work at the BTP. She was about 10 years older than Butch.

One Saturday during the summer of '63, Butch invited me to go out for pizza, and my parents approved instantly (Butch had taken his place, after all). When he pulled up to our home in his car and I rushed out to join him, I was mightily surprised to find that Stearly was already sitting in the front seat next to Butch, while Mary Lou, of all people, was in the back, waiting for me to join her. (The Dentons were out traveling somewhere.) I was still more surprised when Stearly scooted over right next to Butch, after he pulled away from our home, and then I realized that Butch wasn't heading to a pizzeria at all, but to the remotest parking lot he could find in Thatcher Woods. Once we got there, Butch and Stearly seemed to forget they weren't alone in the car and began doing some serious necking, which appeared to have been far from their first time.

Meanwhile, in the back seat, Mary Lou scooted right over to me, and began showing me how badly she wanted to be kissed. I drew back, asking her what about Norm, and weren't they together? But she assured me that it was over and told me not to think about it. I didn't need a lot of convincing; Norm had never told me anything to suggest that she was "his" or that he was in love with her or anything like that. I don't remember whether we ever got any pizza that day.

A week or two later, when the Dentons returned, Mary Lou returned to Norm. Just like that. I never discussed it with Norm. If I'd known they weren't through, I don't think I would have given in to her, at least I wouldn't have wanted to, but who can ever know? In fact, I was still such a fool for Linda. Throughout that summer, every time I had the use of Dad's car to run an errand, I would swing by her house on Clinton, hoping to catch a glimpse of her, hoping for a word, hoping for a chance to show her that standing her up was the last thing on the mind of such a hopeless romantic. But I never saw Linda, ever again.

In my next three paintings, I explored the swirls further with both palette knife and brushes, on larger canvases than any I'd used so far. The first two, *Impressions of the Sun #1* and *#2*, became my only two completely abstract works.[8] In the third, *Decision* (painting #5),[9] I added a person for the first time. The decision of the title concerned one of the biggest milestones or turning points in my life, a heart-wrenching struggle between all I'd known and a great *un*known, between the only people I'd loved and a rather frightening, indifferent world, but that also meant the difference between endless coercion and freedom.

Mom, however, offered a simplistic, fundamentalist Christian explanation of *Decision*, which almost caused me to scrape the canvas and paint something else on it, as I had done with a couple of others. One of those I scrapped/scraped was a vertical rectangular format with a totally bare landscape whose only feature was a tree in the process of losing its remaining leaves in a high wind. When Mom started proclaiming its "meaning" – standing firm in the Faith, against life's storms, looking only unto Jesus in this wilderness wide, clinging steadfastly to Him – I could take no more, and the paint was gone before it had dried. (A better interpretation would have been *Dare to Be a Daniel*, my version.)

Regarding my continued schooling, once my parents finally realized the futility of their attempts to bribe or blackmail me emotionally, they changed their tune. Mom wrote in her cliché-filled anniversary diary in October 1963 that *"We don't want [Stan] to further his education until he can do it heartily as unto the Lord"* – as if it were their decision. (The turn of the millennium would pass before I would ever see that diary entry. It didn't shock or even surprise me, but it saddened me greatly to realize how much time, energy, and even love, my parents wasted by making so much of their lives contingent on ancient books written by frightened, superstitious people.)

Sometimes I'd have a cigarette at Gregg-Moore, advancing from my earliest

---

8   Paintings #3 and 4, respectively (see Appendix 2)
9   Painting #5 (see Appendix 2)

explorations at home in my upstairs bathroom, where I would light a match (legitimate for neutralizing stinkers), quickly blow it out, then place it close to my mouth and inhale the smoke from it, stupidly thinking I'd look cool. From there I progressed to an occasional butt (if it was from a reliable source), then to the rare cigarettes Norm and I bought in three-packs (mostly Salem or other menthol cigarettes that we thought wouldn't smell as much) to smoke during walks to the park across Austin Boulevard at the end of Harrison on Tea Meeting Sundays. It was a way to rebel, which made it exciting. In fact, I was getting incredibly many more kicks out of life than most of the kids my age, since I got kicks out of anything that was prohibited – and nearly everything was – whereas such things had long since become commonplace and even boring to my peers.

Perhaps it was because my parents often smelled smoke on me when I came home from Gregg-Moore, even though I claimed it was second-hand, or perhaps because Dad was seeking more contact with me, or perhaps it was because he wanted to keep a closer eye on me, or maybe because they had given up on the vain thought that I might give in and start at a local college in the fall. Whatever the reason(s), in September Dad told me there was a place for me in the purchasing department at Link-Belt, an office job with about double the pay, and a much more social environment. Al had also worked there one summer.

Around the time I was going to start at Link-Belt, the Meeting's jungle telegraph lurched into action with the shocking news that Butch and Stearly had eloped to Idaho. Mary Lou and I weren't at all surprised. But this was not just a matter for gossip; it was about discipline, about why they would run off "like thieves in the night", if everything were above-board and righteous? The outcome was that, on their return from Idaho, Butch and Stearly were commanded to "stand down"; they weren't technically being put away from the Lord's Table, but they wouldn't be allowed to break bread either, for a period of three months. I was still naive enough to believe that the three months were a more or less random "sentence" for not fulfilling some unspoken, unwritten policy of asking the Meeting for permission to marry. I didn't realize that it was a period of observation and judgmental scrutiny, to determine whether Stearly came up pregnant "too soon".

After the three months had passed, and Stearly's non-bulging abdomen passed inspection, they were again "received in fellowship" – and I was allowed to visit them in their new home, where they let me have a preview sip of wine and listen to Dave Brubeck and other jazz. They ended up buying two of my paintings: *Impressions of the Sun #2* and *Decision*. Al bought *Impressions of the Sun #1* in 1964. It hung on his living room wall for many years. At some point after 2001, however, it was relegated to the damp floor of his garage, where I discovered it and rescued it to a dry basement closet during a visit in 2003. It remained out of view until after 2013, when I "threatened" to buy it back from him unless he displayed it. Sometime thereafter, he hung it on the wall of his basement recreation room where it currently (as of 2017) resides.

The purchasing department at Link-Belt, 310 West Pershing Road, was a totally new experience for me on many levels. The entry inside the front door led up half a flight of stairs to a spacious reception area with a long counter. A large doorway to the right led into a huge open landscape, partially split into sections by various low walls or partitions. The ceiling may have been nearly 20 feet high, but the partitions were no more than 6-7 feet tall. Directly inside the main doorway to the right from the reception area was the purchasing department. Just inside that were two large glass "cubicles" (too large to be called cubicles, but as they lacked walls of ceiling height, I'll make an exception). The first was occupied by the Purchasing Manager (whose name I've forgotten), the second by his assistant, Mr Frank McWethy. I had to pass both cubicle doors to get to the 12 desks of the staff of the purchasing department, arranged in four rows of three desks each, perpendicular to the one long-side of Mr McWethy's cubicle. The Purchasing Manager was aloof in a preoccupied way, and was insulated from the desk jockeys by Mr McWethy's two glass cubicle partition walls.

Mr McWethy seemed to me to be a pleasant-looking elderly gentleman ("elderly" being anyone my dad's age or more), but my colleagues regarded him with some awe; he was allegedly independently and unfathomably wealthy, and only held the job to give himself something to do. In fact, they referred to him as Mr McWealthy behind his back.

My colleagues were a motley crew. The supervisor was Jerry, who reminded me a lot of my homeroom teacher, although Jerry was much more jaded, as were all my new colleagues. Perhaps the most colorful – and most jaded – was John Zon, a Polish guy in his 40s whose surname reportedly began with "zon", but consisted of numerous unpronounceable Polish syllables, hence the short form. At least two of the others were Poles, and they immediately started calling me by a Polish nickname: *Stosh*, my seventh moniker (Stan, Stanley, Yelnats, Red Eagle, Injun, Pancho, Stosh). It didn't take these jaded guys long to figure out a lot of things about me: that although I was the son of the pious Chief Engineer, who sat upstairs, I was not pious; that I could be counted on not to spill any beans to my dad about their antics; that I was exceptionally naïve and inexperienced in a number of key areas; that I was pretty smart and learned quickly; that I was leaving home for California in less than 300 days; that I was a rebel with a cause; that I had a good sense of humor and hadn't heard any of the jokes they were longing to tell to someone who hadn't heard them even once before; and that I could take a joke and laugh at myself.

During my first weeks in the office, John Zon wanted to confide something to me one afternoon, but he wanted the others to know what he was confiding to me, so he gathered them all around me, looked nervously around, and addressed me slowly and said most solemnly in a muted half-whisper: "*A piece of advice, Stosh: Never look at it, Stosh. Never look at it. It'll scare you to death!*" I could see that the others were fighting to hold back their laughter. When I innocently asked "*Look at <u>what</u>?*" they could hold back no longer.

Jim Driscoll insisted that I looked and acted just like James Dean, and all the others agreed, but I didn't know what they meant by that either; James Dean had been killed four years before I started going to the movies, so it wasn't until many years later that I saw my first James Dean movie (and I thought he looked more like Norm than me).

My work consisted of expediting orders. Each of us had a large old oak desk, a typewriter (mechanical, of course), a supply of forms and letterhead paper and carbon paper, a telephone, and an accordion file-holder in which we had copies of the purchase orders that were due for delivery or already late. We were supposed to phone the suppliers and remind them of upcoming deliveries or complain about overdue shipments. John Zon could be ruthless. To give me an idea of how it worked, he had me sit by his desk and listen in on an extra earpiece while he phoned to complain about a shipment that had failed to arrive on schedule. When the supplier told him that the reason for the delay was that the dispatcher had taken ill, John shot back in his thick Chicago accent, "*So whaddya gonna do if he dies? No delivery?!*"

But one piece of advice I got from those jaded guys turned out to be useful indeed. One day, one of the big Link-Belt bosses was passing through the Purchasing Department. I recognized who he was and became nervous, not wanting to do anything that could make a bad impression. Jerry saw my reaction, came over and put his hand on my shoulder, looked me in the eye and said: "*One leg at a time, Stosh, one leg at a time.*" I looked up with another big question mark written all over my face, and he smiled knowingly and explained, "*He puts his pants on one leg at a time, just like you.*" (But my colleagues apparently felt that Mr McWealthy did otherwise.)

Within a few days after my 18th birthday, I was required to go to the local draft board in Forest Park to register. It didn't seem like a big deal at the time – it wasn't as though there was any real war going on. The presence of our "military advisors" in Vietnam was never mentioned in conversation, seldom showed up in the newspapers, and never in the headlines. Some guys were getting drafted, however, but I was still intending either to seek conscientious objector status (even though I wasn't a member of any religious organization that was officially opposed to combat service in the military, like the Quakers or the Meeting) or to go kill Commies. My brothers were both married, and married men were automatically exempted from the draft at that time, so it never became an issue for them. But I had a strange feeling in that Selective Service office, one that somehow didn't correspond to the excitement Norm and I had felt at the prospect of joining the Navy a year or two earlier, nor the thought of rushing forth to kill anybody.

The work at Link-Belt was kind of fun, and I was learning to deal with tricky situations (including my discovery of Linda's dad's company among the suppliers in the Link-Belt purchase orders). One day, we'd been asked by the accounting department to dispute a surcharge on an invoice a supplier had sent for some allegedly valuable packaging material that had not been returned, but discarded on the site. The chief purchasing manager apparently felt it would be a good test for me. I wrote a salty letter to the supplier, pointing out that the purchase order had failed to indicate that any such charges might be levied, nor any instructions as to the recovery of any packaging material, and that I presumed that neither their company nor the recipient of my letter personally made it a habit to retain possession of packaging materials in the unforeseeable event that unknown monetary claims against such materials might be forthcoming at some point in time in the future. The extra charge was dropped immediately, and even the chief purchasing manager came over to my desk to tell me he'd been impressed by my successful argumentation.

But there were dark sides as well. During the afternoon of Friday, November 22nd, somebody rushed over to the purchasing area and shouted out the news that Kennedy had been shot. A few short cheers erupted. In spite of my strong right-wing leanings, this reaction sickened me; and despite Keith Sartorius's efforts, I was sickened by the assassination itself. Something fishy was going on, and I couldn't figure out what. After all, it was Kennedy who had forced the Russians to get their missiles out of Cuba (despite the US having missiles near the Soviet border in Turkey), and saw the shooting down of a US spy plane over Cuba as an act of aggression – on Cuba's part! – even though it would certainly been regarded as an act of aggression (also on Cuba's part, obviously) if the Cubans had a spy plane flying over the US. (In fact, in 1960, another US spy plane was shot down over Russia, and its pilot, Francis Gary Powers, was captured and imprisoned.) And it was Kennedy who had started sending combat troops to this Vietnam place to support the South's corrupt dictatorial President Diệm, all in the name of freedom – as long as Commies were killed. But when Buddhist monks began immolating themselves to protest Diệm's oppressive Catholic minority rule, the US got as tired of him as the South Vietnamese people had long been, and my country supported his overthrow and assassination in early November. Then Kennedy began talking about withdrawing troops, only to be assassinated himself.

At the time Johnson became president, he'd been primarily concerned with progressive social programs, but he soon made the fatal mistake of sending more troops to Vietnam too. Diệm had been replaced by generals who welcomed this, so of course we were only helping an ally, weren't we? And Vietnam was suddenly making headlines on a daily basis.

In early 1964, the presidential election year, a prominent Republican contender named Barry Goldwater was talking in favor of using nuclear weapons to bomb the Vietnamese Commies out of existence, suddenly making Johnson the *peace* candidate, not what my current jingoism was ready for. Goldwater's right-wing hatred seemed to me to fit well with the stuff that Keith Sartorius had got me started on. But something wasn't quite right about that either. It was fine with me that the Republicans wanted to do some no-holds-barred Commie-bashing, but the GOP guys were also the ones who were balking at all the civil rights protests. And the murder of Medgar Evers the week after I graduated had made me sad and furious. Keith's indoctrination efforts never mentioned civil rights, and yet it was the "pinko" Democratic liberals who were the only ones making any sense in terms of finally doing something, however small, about the generations of injustice endured by black people even after slavery had been officially abolished. I had nobody to talk to about it, politics being a more-or-less off-limits topic for the Chosen Few, whose ranks I had never joined and with whom by this time I was not greatly inclined to talk to about anything anyway.

Link-Belt had an entire, huge room – almost big enough to play full-court basketball in – solely for its automatic data processing machines, which processed small amounts of data using a huge amount of punch cards and a huge amount of energy, thus necessitating a second, almost equally large room for the coolers needed to cool off the huge amounts of heat those forerunners to the computer were generating. At that point, I'd never even used an electric typewriter. The only sources of up-to-date information readily available to me were the newspapers (in our case, the highly conservative, Republican-biased *Chicago Tribune*) and the radio, to which we only rarely listened to anything like news, and the even more conservative station WMBI, the voice of the Moody Bible Institute.

I sometimes rode in the car to and/or from work with Dad. I only took the L and bus when I had to, because the commute between Euclid Avenue and Pershing Road was very long and boring. But there were exceptions to the boredom. Once on the bus on my way to catch the L home from work, two pretty teenage girls got on after me and were looking at me and giggling as they sauntered past and took seats directly behind me. They began talking to each other – but clearly for my benefit – about their dates the previous weekend, becoming more and more explicit, while I sat there rigidly, trying not to let on that I was interested or could hear a word, but when one of them told the other that she'd gone all wet when her boyfriend put his hand *down there*, my ears gave me away by turning bright red, and the girls laughed and made eyes at me as they got off the bus two stops before my transfer point to the L.

With Dad it was a different story. Sometimes we had nice chats about work or the traffic, and Dad often had the radio on to hear the traffic reports and some actual news. But with the countdown clock ticking louder every day, there was a whole lot of tension. Dad seemed to feel the pressure of his self-imposed duty to preach to me, and when he did, or turned on WMBI instead, I slouched towards the window and pretended to sleep.

By the late fall of '63, with fewer than 200 days to go on our countdown, Norm and I were firmly committed to San Francisco as our destination, despite neither of us knowing anything more about it than that it was a major city in California, on the ocean, with a mild climate, and with a good public transportation system. We had now figured out our means of getting there: a Greyhound bus from downtown Chicago to downtown San Francisco, whatever that looked like. The ride would take just over 50 hours, but the baggage allowance was considerable. And it was affordable. In the early months of 1964, I bought a black steamship trunk, about 38 x 22 x 24", from a luggage store in Chicago that I had found via the Yellow Pages. I brought it home on the bus, more than two months before our departure.

The appearance of my trunk in our house suddenly brought home the reality of what was rapidly approaching. I needed time to plan what would fit in the trunk, but I also thought we all might need some time to adjust. I hated causing my parents such obvious anguish, but I don't think they had a clue about the anguish I was experiencing for having been allowed no other options. I could hardly tell them I loved them without immediately getting back, *"But if you did, you wouldn't be like this or do this way..."* – pure emotional blackmail. Then the usual ranting would start, especially from Mom. They thought (and told me so) that I was hard-hearted, without ever asking me what I thought or felt, because they gave every impression that my thoughts or feelings had no merit whatsoever. *My* thoughts were simply wrong; they were not *His* thoughts.

In all the months and years Norm and I spent on detailed planning for the Great Escape, one thing stands clear. Despite the monumentally life-changing nature of the move we both realized was about to happen, and despite the many obstacles and pressures, neither Norm nor I *ever* wavered. Maybe we were too naïve to be afraid, but we never got cold feet. We never felt uncertainty in the face of the tremendous Unknown. We never had to persuade each other, or convince each other. It was what we *had* to do, and we were going to do it.

I sold my three fairly large paintings – the one to Al and the other two to Butch and Stearly – which was just as well, because I couldn't have taken them with me anyway (nor could I bring *The City*, which I feared might not be sufficiently dry – the paint was pretty thick). I still had five blank canvases, and one special idea. I knew that if I painted a painting as big as I needed for the motif I had in mind, I wouldn't be able to take it with me either when Norm and I moved, but big canvases were not among the five blank ones anyway. However, if I took my biggest blank canvas (36 x 22"), which would just fit into my trunk, and bolted it together with two of the smaller ones (18 x 22" each), I could make a single larger painting (36 x 44"), just the right size for my idea, but still possible to take apart and fit into the trunk. I intended to use basically the same style I had used for my first painting (*Guitar and Bottle*), but had temporarily abandoned. And it would dry quickly. Before starting, however, I wanted to practice on two others.

In the first small one (10 x 28"), randomly shaped planes in muted greens, grays and blues form a bottle.[10] I used my next canvas, also fairly small (36 x 18"), to practice painting hands – one open and one clenched as if around a pole. I had seen a number of different artists' studies of hands and wanted to see where "my" style could take such a motif. The open fingers were echoed in the background just above the fist, while the fist was echoed to the far left, beyond the open hand.[11]

At the time I painted this one, a Meeting guy I knew from Wisconsin, Ken Keisling, was staying for some months at our home in Oak Park. He was several years older than me and was studying biology at a university in the Chicago area, and needed a place to board. Then in the spring of '64 he was drafted into the army to do some kind of biological weapons shit at a base in Utah. He bought *Hands* before I left Oak Park. It was essentially a study for my final work in Oak Park – and, as it turned out – in the United States: the three-section *Man with Guitar*,[12] with a solitary guitar player sitting on a bed with a purple/green bedspread like the one I had at home, one that Mom had crocheted. The man is not playing for an audience, only for his own tranquility. This painting was done under conditions of extreme psychological stress and excitement for me – just a couple of months before I would leave home for a totally unknown new life in San Francisco – and just enough time for the painting to dry. I knew that this was what I wanted to do. Forget about acting, forget about Hollywood. I was going to study art and be a painter.

---

10   *Bottle is painting* #6 (see Appendix 2)
11   *Hands is Painting* #7 (see Appendix 2)
12   Painting #8 (see Appendix 2)

The last month at my parental home was like living in a daze; I was mostly numb. My only real contact was with Norm, since I was no longer at school and had no social contacts with anyone at work; in fact, no contacts outside the Meeting, and Norm and I were already pretty much pariahs in that context. I couldn't talk to anybody in my family about anything that mattered deeply to me, nor about how exciting the prospect of living in San Francisco was. I was just working, saving, keeping my head down, counting off (or down) the days, trying to be pleasant, thinking about what to bring and what to leave behind. It was easiest to decide about the things. Mental baggage takes more work and time to leave behind, especially since I was still unaware of any but the outermost layers of my indoctrination.

I practiced packing the black trunk with my four paintings and my paints; clothing and some books; my arrowheads and eagle feathers (I would have to leave my moose antlers behind for the time being); clothes for summer and for a bit chillier weather; a few kitchen utensils and a waffle iron that Norm and I might be needing; some towels; the blue portable Royal manual typewriter I had acquired for writing term papers; a few important documents and other papers. I would also take the small brown Samsonite suitcase I used for my trip to La Habra, and my guitar case. Norm was just bringing one suitcase. We got the Greyhound tickets several weeks in advance; the departure time would be in the late morning on Saturday, June 6th, 1964, the final day of our countdown.

On my last day at Link-Belt, all the guys in the purchasing department took me out for a fantastic steak lunch at the Stock Yard Inn. Their well-wishing and back-slapping felt genuine. It was the only warm send-off I would get from anyone. My time with them had been enjoyable, and I now felt I had a nest egg that would see me and Norm through until we could find work in San Francisco.

My parents and I didn't go to the Des Moines Conference during the Memorial Day weekend that year. I went with them to Meeting that Sunday morning, May 31st, for the last time, and I was determined to be friendly and pleasant when I said goodbye to everyone after Meeting. Clem Dear, my Sunday School teacher, who was accustomed to talking to "his" boys while giving them a firm left-handed massage at the base of the neck while shaking the right hand in a way that prevented escape, was feeling his adrenalin and seemed determined to pinch a few tendons in my neck as he informed me repeatedly and with the greatest solemnity, shaking his head, and dramatically closing his eyes, that *"all that is not of God will come to naught!*" I debated with myself, as he went on and on, whether I should start giving *his* neck an equally painful massage, but decided to let it pass.

Others displayed vague scowls of disapproval and avowals to pray for us; only a couple even wished us a safe trip. *Nobody* wished for us what we were wishing for ourselves: an exciting adventure, the start of an independent adult life, the ability to learn and take responsibility. Not even good luck. Meeting people didn't believe in luck, since He not only controls everything but also knows what's to come (which in that case should have included our move and made it part of His Divine Plan). Here I was, actually daring to be a Daniel, and nobody seemed to realize it, much less appreciate it. Those who failed to appreciate it would have to include *me* for many years, because in 1964, all I was aware of having done was to question the Meeting enough to recognize my need to get away from it. It would take a lot more living and learning to realize that I had in fact *only begun* to learn to question. Anything and everything. *Not* to submit blindly to things – including orders – but to demand that they first be made sensible to me, that they convinced me that they were fair, worth following, worthy of following.

The countdown was now into the final weird week. I was all packed, days in advance. On the morning of our departure, Mom gave me some fruit for the trip, and some BTP stuff which I would discard in a trash can at the first bus stop along the way, together with the fruit peels. Hardly a word was spoken about the trip, or about anything. But Norm's dad had decided, whether in consultation with my parents or independently, that he would drive Norm and me to the Greyhound bus depot in the Loop on Saturday morning, and would collect me shortly before 10 AM. Mom and Dad would stay at home, as would Norm's mom, who was too emotional. My parents were just agonizing. And I felt so torn.

Norm and his dad pulled up on schedule and Norm helped me get my trunk to the car and into it, while Mom and Dad waited in the house. I went back to get my suitcase and guitar, gave my parents big hugs amid Mom's angry sobs and Dad's anxious tears. Then I turned and walked back to the car and we drove off.

Hardly a word was spoken on our way to the Loop. At the bus terminal, Norm and I somehow got all our stuff from the car over to the right place for the right bus. I shook hands with Norm's dad and thanked him for the lift. He forced a grim half-smile and a curt nod, but didn't say a word. Norm and I got on board and found a couple of seats together somewhere in the middle and waited euphorically for the bus to pull out. Norm and his born-again right-wing virgin friend were about to enter the real world.

END OF BOOK ONE

APPENDIX 1 – my boyhood home

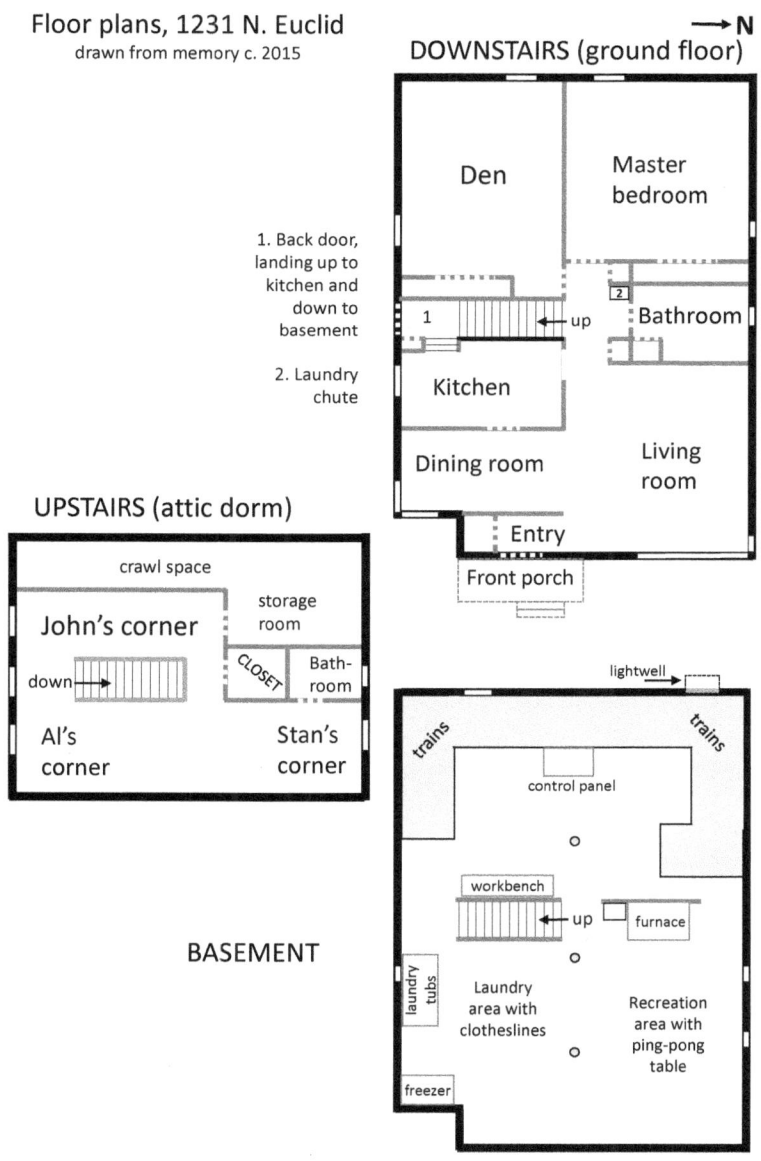

APPENDIX 2 – paintings 1 to 8

#1 Guitar and Bottle

#2 The City

#3 Impressions of the Sun #1

#4 Impressions of the Sun #2

#5 Decision

#6 Bottle

#7 Hands

#8 Man with Guitar

Hindsights
the six-part autobiography of an unknown artist

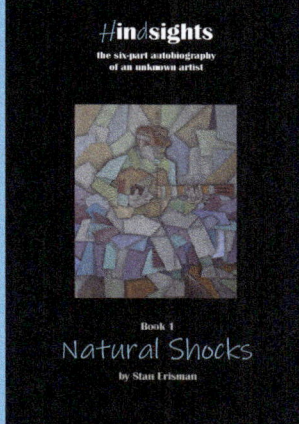

Book 1
Natural Shocks
by Stan Erisman

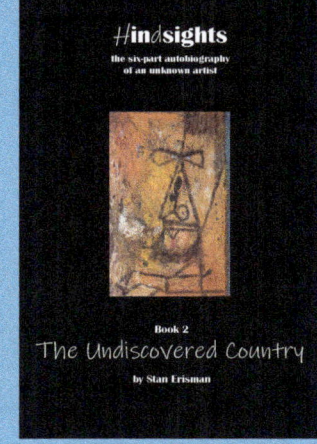

Book 2
The Undiscovered Country
by Stan Erisman

Book 3
No Traveller Returns
by Stan Erisman

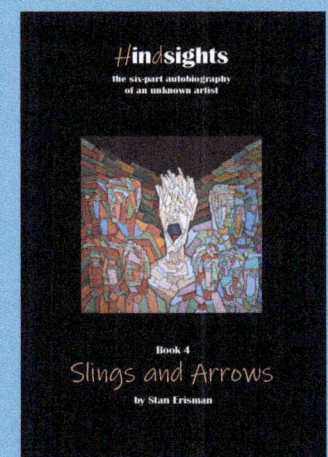

Book 4
Slings and Arrows
by Stan Erisman

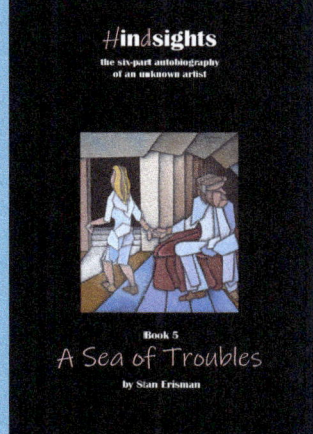

Book 5
A Sea of Troubles
by Stan Erisman

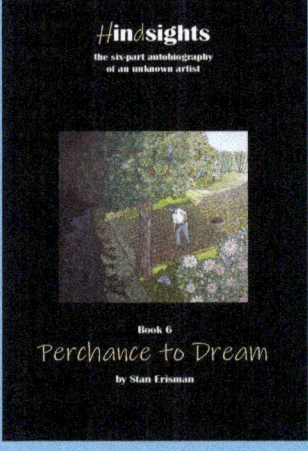

Book 6
Perchance to Dream
by Stan Erisman

www.ingramcontent.com/pod-product-compliance
Lightning Source LLC
Chambersburg PA
CBHW040306170426
43194CB00022B/2911